PATHS TO INTERNATIONAL JUST

This volume focuses on the everyday social relationships through which international justice is produced. Using case studies from the International Criminal Court, the European Court of Human Rights, the UN Women's Convention Committee and elsewhere, it explores international justice as a process that takes place at the intersection of the often contradictory practices of applicants, lawyers, bureaucrats, victims, accused and others. With a sensitivity to broader institutional and political inequalities, the contributors ask how and why international justice is mobilised, understood and abandoned by concrete social actors, and to what effect. An attention to the different voices that feed into international justice is essential if we are to understand its potentials and limitations in the midst of social conflict or full blown political violence.

MARIE-BÉNÉDICTE DEMBOUR is a Professor of Law and Anthropology at the Sussex Law School, University of Sussex.

TOBIAS KELLY is a Lecturer in Social Anthropology at the School of Social and Political Studies, University of Edinburgh.

CAMBRIDGE STUDIES IN LAW AND SOCIETY

Cambridge Studies in Law and Society aims to publish the best scholarly work on legal discourse and practice in its social and institutional contexts, combining theoretical insights and empirical research.

The fields that it covers are: studies of law in action; the sociology of law; the anthropology of law; cultural studies of law, including the role of legal discourses in social formations; law and economics; law and politics; and studies of governance. The books consider all forms of legal discourse across societies, rather than being limited to lawyers' discourses alone.

The series editors come from a range of disciplines: academic law; socio-legal studies; sociology; and anthropology. All have been actively involved in teaching and writing about law in context.

Series editors

Chris Arup *Victoria University, Melbourne*

Martin Chanock *La Trobe University, Melbourne*

Pat O'Malley *University of Sydney, Australia*

Sally Engle Merry *Wellesley College, Massachusetts*

Susan Silbey *Massachusetts Institute of Technology*

Books in the Series

The Politics of Truth and Reconciliation in South Africa
Legitimizing the Post-Apartheid State
Richard A. Wilson

Modernism and the Grounds of Law
Peter Fitzpatrick

Unemployment and Government
Genealogies of the Social
William Walters

Autonomy and Ethnicity
Negotiating Competing Claims in Multi-Ethnic States
Yash Ghai

Constituting Democracy
Law, Globalism and South Africa's Political Reconstruction
Heinz Klug

The New World Trade Organization Agreements
Globalizing Law through Services and Intellectual Property
Christopher Arup

The Ritual of Rights in Japan
Law, Society, and Health Policy
Eric A. Feldman

The Invention of the Passport
Surveillance, Citizenship and the State
John Torpey

Governing Morals
A Social History of Moral Regulation
Alan Hunt

The Colonies of Law
Colonialism, Zionism and Law in Early Mandate Palestine
Ronen Shamir

Law and Nature
David Delaney

Social Citizenship and Workfare in the United States and Western Europe
The Paradox of Inclusion
Joel F. Handler

Law, Anthropology and the Constitution of the Social
Making Persons and Things
Edited by Alain Pottage and Martha Mundy

Judicial Review and Bureaucratic Impact
International and Interdisciplinary Perspectives
Edited by Marc Hertogh and Simon Halliday

Immigrants at the Margins
Law, Race, and Exclusion in Southern Europe
Kitty Calavita

Lawyers and Regulation
The Politics of the Administrative Process
Patrick Schmidt

PATHS TO INTERNATIONAL JUSTICE

SOCIAL AND LEGAL PERSPECTIVES

Marie-Bénédicte Dembour
Tobias Kelly

CAMBRIDGE
UNIVERSITY PRESS

CAMBRIDGE UNIVERSITY PRESS

Cambridge, New York, Melbourne, Madrid, Cape Town, Singapore, São Paulo, Delhi

Cambridge University Press
The Edinburgh Building, Cambridge CB2 8RU, UK

Published in the United States of America by Cambridge University Press, New York

www.cambridge.org
Information on this title: www.cambridge.org/9780521709200

© Cambridge University Press 2007

First published 2007

Printed in the United Kingdom at the University Press, Cambridge

A catalogue record for this publication is available from the British Library

ISBN   978-0-521-88263-7   hardback
ISBN   978-0-521-70920-0   paperback

For Bob

For Faye

CONTENTS

PLATE

ACKNOWLEDGMENTS

We are indebted to Anne Griffiths who secured funding from the ESRC for a seminar series on 'Developing Anthropology of Law in a Transnational World', spurring Marie Dembour to convene a workshop in this series, on 'Paths to International Justice', in Brighton on 1–3 September 2005. Jane Cowan helped to develop this idea and was generous with advice from beginning to end. Funding from the British Academy made it possible for Kamari Clarke and Lisa Laplante to visit the English seaside and offer contributions. The workshop also greatly benefited from the participation of Richard Wilson and Nigel Eltringham. Thanks to the Sussex Institute, the Sussex Law School and the School of Social Sciences and Cultural Studies of the University of Sussex, we were able to relax and taste, amongst other things, the delights of North African food. Katherine Tomlinson's administrative skills ensured the smooth running of these three days. Later on, Theowen Gilmour edited the manuscript, with the financial help of the Sussex Law School and the School of Social and Political Studies at the University of Edinburgh. We thank the staff at Cambridge University Press for their warm-hearted professionalism, especially Finola O'Sullivan who was encouraging and supportive from the very beginning. Their anonymous reviewers made perceptive comments on each of the contributions initially submitted and thus also directly contributed to this volume.

CONTRIBUTORS

SAL BUCKLER is Research Associate in the Department of Anthropology at the University of Durham and also works as policy and research advisor for local and national government in the UK, specialising in multiculturalism, diversity and equalities. Her PhD fieldwork was carried out with Romany Gypsies in England. She is the author of *Fire in the Dark: Telling Gypsiness in North East England* (Berghahn 2006) and has acted as specialist advisor and expert witness regarding Gypsy and Traveller issues in England.

BAŞAK ÇALI is Lecturer in Human Rights at the Department of Political Science, University College London and a Council of Europe expert on the European Convention on Human Rights and Fundamental Freedoms. Her main area of research is international legal theory and practice focusing on human rights, humanitarianism and laws of war. She has published on legal cosmopolitanism, transnational adjudication of human rights and the interplay between domestic and international formulations of human rights. She is the co-editor of *The Legalization of Human Rights: Multidisciplinary Perspectives on Human Rights and Rights Law* (Routledge 2006).

KAMARI MAXINE CLARKE is Associate Professor of Anthropology at Yale University and research associate at the Yale Law School. Over the years, her research has ranged from studies of social and religious movements in the United States and West Africa to related transnational legal movements, to inquiries into the cultural politics of power and justice in the burgeoning realm of international tribunals. She is the author of *Mapping Yoruba Networks: Power and Agency in the Making of Transnational Networks* (Duke University Press 2004), *Globalization and Race: Transformations in the Cultural Politics of Blackness* (Duke University Press 2006) and *Justice in the Making: The Cultural Politics of the International Criminal Court* – a book on an emergent international Rule of Law regime and its challenges.

JANE K. COWAN is Professor of Social Anthropology at the University of Sussex. She is the author of *Dance and the Body Politic in Northern Greece* (Princeton University Press 1990), editor of *Macedonia: the Politics of Identity and Difference* (Pluto Press 2000) and co-editor of *Culture and Rights: Anthropological Perspectives* (Cambridge University Press 2001). She has also published extensively on gender relations, ritual, popular music, the politics of language and 'tradition' and the emergence of minority identities and claims. She is currently writing a book on the League of Nations' supervision of minorities treaties with respect to the contested territory and populations of Macedonia. She is Associate Editor of *Anthropological Theory*.

MARIE-BÉNÉDICTE DEMBOUR is Senior Lecturer in Law at the University of Sussex. Her doctorate, in Social Anthropology, provided the research ground for her monograph *Recalling the Belgian Congo: Conversations and Introspection* (Berghahn 2000). Her more recent interests include human rights, migration and multiculturalism. She is particularly interested in offering and/or encouraging anthropological understandings of rights and law. She co-edited *Culture and Rights: Anthropological Perspectives* (Cambridge University Press 2001). She is the author of *Who Believes in Human Rights? Reflections on the European Convention* (Cambridge University Press 2006).

EMILY HASLAM is Lecturer in International Law at Kent Law School and the Brussels School of International Studies, University of Kent. Her recent articles include 'Victim Participation at the International Criminal Court: A Triumph of Hope Over Experience' in McGoldrick *et al.* (eds.) *The Permanent International Criminal Court: Legal and Policy Issues* (Hart 2004) and 'Silencing Hearings: Victim-witnesses at War Crimes Trials' (*European Journal of International Law* 2004) (with Marie-Bénédicte Dembour). She is currently completing a doctorate on the role of civil society in International Criminal Law.

TOBIAS KELLY is Lecturer in Social Anthropology at the University of Edinburgh. He is the author of *Law, Violence and Sovereignty among West Bank Palestinians* (Cambridge University Press 2006), based on fieldwork carried out amongst West Bank Palestinians during the second *intifada*. He has also published on rights claims, identity documents, and forced migration. His current research interests include law and development, the legal recognition of suffering, and techniques of identification. He received a PhD in Anthropology from the London School of Economics in 2003, and has previously worked at Birzeit University, the LSE and Oxford University.

LISA J. LAPLANTE is Legal consultant for Liberated Innocents in Lima, Peru, and Deputy Director at Praxis Institute for Social Justice. Since 2002, she has followed Peru's political transition and her observations covering different topics related to transitional justice and human rights, appear in *Human Rights Quarterly*, *Yale Human Rights and Development Law Journal*, *Michigan Journal of International Law*, *Health and Human Rights: International Journal*, among others. She focused on the Inter-American System and Peru in the article 'Bringing Effective Remedies Home: the Inter-American Human Rights System, Reparations, and the Duty of Prevention' (*Netherlands Human Rights Quarterly* 2004).

SALLY ENGLE MERRY is Professor in Anthropology at the Institute for Law and Society at New York University. She was the Marion Butler McLean Professor in the History of Ideas and Professor of Anthropology at Wellesley College. She is the author or editor of six books, including *Colonizing Hawai'i: the Cultural Power of Law* (Princeton University Press 2000), which received the 2001 J. Willard Hurst Prize from the Law and Society Association, and *Human Rights and Gender Violence: Translating International Law into Local Justice* (Princeton University Press 2006). Her work focuses on the anthropology of law, colonialism and transnationalism. She is past-president of the Law and Society Association and the Association for Political and Legal Anthropology.

JELENA TOŠIĆ is a Lecturer in the Department for Social and Cultural Anthropology at the University of Vienna. Her doctoral thesis was concerned with 'Global Rights and Local Contexts: Human Rights and Globalization in the Postsocialist Transformation of Serbia and Montenegro' (2005). She is the author of 'Beyond the False Dilemma between Nationalism and Reform-Democracy' which appeared in *Cultural Dynamics of Globalization*, edited by Johanna Riegler (Austrian Academy of Sciences 2005).

FILIPPO M. ZERILLI is Lecturer in Cultural Anthropology at the University of Cagliari. His research interests include the history of anthropology, postsocialism, property relations and the ethnography of law and human rights. He is author of *Il lato oscuro dell'etnologia* (CISU,

Rome 1998) and editor of *Dalle 'Regole' al 'Suicidio'. Percorsi durkheimiani* (Argo, Lecce 2001). He has co-edited *Incontri di etnologia europea. European ethnology meetings* (ESI, Naples 1998) and *La ricerca antropologica in Romania* (ESI, Naples 2003). He is currently finishing a book provisionally entitled *Diritti postsocialisti. Etnografia della restituzione della proprietà in Romania.*

ABBREVIATIONS

ADAD	Association des Avocats de la Défense auprès du Tribunal pour Rwanda
ASP	[UN] Assembly of State Party
ARVs	anti-retrovival
CBO	Community Based Organisation
CEDAW	Convention for the Elimination of all forms of Discrimination Against Women
CSW	[UN] Commission on the Status of Women
DOS	Democratic Opposition of Serbia
DRC	Democratic Republic of Congo
ECHR	European Convention on Human Rights
ECtHR	European Court of Human Rights
ECOSOC	[UN] Economic and Social Council
FAO	Food and Agriculture Organisation
FIDH	Fédération internationale des droits de l'homme
IACHR	Inter-American Commission on Human Rights
I/A Court H.R.	Inter-American Court of Human Rights
IAS	Inter-American System [of human rights protection]
ICC	International Criminal Court
ICDAA	International Criminal Defense Attorney's Association
ICTJ	International Centre for Transitional Justice
ICTR	International Criminal Tribunal for Rwanda
ICTY	International Criminal Tribunal for the former Yugoslavia
ILO	International Labour Organisation
IWRAW	International Women's Rights Action Watch
IWRAW-AP	International Women's Rights Action Watch-Asia Pacific
KLA	Kosovo Liberation Army
LRA	Lord's Resistance Army

MINJUS	[Peru's] Ministry of Justice
NGO	Non-Governmental Organisation
NRC	National Resistance Council [Uganda]
NRM	National Resistance Movement [Uganda]
OAS	Organisation of American States
OTP	Office of the Prosecutor of the International Criminal Court
PIR	Plan Integral de Reparaciones
RPE	Rules of Procedure and Evidence
RPF	Rwandan Patriotic Front
SCR	[UN] Security Council Resolution
TRC	Truth and Reconciliation Commission
UAC	Ugandan Amnesty Commission
UDHR	Universal Declaration of Human Rights
UK	United Kingdom
UN	United Nations
UNDP	United Nations Development Programme
UNICEF	United Nations Children Fund
UNIFEM	United Nations Development Fund for Women
US	United States of America
VMRO	Macedonian Revolutionary Organisation
WTO	World Trade Organisation

CHAPTER 1

INTRODUCTION: THE SOCIAL LIVES OF INTERNATIONAL JUSTICE

Tobias Kelly and Marie-Bénédicte Dembour

For many years a woman could be seen sitting almost daily on the steps of the European Court of Human Rights with a placard protesting the lack of justice she had met at Strasbourg.[1] Court employees, lawyers, other applicants and members of the public would pass her without paying much attention.[2] Her presence and silent protest were tolerated as if they were part of the picture, embodying the recognition that the Court was unfortunately not equipped to ease the pain of all those who had invested their hopes in human rights law. Less tolerable for the Court was the throwing of stones at its entrance on a quiet Sunday afternoon in April 2001. The attack was rumoured to be the act of a lone, disappointed and reportedly deranged applicant. For a few days, the glass-panelled structure of the Court, intended by its architect to challenge 'the notion of law as a closed, formal and intimidating insti-tution' (Rogers of Riverside 2000: 1213), bore the physical marks of the exclusionary character of law, unable to rise to the claims of all who come before it.[3]

International Justice today is caught on the horns of a dilemma. On the one hand, international conventions, committees, tribunals and courts are proliferating as never before, seemingly holding out the promise of establishing a global order based on law, justice and human

---

[1] The editors thank Başak Çalı, Jane Cowan, Kim Coles, Emily Haslam and Simon Halliday for their insightful comments on earlier drafts of this introduction.
[2] Dembour's fieldnotes. The former Registrar of the ECtHR also refers to the woman sitting on the Court's steps (Petzold 2000: 1578).
[3] The legal philosopher Wolcher (2006) argues that the principle task of law is to distinguish between suffering that does and does not merit legal attention.

rights. On the other hand, the effectiveness and legitimacy of the institutions of international law are widely questioned – not just by politicians and academics, but also by many potential applicants. Stories such as those of the two women described in the opening paragraph are typically left unrecorded in conventional legal scholarship, dismissed as anecdotes irrelevant to the larger scheme of international law. This volume is built on a different view. We take it for granted that such experiences testify to the limits of international justice for the people directly concerned, and as such need to be reflected upon. If international justice is to be meaningful, and we are to understand the relationship between the proliferation of its claims and the widespread disenchantment with its achievements, we cannot understand it solely as an abstract moral principle or a series of legal texts. Instead we must explore how international justice is manifested and made real through complex social processes.

This collection asks how and why international justice is mobilised, understood and abandoned by concrete social actors and to what effect. International justice is as much a social and cultural process as it is a legal and political one, and it takes place at the intersection of the often contradictory practices of petitioners, litigants, bureaucrats, lawyers, victims,[4] witnesses, accused, judges and third parties. The title of this volume is adapted from Hazel Genn's book *Paths to Justice* (1999), which examines how ordinary people view, relate to, and either use or do not use civil justice mechanisms in the United Kingdom. Genn asks why people turn to law, which strategies they adopt in doing so, and what they want out of the process (see also Nader 2002). This volume extends Genn's questions to the sphere of international justice, exploring them through nine case studies of various international judicial or quasi-judicial institutions, conducted through anthropological fieldwork or socio-legal analysis. In doing so the book examines why people – applicants and defendants, but also bystanders and officials – choose to turn to (or avoid) international justice and what they expect from it. Understanding how people relate to international justice *must* inform our understanding of international justice. If its aim is to guide political and social life, how people access and receive international justice must be of fundamental concern to everybody, including the most black-letter lawyer and abstract political scientist.

---

[4] The term 'victim' is problematic, not least in that it may be taken to deny agency (Hirsch 2007; Clarke, this volume).

UNDERSTANDING 'INTERNATIONAL JUSTICE'

The expression 'international justice' can be understood in a variety of ways. In the first instance, its appearance in the title of this volume signals our intention to examine processes of adjudication which happen in structures set up by international law. This does not mean that we are not interested in the other ways in which the expression is used, including a sense of political and moral accountability, or the possibility of a distinctively post-national order.[5] Indeed we think the latter two senses are of crucial importance for an appreciation of how the institutions of international law develop, are given meaning and take purchase in people's lives. But we also believe that international justice, however broadly conceived, only takes shape in the context of the seemingly prosaic settings which are therefore put at the heart of this volume. We have restricted ourselves to studying international human rights and international criminal courts (a term which we use broadly to cover both judicial and quasi-judicial institutions).[6] Before we explain why we feel entitled to do so, we present a brief history, primarily intended for the non-lawyer, of the way these courts have developed.

For centuries, international law was widely understood as concerned with relationships between states – and states only. Individuals were denied the ability to make direct claims. This conception of international law prevailed virtually unchallenged for centuries. It is present in works historically as distant as Grotius' *On the Law of War and Peace* and Oppenheim's *International Law*, first published in 1625 and 1905 respectively. It was only with the development of the human rights regime after World War II that the individual started to be in a position to *directly* defend individual interests under international law (McCorquodale 2006).[7] With its mention of human rights for all, the adoption of the Charter of the United Nations (UN) represented a key

---

[5] Such considerations are rarely examined under the term 'international justice'. Favoured expressions include 'global justice' (Pogge 2001; Nagel 2005), justice 'beyond borders' (Caney 2005), 'justice without borders' (Tan 2004) and 'cosmopolitan justice' (Hirsh 2003). For an appearance of the term 'international justice', as we use it in the first instance in this volume to refer to international courts and tribunals and without restricting it to international *criminal* justice, see Lauterpacht (1991).

[6] Thus, we have not sought contributions dealing with international adjudication concerned for example with more economic matters, such as the European Court of Justice or the WTO system of dispute settlement.

[7] Cowan's contribution (this volume) shows, however, that the League of Nations' minority petition procedure paved the way for this individual encounter with international law, since it allowed anyone – individual or group – to submit a petition. Admittedly, this was very circumscribed – considered as it was as 'information only' and thus not seen as an individual

watershed. It was soon followed by the proclamation of the Universal Declaration of Human Rights (UDHR) on 10 December 1948 and, in time, the adoption of the two UN Covenants and another four human rights conventions.[8] The European Convention on Human Rights, signed in 1950, constituted the first so-called 'regional' system of human rights protection and proved a model for subsequent American and African initiatives. In parallel to the post-World War II development of international human rights law, a revolution in the way international criminal law is conceived was instigated by the Nuremberg and Tokyo trials. The treaties which established the Nuremberg and Tokyo tribunals at the end of the war allowed the prosecution of individual Nazis and Japanese before international military courts for war crimes, crimes against peace and crimes against humanity (Taylor 1992). This unique historical experience was revived in the 1990s when international criminal law suddenly developed in an unexpected way: first two ad-hoc international criminal tribunals were established in respect of the former Yugoslavia and Rwanda, and then the Rome Statute adopted in 1998 gave way to the establishment of the International Criminal Court.

In 1945, there was only one international court: the International Court of Justice, established by the UN Charter to decide cases brought by a state against another state.[9] In stark contrast, multiple international courts exist today. On the human rights front, there are the European Court of Human Rights, the Inter-American Court of Human Rights and the African Court on Human Rights and Peoples' Rights. There are also quasi-judicial institutions, such as the committees established to monitor the six UN human rights treaties.[10] In terms of international criminal law, there are currently two ad-hoc tribunals, the International Criminal Tribunal for the former Yugoslavia

---

Footnote 7 (cont.)

    litigation – but at the time, the treaty-bound states saw it as violating precisely this foundational idea that only states had the right to 'speak' in the international arena.

[8] International Covenant on Civil and Political Rights (1966); International Covenant on Economic, Social and Cultural Rights (1966); Convention on the Elimination of Racial Discrimination (1966); Convention on the Elimination of all forms of Discrimination Against Women (1979); Convention against Torture (1984); Convention on the Rights of the Child (1989). For an excellent black-letter law introduction to international human rights law, see Smith 2003.

[9] The International Court of Justice is a successor to the Permanent International Court of Justice, established in 1920 through the League of Nations.

[10] Other courts, such as the European Court of Justice (established to rule on what was originally called European Economic Community matters), are also sometimes listed amongst the international courts which deal with human rights issues.

and the International Criminal Tribunal for Rwanda. The Special Court for Sierra Leone established in 2002 was soon followed by further 'hybrid' courts that similarly mixed international and national elements in Cambodia, Ethiopia, Kosovo and East Timor (Orentlicher 2003; Romano, Nollkaemper and Kleffner 2004). Most striking of all perhaps is the International Criminal Court (ICC) established in the Hague in 2002 (Schabas 2001; Glasius 2006).[11]

The proliferation of treaties, tribunals and courts has gone hand in hand with increasing disenchantment, perhaps inevitable given the various high hopes invested in international justice. Academic critiques of the principles and practices of international law are of course long standing (see, for example, Charlesworth and Chinkin 2000; Kennedy 2004; Koskenniemi 2005; Anghie 2006). However, further critiques are emerging. While the end of the cold war seemingly heralded a new world order based on human rights, in practice the 1990s and the new millennium have been marked by as much violence and suffering as previous decades. The existing architecture of international criminal and human rights law is facing new challenges in the shape of the invasion of Iraq, the War on Terror and the increasing number of states who have signed bilateral opt-outs with the US over the ICC. This has seen powerful voices calling for the complete reordering of international law. For many others, the existing order has already been overcome by the economic and political self-interests of a few powerful states. In the meantime violence and impunity seem set to continue in Sudan, the Congo, Iraq and elsewhere in the world, as those mechanisms that do exist seem unable to respond. In this context, although an increasing number of claims are made in the name of the justice of international law, many people, including many making these claims, are deeply sceptical about its possibilities.

At a formal level, human rights and criminal courts are very different institutions. International human rights courts typically adjudicate upon complaints brought by individuals against states; the applicant is the victim of the alleged human rights violation and seeks 'reparation'.

[11] It is worth stressing that these international courts have all been set up under international law, but in different ways. To give only a few examples here, the European Court of Human Rights was established in 1959 according to the provisions of the European Convention on Human Rights which was open for signature in 1950 to any state belonging to the Council of Europe and thus subscribing to its ideals; the two ad-hoc tribunals were created in 1993 and 1994 respectively by a UN Resolution from the Security Council adopted under Chapter VII of the UN Charter as a means of maintaining international peace and security; the Independent Special Court for Sierra Leone was established following an Agreement in 2002 between the UN and the Government of Sierra Leone.

By contrast, an international criminal court exists to decide whether an individual is guilty of the (most serious) crimes which he/she is alleged to have committed; the case is brought by the prosecution in order to achieve punishment. In a human rights trial, the defendant is a state; in a criminal trial the defendant is an individual. Understandably, the procedures which are followed, including the standard of proof which is required, do not stem from the same philosophy in one type of tribunal as in the other. In the eyes of many lawyers, international human rights law and international criminal law are so different – both in the aims which they pursue and the methods which they follow – that they hardly belong to the same family. This fundamental difference between these two types of international law (not to mention others such as international environmental law, the law of the sea, international economic law, private international law) has resulted in a legal practice and scholarship which often relates to either one or the other, but seldom embraces both.

It is clear, however, that both human rights law and international criminal law have emerged from a similar concern: protecting people against abuses perpetrated by states. Some commentators have gone so far as to suggest that the recent evolution in international criminal justice is the direct result of the failure of the post-World War II human rights regime to deliver protection (Lattimer 2003: 387). This approach implicitly recognises that the two 'separate' areas of international law share a common set of political and philosophical assumptions about the nature of justice, sovereignty and responsibility. Furthermore, and perhaps most importantly for most people around the world, the two forms of international law are inseparable, both sociologically and politically.[12] This, we think, amply justifies treating them together, or at least alongside each other, in this volume.

INTERNATIONAL JUSTICE AS A SOCIAL PROCESS

International criminal law and international human rights law are not just part of some order that exists above and beyond the 'local', but are inherently given shape and meaning in specific local contexts. The dominance of anthropologists in this volume should therefore be

[12] The confusion between international human rights and criminal law is a daily fact in the media. For example, Alex Duval Smith describes the ICC as 'the first permanent home for international human rights justice' in *The Independent* on 10 November 2006 (in an article entitled 'Warlord in court over use of child soldiers in Congo').

particularly welcome given their discipline's commitment to long-term empirical analysis and close observation of social interaction through fieldwork. Suspicious of gatekeepers or social brokers who claim to represent the whole society, anthropologists are interested in exploring the multiple tensions and layers which form social processes. As Hastrup has argued, the specific contribution of anthropologists often expresses itself in ethnographies of 'the unsaid' (2003: 30). Central to this approach is an emphasis on the unexamined undersides and complexities of legal claims. In doing so anthropologists have sought to examine not only how legal claims are often invested with multiple and often contradictory normative assumptions, but can also be used instrumentally in ways not imagined by the framers of the law. Such an approach allows us to confront the sense that the law is the only way of dealing with political and economic conflicts. It also allows us to challenge the assumption that a case ends with a legal decision, by examining the unforeseen social consequences of legal processes.

The focus on the locally embedded meanings of legal claims has resulted in numerous empirical studies of the implications of human rights claims on the ground (see, for example, Wilson 1997). However, the emphasis on human rights as an interpretative process has also resulted in a tendency to ignore the material and institutional location of human rights claims, let alone the processes of international – both human rights and criminal – adjudication. Legal claims do not just exist out there in a neutral normative space to be freely interpreted and used, but rather take shape in the context of unequal social and political relationships. Treating human rights as whatever people say they are ignores the history of institutional and political attempts to produce human rights texts and to impose particular authoritative readings. As Strathern has argued, what might be called the 'empirical approach' to the study of human rights reproduces a particular – western derived – conception of the autonomous individual (2004). Such approaches are in danger of treating individual claims as existing prior to the social relations within which they are constituted.

This volume focuses specifically on institutions of international justice. Whilst bringing a long-standing anthropological sensitivity to specificity, texture and context, it recognises that not all voices are equal in the creation of international law. The implications of the claims of a judge sitting in Strasbourg at the European Court of Human Rights (ECtHR) or of a UN official in Geneva are very different from those of a peasant farmer in Guatemala or a homeless labourer in Delhi.

A particular focus on institutions can serve to highlight social, political and cultural inequalities. It is, after all, in courts (a term which we have already said we use in a broad sense) that legal claims are given legitimacy (or not), defined and made real. It is also there that alternative interpretations are overruled and 'official' lines are created. An emphasis on such processes allows us to keep an eye on the particularities of international human rights and international criminal law as a very specific path to justice. This does not mean that we should treat places such as the European Court of Human Rights or the International Criminal Tribunal for Rwanda (ICTR) as unitary operations, with hegemonic cultures or omnipotent powers (see Coles 2007). Their boundaries are always porous, their projects incomplete and their goals contested. The personnel and experts who staff international courts cannot be assumed to share the same justice project – they may have different goals and assumptions. At the same time, international bodies are far from autonomous entities, but interact in complex ways with the interests of states, activist organisations and also individual actors (Rajagopal 2003; Keck and Sikkink 1998). It is therefore crucial to view the institutions of international law, not merely as abstract entities, but as complex social processes.

Social scientists often seem reluctant to study the technicalities of the law. In contrast, the contributors to this volume seek to engage directly with positive law. In their exploration of international justice as a social process, they refer to cases, they cite law, they quote legal authorities. They do so in order to illuminate wider social processes by reference to the significance of the particularity of the law. What lawyers say and do structures the conditions of possibility for political and social action (Riles 2001; Latour 2004). Such an approach forces us to recognise the specificity of legal processes and demands that we do not treat law as simply another normative frame among many. However, not everything can be said in the language of law, and not everything can be done through legal means, creating important limitations and constrictions for those who make claims upon it.

This volume is an invitation for legal scholars to acknowledge the unseen, the unsaid and the unexpected meanings and consequences of legal processes, and for social scientists to explore how the technical, the institutional and the formal shape the possibilities of international justice. The book is divided into three parts which each contain three chapters (which admittedly could often belong to either of the other two parts of the book). The first part pays attention to various paths which

lead towards and away from international judicial or quasi-judicial institutions. These paths can be smooth, indirect or dead-ends. Whatever
the case, they involve a variety of social actors and organisations which
stretch far beyond courts and lawyers. The second part examines
how and why these paths lead to something which is called the 'international', and the implications this has for all those subject to its force
or for those who rely upon its protection. It asks what difference it
makes, if any, that the procedures are said to be 'international', rather
than national or local. The third part is concerned with the multiple
notions of justice which may be said to be involved in these processes.
Adopting a view of justice as a contested and constantly negotiated
concept, it stresses that justice is often invoked but rarely defined.

THE MANY PATHS TO INTERNATIONAL JUSTICE

One of this volume's central messages is that the paths to and from
international justice take many forms. People turn to international
courts for multiple reasons. As we shall demonstrate, these sometimes
have very little to do with the formal aims and objectives of adjudication. Moreover, access can never be taken for granted. It depends on
local political configurations and struggles, within which states, political movements and non-governmental organisations (NGOs) can play
important roles. Once the judicial or quasi-judicial process is legally
activated, experiences are shaped by social actors well beyond those
directly involved in the setting up or running of the formal institution.
The wider implications of the resulting institutional decisions, rulings
and actions are sometimes unpredictable, being misunderstood, sub-
verted or instrumentalised in particular local settings. The institutions
of justice therefore exist at the intersection of multiple and often contradictory processes, involving different and sometimes irreconcilable
senses of justice.

The first contribution we present in this volume is by Cowan, who
examines the minority supervision system devised at the League of
Nations in the 1920s. The point of departure for the paper is a spate of
petitions submitted to the League's Secretary-General concerning the
fate of the so-called 'Bulgarian minorities' in post-World War I Europe.
Intriguingly the 'failure' of these petitions was entirely predictable,
given that they had been submitted beforehand, more or less in the
same form, without success. Cowan is interested in why these 'impenitent complainants' continued submitting almost identical petitions

over and over again, despite clear advice given by League Minorities Section officials to alter their format and content. She finds an answer by placing these actions in their larger social and political context. Drawing on evidence from non-legal sources, including pamphlets and newspapers, she argues that the petitions were politically successful, from the perspective of the petitioners, in stirring nationalistic sentiments and in drawing attention to what the petitioners regarded as the failure of the international system to render justice to the suffering Macedonian Bulgarians living in Greek and Serbian lands.

There are three reasons to open the volume with this contribution. Firstly, Cowan's focus is on the League of Nations, the precursor to the current international system examined by the other contributors. Secondly, Cowan explicitly puts to the fore the question of what the success or failure of international justice may mean, a question central to this volume. Thirdly, she explores the interests and strategies of petitioners – thus addressing a key issue in the development of anthropology of law and social-legal studies more generally, namely litigants' roles and perspectives (Nader 2002; Moore 2005: 352–3). In doing so, Cowan grapples with the details of judicial (or rather, to be precise, quasi-judicial) procedures of litigation, but without limiting her analysis to a legal framework. She not only studies the fate of particular individual petitions but also questions the way the League has long been remembered as a 'failed' institution. This leads her to distinguish between two levels of success/failure. On the one hand, the petitioners she talks about failed in a narrow technical legal sense but succeeded in their broader aim of spreading propaganda and even undermining the League. Failure in one sphere produced success in the other. On the other hand, the almost universal image of the League as a historical failure does not acknowledge its success in laying the ground for future attempts to go beyond state sovereignty: without the precedent of the League of Nations, the United Nations system simply would not have been born. The two levels of Cowan's analysis are crucial, for they indicate that we must look beyond narrow institutional configurations if we wish to understand how international justice takes effect and is given meaning on the ground.

The importance of understanding the institutions of international justice in a broad context is taken up in an altogether different vein by legal scholar Haslam. Her paper offers an understanding of how international law is created, in all its specificity. Imagining that the answer lies exclusively in men who wear suits, represent governments and sign documents in official buildings is short-sighted. Haslam argues that we must consider the impact of civil society, here understood as agents acting outside the traditional state-derived frameworks of international law. To make her case, she discusses the interests, motivations and impact of two groups who, without necessarily being litigants or *amici curiae*,[13] have come in direct contact with the International Criminal Tribunal for Rwanda, either because they were called to testify or because they represented defendants or were defendants. She traces how associations speaking for these two groups have contested the way the ICTR works, forcing it to revise its methods and rules and, in turn, influencing the development of international law. Haslam's contribution complements the literature exploring how international NGOs play a crucial role in transforming notions of justice and creating new forms of accountability (Keck and Sikkink 1998; Duffield 2001; Rajagopal 2003). Its novelty lies in the fact that her paper stresses how the actions of small, locally based associations, not normally regarded as repositories of power, can be closely connected to the development of *actual* rules found in international law. Even though the associations and actors she talks about have no formal legitimacy to adjudicate or to develop international law, and are accordingly bypassed in accounts of sources of international law, they directly influence the paths of international justice.

The next contribution in the volume, by Tošić, is concerned not so much with the paths which lead towards international justice as with those that lead away from it. Based on anthropological fieldwork, Tošić's paper examines how the Milošević trial at the International Criminal Tribunal for the former Yugoslavia (ICTY) in the Hague, which was broadcast live on Serbian TV, was received back 'at home'. Tošić thus leaves aside the figures (litigants, lawyers, witnesses, judges or decision-makers) who directly feed into the process of making international adjudication happen, in order to explore how the ICTY process was understood in Serbia. She documents how attempts to make international justice 'transparent' through daily television broadcasts of the judicial proceedings taking place at the Hague created their own senses of conspiracy (compare West and Sanders 2003). The errors, procedural problems and omissions of the tribunal, part and parcel of any legal proceeding but usually hidden from view, were all too obvious

---

[13] *Amici curiae* are submissions by a party who is neither an applicant nor a defendant and who is allowed by the court to present information and opinions on a point of law or another aspect of the case.

to those watching. Instead of the tribunal being a grand theatre of truth, the ICTY was reduced to a day-time soap opera. For those who did take the tribunal seriously, the daily presence of the trial on their screens was testament to the collapse of international justice into a form of victor's justice through its hijacking by specific interests, rather than the neutrality of international governance. The very attempts to make the process transparent therefore added to a sense of a wider conspiracy to impose collective guilt on the Serbs. Rather than encouraging people to come to terms with the abuses and war crimes committed during the wars in the former Yugoslavia, the tribunal has deepened divisions within Serbia, and even fuelled Serb nationalism. Tošić is very careful not to lay the blame for the reception of the Tribunal at the doors of the Tribunal itself, but rather seeks to explore how Serbian understandings of the ICTY have been produced through conflicts between local elites.

International justice, then, does not start at the court's door nor end with a decision, judgment or recommendation. To discuss international justice meaningfully, we must always ask who is involved in it, as well as why, where and when, rather than envisaging what it is and does in the abstract. International justice operates on a ground produced by multiple overlapping and conflicting coalitions and networks, where states, international organisations, NGOs and other actors all play an important role in shaping the possibilities for action and inaction. As international justice is invoked, understood and takes hold, it is produced through competing political agendas and normative claims, explored further in the second and third parts of this volume.

CONSTITUTING THE 'INTERNATIONAL'

'The International' is the second theme we explore in this volume. We capitalise the term in its first use (only) in order to draw attention to the fact that it is commonly conceived as being 'above' the national. This sense of transcendence also means that the international is often seen as the ideal place to deliver justice, representing universal and non-partisan values. In opposition to this view, we stress that the international does not stand above anything else, at least not in an immanent or disincarnated way: international justice is enmeshed with national and local processes, legally, politically and socially. As such, the international is not one constant phenomenon. For example, the multiple international courts that now exist have been established in very different historical conditions and according to various legal methods, affecting their aims and the ways they function. It cannot be assumed that the European Court of Human Rights is equivalent to the Inter-American Court of Human Rights (I/A Court H.R.), is equivalent to the ICC, is equivalent to the Convention for the Elimination of all forms of Discrimination Against Women (CEDAW) Committee. One site of international justice is not another. The contributions to this volume treat the international as a form of political imagination that is always rooted in specific institutional and political contexts, even when gesturing beyond the here and now and aspiring to some form of transcendence.

One of the central consequences of the assumption that the 'international' exists in a higher sphere is that many people perceive it as being better placed to deliver justice than the national. Symptomatic of this trend is for example the fact that much socio-legal scholarship on human rights law treats the international as given. The common focus on *implementation* of international law into the national arena (Risse, Ropp and Sikking 1999; Halliday and Schmidt 2004) takes it for granted that the international exists in a separate superior domain. One edited collection, for example, examines 'the linkages in domestic contexts that support the acceptance of international norms' (Schmidt and Halliday 2004: 4) assuming that the international is of superior quality, without having demonstrated or even questioned this proposition. With reference to international criminal law, anthropologist Wilson (2005) has persuasively argued that international courts such as the ICTY are able to produce historical accounts which are not tainted by nationalism and efforts towards nation-building. Without denying that politics are at play in international justice, Wilson puts forward the idea that these politics are of a different nature from those one would find on the domestic scene. Others are less convinced by the value of international justice. For example, Stover and Weinstein (2004) have criticised the two ad-hoc tribunals for having been set up in geographical, cultural and linguistic remoteness from the regions of conflict in which the crimes to be tried had taken place, thus being largely counterproductive in effecting change 'at home' (see also Tošić, this volume).

The first contribution to the second part of the volume also challenges the guiding role of the international. Legal scholar Çalı specifically offers her essay as an interrogation about the presumed added value of having a judicial system which is international in character. She focuses on the European Court of Human Rights's resort to the doctrine of the margin of appreciation, through which national states are deemed better placed – to the extent of the margin of appreciation granted them – to assess what local circumstances require. The application of this doctrine often allows the Court to find that the European Convention on Human Rights (ECHR) has not been violated. It does so without forcing the Court to spell out whether this is *either* because of due respect for state sovereignty *or* because of the absence of a normative consensus. The former motivation would be based on a functional conception of the Court's role linked to a 'society of states' logic; the latter on substantive concerns inspired by (in this case, the absence of) cosmopolitan ideals. By failing to clarify which of the two logics it adheres to, the Court risks being seen as strengthening state control rather than transcending national sovereignties. To illustrate this argument, Çalı discusses the case of *Leyla Sahin v. Turkey* in which the applicant complained that she could not wear a headscarf at University. The European Court simply deferred to the arguments of the Turkish Constitutional Court in support of the ban of the headscarf, without taking into consideration (and a fortiori responding to) either the experience of the applicant or the political debate which the ban had caused in Turkey – leading the President of the European Court to visit Turkey to explain to the national authorities why their state had not been found in violation of the European Convention. Çalı concludes that the Court was unable to contribute anything to the debate raging at the national level.

The next contribution also seeks to challenge the idea that the international is a uniquely promising model of justice but does so in a different vein. Anthropologist Clarke focuses on the politics of the complex relationship which developed (and will no doubt continue to develop even after this volume is published) between international, national and local actors in relation to the international prosecution of crimes which were committed in Uganda by the Lords' Resistance Army. Her case study documents how the proceedings initiated by the ICC against people accused of crimes sideline local notions of justice (see also Ratner and Bischoff 2004; Allen 2006). She interrogates the notion of victim which is at the heart of the ICC's concepts and practice, and denounces it for denying agency, consciousness and humanity. As Clarke explains, the ICC has jurisdiction only if crimes are not prosecuted at the national level. The relationship between the international and the national is therefore seen as one of complementarity. This assumes there is a 'natural harmony' of judicial interests between the national and the international in the protection of victims. Clarke demonstrates that such an assumption is not warranted. In Uganda, ritual ceremonies where the perpetrator acknowledges wrongdoing and offers compensation have emerged as an alternative attempt to deal with the crimes committed by the Lords' Resistance Army. Alongside national laws declaring amnesty, such attempts at reconciliation have made the retributional path of the ICC deeply controversial. While some international (and local) actors are adamant in their demand for the ICC to override national amnesties, other local (and international) actors see the way forward for the region and the country as being through local rituals and national amnesties.

Without wishing to romanticise the setting up and effects of the 'traditional' atonement rituals, Clarke finds it crucial to question the neutrality and universality which the ICC model claims for itself. To do so, she relies on Agamben's understanding of sovereignty and his figure of the 'homo sacer'. For Agamben (1998), homo sacer has 'bare life' in that he can be killed with impunity without his death having any sacrificial value; the sovereign is the person 'who decides the state of exception' by being able to suspend the rule. In Clarke's analysis, the ICC wants to suspend the Ugandan way of doing things (through amnesties and reconciliation rituals) and to impose its own rule. Thus, victims are not allowed to act, interpret and exercise legal power in their own right (other than testifying in legal proceedings when called upon). Instead of being recognised as political agents, they are treated as docile beings that need to be saved by the West; the Rule of Law thus serves to perpetuate exclusion. Clarke does not call for the ICC to be disbanded, but she presses for Africans to be given back their sovereignty by expanding the basis within which we locate political beings, including not only victims but also perpetrators of the Ugandan conflict. Her argument is not one about moral or cultural relativism; it is a historical and political point about the relative power of those who are involved in the writing of international law.

Universal claims are historically and politically located; seemingly global emancipatory narratives always express particular experiences and interests. For example, while asserting to declare the universal rights of mankind, the UDHR, proclaimed in 1948, embodied a particular vision of humanity, politics and sociability, to which non-western states (many of which remained colonised at the time) hardly contributed. Contrary to the mantra of international law, the national politics which create the international are not played by equal and sovereign states (Simpson 2004; Cowan 2007). Such inequalities have enormous implications for the way international human rights law and international criminal law develop. This is a theme that runs through Merry's contribution, which focuses on the UN CEDAW. Merry analyses CEDAW's mechanism of enforcement, which mainly consists in a monitoring process whereby state parties must submit reports to the Committee established by CEDAW.[14] She points out that some states say, not wholly unconvincingly, that they do not have the necessary resources to submit – let alone defend – their report to the CEDAW Committee. She also stresses that NGO participation in the process is almost exclusively the preserve of organisations which are big, North-based and mainstream (conservative); small, South-based and/or leftist NGOs tend not to be able to participate. Furthermore, Merry remarks that members of the Committee are chosen in a way which ensures a formal representation of the various regions of the world, but without any attention being paid to the representation of various socio-economic, cultural and religious backgrounds. Not surprisingly, therefore, those who work for CEDAW are found to share a similar outlook in terms of social class, education and cosmopolitanism. They do not conceive of the international as a mosaic of different cultural practices but by reference to an agenda which can be described as an expression of secular global modernity.

Any sense of the over-arching transcendence of international justice should be seen as the product of specific local concerns and political conflicts. The international, like all claims to justice, is always located in concrete localities. As Cowan shows in this volume, for example, the international order established by the League of Nations was the direct concern of a relatively small number of bureaucrats. What is it, then, that gives the sense that the international hovers above the local or the national? To answer this question we wish to transpose to the international Wastell's argument (2001) that the global is above all a language and practice of scale. The very claim that the international stands above the local/the national is the product of what might be called the 'urge to measure', and thereby creates a hierarchical distinction between forms of action. Yet, all such practices are concretely grounded and there is no bird's eye view from which to appreciate the supposed difference of scale. The global claims of international law should therefore be seen as a series of circulating localities (Merry 2006).

---

[14] Merry does not examine as such the way the CEDAW Committee has started to deal with individual complaints, a function which became open to it when CEDAW's optional protocol came into force in 2000. What she says is nonetheless directly relevant to the quasi-judicial work which the Committee can now do – as well as to international justice more generally.

THINKING ABOUT JUSTICE

The third part of the volume is about justice, which we approach as an essentially contested concept. Our position is that justice is always embedded within specific social relationships rather than being the product of an abstract set of principles derived from an ahistorical human nature. In our view, no model of justice can ever be attained in an absolute and uncompromising way.[15] This inevitably posits law in an awkward and controversial relationship with justice. As Haslam argues in this volume, taking her cue from Derrida, the ultimately unobtainable nature of justice runs up against the finality of legal determinations. Law can never provide justice, precisely because justice is always just beyond reach, part of a project that is never ending. This does not mean, however, that law has nothing to do with justice. Many of the people who work in the institutions of international law, who make claims upon it, or are subjected to its force, make considerable investments in trying to bring law and justice closer together. How then are we to understand the justice (or injustice) of international judicial processes?

Lawyers tend to assess justice by reference to retributive, restitutive and reparative functions, associated with different areas of law.[16] They commonly evaluate international justice on the basis of the goals publicly stated for the courts in the preambles of the treaties which establish them and in the case law they develop (Swaak-Goldman 1997; Beresford 2001; Meernik and King 2001). However, along with others, lawyers also often subject the practice of international law to critiques based on extra-legal ethical or political principles (Barria and Roper 2005; Nsanzuwera 2005). This is not surprising: justice refers not only to (relatively) narrowly defined legal aims but also to broad political and social aspirations related to accountability, stability, fairness and economic distribution, to cite but a few.

In practice, lawyers, officials, victims, defendants and other actors often invoke contradictory combinations of all these aspects of justice

---

[15] Our position is therefore in direct contrast to that expounded by Rawls in his highly influential *A Theory of Justice* (1973). Rawls argues, for example, that: 'Justice is the first virtue of social institutions, as truth is of systems of thought . . . truth and justice are uncompromising' (1973: 3–4). He also writes: 'law and institutions no matter how efficient and well-arranged must be reformed or abolished if they are unjust' (ibid.) suggesting both a possible test on whether justice is achieved and a faith that law can be just.

[16] In the field which interests us, criminal law, human rights law and 'transitional justice' mechanisms such as national truth commissions, respectively.

in the course of their claims. As such, the contributors to this volume are committed to produce an analysis of justice attentive to the full complexity of the claims made by people directly or indirectly involved in international adjudication processes. They seek to understand the meanings and implications of the claims of those who invoke international justice. However, paying attention to their desires and fears does not necessarily mean siding with their aims and objectives. It is not difficult to imagine situations where scholars would feel impelled to distance themselves from the claims of the people they study. Without going so far, Haslam expresses, for example, some reservations about the demands made by the activists whose actions she traces at the ICTR. The potential pitfalls of ethical nihilism involved in cultural relativism are well learned (Dembour 2001).[17]

Several contributors to this volume directly engage with the normative assumptions, aspirations and consequences of international legal regimes. Some implicitly express their support for them. For example, Merry celebrates the cultural success that CEDAW has achieved in altering the meanings of gender and of state responsibility for gender equality. This is not to say that she is unaware that CEDAW's commitment to universalism is controversial. Citing Fanon, she even suggests that the idea of civilisation which CEDAW embodies can be read in a postcolonial framework. Nonetheless, she overall supports the cultural conversion which she sees CEDAW having initiated towards gender equality (see further Merry 2006). By contrast, other contributors are highly critical of both the substantive premises on which international human rights and international criminal law are built, and the ways in which international judicial institutions meet the needs and desires of the people who make claims on them. One striking example is Clarke, who refers to the excluding effect of the universalist language deployed around the International Criminal Court, which not only compromises the national amnesties and reconciliation rituals set up in Uganda but more importantly fails to treat victims as social/political beings. Still other contributors to this volume are more or less silent about their own ethical commitments. This is entirely justifiable, for empirical research has a value in and of itself, and should not be reduced to the demands of normative interrogation (Jean-Klein and Riles 2005). However, at

---

[17] This is so even though anthropologists are often taken by non-anthropologists to be adamantly relativist (Engle 2001). Such a description of the discipline is somewhat of a caricature as anthropologists increasingly engage politically with human rights claims (Scheper-Hughes 1995; Goodale 2006).

the same time, the empirical issues that we choose to research are themselves underlined by ethical concerns, and seemingly abstract philosophical questions are also often motivated by pressing political or social issues. The line between description and prescription should not be drawn too sharply (Cowan 2006).

The ubiquity of human rights claims and international criminal prosecutions may make them appear as mere instrumental attempts to gain advantage in particular disputes. Yet, even seemingly pragmatic claims can be shot through with complex normative assumptions. In the first contribution to the third part of this volume, Zerilli and Dembour describe one such situation, relating to the case of *Brumărescu v. Romania* before the European Court of Human Rights. The case was the first in which the ECtHR ruled against a postsocialist state in relation to claims arising from the expropriation of property by the previous regime. What could be considered a 'thick description' of the house at the centre of the case leads Zerilli and Dembour to examine how the dispute resonated with hopes and fears concerning the post-socialist transition, kinship relations and the nature of responsible citizenship. Although for many Romanians *Brumărescu v. Romania* was emblematic of wider disputes between would-be self-interested capitalists and tenants, for the claimant the case revolved around his memories of the family home and his idea of what it takes to be a 'good Romanian', whereas for the ECtHR the issue was primarily one of due process. Whilst the European Court's judgment became a symbolic resource in local and national politics, it failed to provide any closure either to the dispute concerning the ownership of that particular house or to the issue of property restitution in Romania more generally. Like Çalı, Zerilli and Dembour conclude that the Court's involvement did nothing to appease the situation. This is particularly interesting given that the Court found a violation of the Convention in this case, as opposed to remaining seemingly uninvolved in the national situation by simply applying the doctrine of the margin of appreciation.

In the next contribution to this volume, Laplante describes a situation where the interaction of international and national processes creates a conflict between claims to justice, albeit in an unexpected way. Writing in the context of attempts to come to terms with over twenty years of brutal civil war, Laplante describes how the work of the Peruvian Truth and Reconciliation Commission (TRC) was supported by the Inter-American System of human rights protection (IAS). She argues that the decisions of the IAS concerning human rights violations in Peru created a form of political consciousness that helped to strengthen local and national claims to restitution. Furthermore, the Peruvian state voluntarily complied with the various decisions adopted in its respect by the Inter-American Commission and Court of Human Rights as part of an attempt to show that it had re-entered the democratic community of nation-states. However, Laplante identifies a tension between the international and the national processes. The IAS, operating according to the individualistic concerns of human rights, granted reparation to victims at a level far above what a national programme of reparations, instigated by the Peruvian TRC and constrained by wider social concerns of economic sustainability, can envisage. The expected result, namely sharply divergent levels of reparation awarded by the two systems, are thoroughly unacceptable within the legal paradigm, offending the key principle of equality before the law. Laplante is left perplexed by the inequalities that the two-track justice paths are likely to produce for victims of human rights violations in Peru. However unsatisfying she finds those, she nonetheless does not question overall, and indeed seems to celebrate, the general principles of international human rights law.

In stark contrast, the final contribution to this volume is *fundamentally* critical of the paradigm of international human rights law. An anthropologist, Buckler focuses on five cases before the ECtHR concerning the rights of Gypsies in the UK to maintain a family life in the face of their eviction by local government officials from land they owned. The Court ruled that the interference with their right to a family life was justifiable in a democratic society due to wider planning considerations. Basing her argument on long-term ethnographic fieldwork, Buckler suggests that the Gypsies she worked with in England (2006) would say that the judgments of the European Court fail to recognise their own sense of humanity, therefore making a mockery of the concept of human rights. She argues that their sense of morality is rooted in known social relationships, rather than in the imagined structures of the state. Extended families, consisting of members who actually meet each other, provide the ground for all moral decision-making. In this context, the Court's implicit assumption that family life is reducible to relationships developed in the home is unacceptable. Buckler's chapter, then, is a fundamental critique of international human rights courts, the ECtHR being only one of its particular manifestations. Through a nuanced and ethnographically informed analysis of a particular form of social agency, Buckler finds that human rights law cannot live up to its promise of protecting moral agency in all its forms. She urges a move away from a legalistic conception of human rights to one which can adequately address multiple forms of socially embedded moral agency.

All eleven contributors to this volume share a focus on multiple and socially embedded claims to justice. Such an approach allows a middle ground between a narrow legal interpretation of justice that would limit claims to what legally 'is' and a perhaps more philosophical approach to justice that would focus on the 'ought'. This approach avoids narrowly predetermining the nature of justice, whilst always rooting justice within broader political and social constraints. The volume also represents an invitation to bring together, and go beyond, two approaches to international justice. The first approach, characteristic of much (though not all) legal and political scholarship, asks how judicial institutions match up with more general legal or political principles. Such forms of analysis are valuable but are in danger of ignoring the fact that international justice comes about through people turning to it, making it necessary to study what goes on beyond the confines of the courtroom. The second and more anthropological approach explores how people understand international law in specific local contexts. Again, such analysis is important, not least because it is in an excellent position to highlight that there is no singular definition of (legal) justice. However, it tends to ignore how rights claims typically get expressed through institutional configurations. In this way, the chapters gathered in this volume seek to bridge legal and anthropological expertise in order to explore the meanings, implications and limitations of international justice on the ground.[18]

REFERENCES

Agamben, Georgio. 1998. *Homo Sacer: Sovereign Power and Bare Life*. Daniel Heller-Roazen, trans. Stanford: Stanford University Press.

Allen, Tim. 2006. *Trial Justice: The International Criminal Court and the Lord's Resistance Army*. London: Zed.

Anghie, Anthony. 2006. *Imperialism, Sovereignty and the Making of International Law*. Cambridge: Cambridge University Press.

[18] One contribution sees an anthropologist and a lawyer working together. Some contributors are anthropologists who were specifically invited to apply their expertise to the field of international justice, which was new to them. Lawyers who are participating in this volume were asked to stress the social dimensions of their material.

Barria, Lilian and Steven Roper. 2005. How Effective are International Criminal Tribunals? An Analysis of the ICTY and the ICTR. In *International Journal of Human Rights* 9(3): 349–68.

Beresford, Stuart. 2001. Unshackling the Paper Tiger: the Sentencing Practices of the Ad Hoc International Tribunals for the Former Yugoslavia and Rwanda. In *International Criminal Law Review* 1: 33–90.

Buckler, Sally. 2006. *Fire in the Dark: Telling Gypsiness in North East England.* Oxford: Berghahn.

Caney, Simon. 2005. *Justice Beyond Borders: a Global Political Theory.* Oxford: Oxford University Press.

Charlesworth, Hilary and Christine Chinkin. 2000. *The Boundaries of International Law: a Feminist Analysis.* Manchester: Manchester University Press.

Coles, Kimberley. 2007. *Democratic Designs: International Intervention and Electoral Practices in Post-War Bosnia-Herzegovina.* Ann Arbor: University of Michigan Press.

Cowan, Jane K. 2006. Culture and Rights after Culture and Rights. In *American Anthropologist* 108(1): 9–24.

2007. The Supervised State. In *Identities: Global Studies in Culture and Power* 14(5).

Dembour, Marie-Bénédicte. 2001. Following the Movement of a Pendulum: Between Universalism and Relativism. In *Culture and Rights: Anthropological Perspectives* (eds.) J. K. Cowan, M.-B. Dembour and R. A. Wilson. Cambridge: Cambridge University Press.

Duffield, Mark. 2001. Governing the Borderlands: Decoding the Power of Aid. In *Disasters* 25(4): 308–20.

Engle, Karen. 2001. From Skepticism to Embrace: Human Rights and the American Anthropological Association from 1947–1999. In *Human Rights Quarterly* 23(3): 536–59.

Genn, Hazel. 1999. *Paths to Justice: What People Do and Think About Going to Law.* Oxford: Hart.

Glasius, Marlies. 2006. *The International Criminal Court: a Global Civil Society Achievement.* Abingdon: Routledge.

Goodale, Mark. 2006. Introduction to 'Anthropology and Human Rights in a New Key'. In *American Anthropologist* 108(1): 1–8.

Halliday, Simon and Patrick Schmidt (eds.) 2004. *Human Rights Brought Home: Socio-Legal Studies of Human Rights in the National Context.* Oxford: Hart.

Hastrup, Kirsten. 2003. Representing the Common Good: the Limits of Legal Language. In *Human Rights in Global Perspective: Anthropological Studies of Rights, Claims and Entitlements* (eds.) R. Wilson and J. Mitchell. London: Routledge.

Hirsch, Susan F. 2007. *In the Moment of Greatest Calamity: Terrorism, Grief, and a Victim's Quest for Justice.* Princeton: Princeton University Press.

Hirsh, David. 2003. *Law Against Genocide: Cosmopolitan Trials.* London: GlassHouse Press.

Jean-Klein, Iris and Annelise Riles. 2005. Anthropology and Human Rights Administrations. In *Political and Legal Anthropology Review* 28(2): 173–202.

Keck, Margaret and Kathryn Sikkink. 1998. *Activists Beyond Borders: Advocacy Networks in International Politics.* Cornell: Cornell University Press.

Kennedy, David. 2004. *The Dark Sides of Virtue: Reassessing International Humanitarianism.* Princeton: Princeton University Press.

Koskenniemi, Martti. 2005. *From Apology to Utopia. The Structure of International Legal Argument.* Cambridge: Cambridge University Press.

Latour, Bruno. 2004. Scientific Objects and Legal Objectivity. In *Law, Anthropology and the Constitution of the Social* (eds.) A. Pottage and M. Mundy. Cambridge: Cambridge University Press.

Lattimer, Mark. 2003. Enforcing Human Rights through International Law. In *Justice for Crimes Against Humanity* (eds.) M. Lattimer and P. Sands. Oxford: Hart.

Lauterpacht, Elihu. 1991. *Aspects of the Administration of International Justice.* Cambridge: Grotius Publications.

McCorquodale, Robert. 2006. The Individual and the International Legal System. In *International Law* (ed.) M. Evans. Oxford: Oxford University Press.

Meernik, James and Kimi King. 2002. The Effectiveness of International Law and the ICTY: Preliminary Results from an Empirical Study. In *International Criminal Law Review* 1: 342–72.

Merry, Sally Engle. 2006. *Human Rights and Gender Violence: Translating International Law into Local Justice.* Chicago: University of Chicago Press.

Moore, Sally Falk. 2005. Certainties Undone: Fifty Turbulent Years of Legal Anthropology, 1949–1999. In *Law and Anthropology: A Reader* (ed.) S. F. Moore. Oxford: Blackwell.

Nader, Laura. 2002. *The Life of the Law: Anthropological Projects.* Berkeley: University of California Press.

Nagel, Thomas. 2005. The Problem of Global Justice. In *Philosophy and Public Affairs* 33(2): 113–47.

Nsanzuwera, François-Xavier. 2005. The ICTR Contribution to National Reconciliation. In *Journal of International Criminal Justice* 3(4): 944–9.

Orentlicher, Diane F. 2003. Striking a Balance: Mixed Law Tribunals and Conflicts of Jurisdiction. In *Justice for Crimes Against Humanity* (eds.) M. Lattimer and P. Sands. Oxford: Hart, 213–35.

Petzold, Herbert. 2000. Epilogue: La réforme continue. In *Protecting Human Rights: The European Perspective. Studies in Memory of Rolv Ryssdal* (eds.) P. Mahoney, F. Matscher, H. Petzold and L. Wildhaber. Köln: Carl Heymans Verlag.

Pogge, Thomas W. (ed.). 2001. *Global Justice*. Oxford: Blackwell.

Rajagopal, Balakrishnan. 2003. *International Law from Below: Development, Social Movements and Third World Resistance*. Cambridge: Cambridge University Press.

Ratner, Steven R. and James L. Bischoff (eds.). 2004. *International War Crimes Trials: Making a Difference? Proceedings of an International Conference held at the University of Texas School of Law, 6–7 November, 2003*. University of Texas School of Law.

Rawls, John. 1973. *A Theory of Justice*. Oxford: Oxford University Press.

Riles, Annelise. 2001. *The Network Inside Out*. Ann Arbor: University of Michigan Press.

Risse, Thomas, Stephen Roppe, and Kathryn Sikking (eds.). 1999. *The Power of Human Rights: International Norms and Domestic Change*. Cambridge: Cambridge University Press.

Rogers of Riverside, Lord. 2000. The Design of the Palais des Droits de l'Homme. In *Protecting Human Rights: The European Perspective. Studies in Memory of Rolv Ryssdal* (eds.) P. Mahoney, F. Matscher, H. Petzold and L. Wildhaber. Köln: Carl Heymans Verlag.

Romano, Cesare, Andre Nollkaemper and Jann Kleffner. 2004. *International Criminal Courts: Sierra Leone, East Timor, Kosovo and Cambodia*. Oxford: Oxford University Press.

Schabas, William A. 2001. *An Introduction to the International Criminal Court*. Cambridge: Cambridge University Press.

Scheper-Hughes, Nancy. 1995. The Primacy of the Ethical: Propositions for a Militant Anthropology. In *Current Anthropologist* 36(3): 409–20.

Schmidt, Patrick and Simon Halliday. 2004. Introduction: Socio-Legal Perspectives on Human Rights in the National Context. In *Human Rights Brought Home: Socio-Legal Studies of Human Rights in the National Context* (eds.) S. Halliday and P. Schmidt. Oxford: Hart.

Simpson, Gerry. 2004. *Great Powers and Outlaw States: Unequal Sovereigns in the International Legal Order*. Cambridge: Cambridge University Press.

Smith, Rhona Howard K. M. 2003. *Textbook on International Human Rights*. Oxford: Oxford University Press.

Stover, Eric and Harvey M. Weinstein (eds.). 2004. *My Neighbor, My Enemy: Justice and Community in the Aftermath of Mass Atrocity*. Cambridge: Cambridge University Press.

Strathern, Marilyn. 2004. Losing (out on) Intellectual Resources. In *Law, Anthropology, and the Constitution of the Social: Making Persons and Things* (eds.) A. Pottage and M. Mundy. Cambridge: Cambridge University Press.

Swaak-Goldman, Olivia. 1997. The ICTY and the Right to a Fair Trial: A Critique of the Critics. In *Leiden Journal of International Law* 10: 215–21.

Tan, Kok-Char. 2004. *Justice Without Borders: Cosmopolitanism, Nationalism and Patriotism*. Cambridge: Cambridge University Press.

Taylor, Telford. 1992. *The Anatomy of the Nuremberg Trials*. New York: Alfred A. Knopf.

Wastell, Sari. 2001. Presuming Scale, Making Diversity: On the Mischiefs of Measurement and the Global/Local Metonym in Theories of Law and Culture. In *Critique of Anthropology* 21(2): 185–210.

West, Harry and Todd Sanders (eds.). 2003. *Transparency and Conspiracy: Ethnographies of Suspicion in the New World Order*. Durham: Duke University Press.

Wilson, Richard (ed.). 1997. *Human Rights, Culture and Context: Anthropological Perspectives*. London: Pluto.

Wilson, Richard Ashby. 2005. Judging History: The Historical Record of the International Criminal Tribunal for the Former Yugoslavia. In *Human Rights Quarterly* 27(3): 908–42.

Wolcher, Louis. 2006. Universal Suffering and the Ultimate Task of Law. In *Windsor Year Book of Access to Justice* 24: 361–99.

PART 1

PATHS . . .

CHAPTER 2

THE SUCCESS OF FAILURE? MINORITY SUPERVISION AT THE LEAGUE OF NATIONS

Jane K. Cowan

For the half century since the descent into war in 1939, few writers dissented from the popular verdict that the League of Nations' minorities regime, like the rest of the Great Experiment in international governance, had calamitously failed.[1] Pundits, practitioners and scholars alike portrayed the 1948 Declaration of Human Rights as a product of a rupture. Historians of human rights, if mentioning the League regime at all, referred to it briefly and ambivalently. Dutifully devoting a few sentences or a few pages to 'antecedents' of the current human rights system, they praised the League regime as pioneering before condemning it for giving too little – or too much – voice to minorities, for its imposed and non-universal character, for its lack of 'teeth' and its gross exploitation by the Nazis.[2] By the mid-1990s, however, post-socialist upheavals and the emergence of new nationalisms in eastern Europe, on the one hand, and on the other, a global burgeoning of political mobilisation around identity and culture were prompting a spate of reassessments.[3] 'Revolutionary,

[1] I thank the participants in the Sussex workshop, especially Başak Çalı, Marie Dembour and Toby Kelly, as well as Keith Brown, Laurie Kain Hart, Antigoni Papanikolaou and one anonymous reviewer, for helpful and stimulating comments on the original draft. I also gratefully acknowledge the support of the John D. and Catherine T. MacArthur Foundation, the Princeton Hellenic Studies Program, the British Academy–Leverhulme Foundation and the University of Sussex for the larger research project.
[2] In Steiner and Alston's (2000) impressive tome of 1,497 pages, a standard teaching text on human rights, just over three pages are devoted to (an excellent) summary of the minorities protection scheme, and an additional sixteen pages to one case study from that era, (Greek) 'Minority Schools in Albania'. Many accounts offer less (see, e.g., Donnelly 1993: 6, Henkin 1990: 14–15).
[3] See, for instance, Maier 1992; Berman 1993; Buwalda 1994; Fink 1995; Finney 1995; Kymlicka 1995; Cornwall 1996; Herman 1996; Mazower 1997; Jackson Preece 1998.

unequalled and underestimated', pronounced one (Herman 1996: 49), articulating an emerging view that – its flaws notwithstanding – the League minorities regime might teach us a thing or two about international management of contemporary minority conflicts.

I, too, take issue with the premises of the argument of 'failure': with the idea that the League institution in its entirety merits such summary disdain. I am perplexed by the spirit of the question several times posed to me when presenting my research at conferences: why was I spending (read: wasting) my time studying, as one interlocutor phrased it, 'one of the greatest failures of the twentieth century'? These are remarkably undiscriminating rejections of a historically unprecedented, multifaceted, contradictory, long-standing and evolving political institution. More importantly, they beg key questions such as what 'failure' means, and what precisely marks, and takes the measure of, this failure.

How does one break out of this repetitive-compulsive line of questioning, which offers only the choice of endorsing or repudiating the adequacy of an international mechanism?[4] I wish here to up-end the tables: to reorganise the furniture of thinking about political and legal processes at the international level within the wider history of claims-making. 'Failure' is my conceptual *agent provocateur*, enabling me to ask: failure at what? For whom? From whose perspective? Focusing on the minority petition procedure – an innovative and highly contentious element of the League of Nations minority protection scheme – with respect to the region of Macedonia, I have two overarching aims. First, I intend to trace out an emergent socio-political space of governmentality of the 1920s and 1930s, one that hovered between the 'legal' and the 'political', and that was constituted through relations between international institutions, states and an increasingly visible and voluble transnational 'public sphere'. The minority petition procedure, I argue, constituted an unprecedented political encounter that radically challenged the state-centric premises of international relations and that cleared the ground for individual citizens' engagement in a universal human rights regime after 1948.

My claim rests on a reframing. Whereas most scholarship on the minorities regime has focused narrowly on the rather constrained, if much contested, institutional procedure that structured the encounter, I insist that the wider extra-institutional context constitutes something

---

[4] Admittedly, a few scholars have posed the question starkly only to define a 'middle' position of mixed success: see especially Robinson et al. 1943, Azcárate 1948.

more than just 'a (socio-political-historical-cultural) *context*'. It needs to be conceived as a *public space* in dynamic interaction with the League *institutional space*. This is essential, not least because this wider, extra-institutional public space is where specific audiences for – and potential respondents to – petitions were located. Thus, my second aim is to demonstrate that an enlarged definition of the space where petitions and claims circulated – a space that was not only transnational, but was constituted by the point of overlap of varying social, legal and political fields and divergent social and cultural codes – enables us to grasp in a fuller sense the multifarious aims and strategies of petitioners vis-à-vis the international institution. As I will argue, petitions that 'failed' might, by that very failure, be rendered 'successful' in the eyes of those who submitted or supported them. Taking into account the wider space where claims and petitions circulated, and thus their longer-term 'career', we are compelled to reconceptualise the pragmatics of claims.

AN EMERGENT SPACE OF GOVERNMENTALITY

Keenly aware that 'persecuted minorities' had too often been the cause or pretext of conflict between states, the Committee on New States at the Versailles peace negotiations after the Great War stipulated that certain states – newly established, significantly expanded or allied with the losing side and, significantly, *not including* any 'Great Power' – agree to be bound by minorities treaties or agreements. Such agreements confirmed the civil and political rights of individual members of 'racial, linguistic and religious minorities' as well as offering certain special rights, relating to language, education and local autonomy. This was not the first time that minorities had been protected by treaty; previous agreements, however, were bilateral, involving an external 'protector' state. With the Versailles treaties, protection of minorities was made a matter of international concern and responsibility. While treaty-bound states (dubbed 'minority states' by some analysts, see Claude 1955, Fink 1995) undertook to fulfil their obligations to minorities, the soon-to-be-created League of Nations was charged to 'guarantee' the treaties.

How this was to work, the Covenant did not spell out. A small team of former national civil servants who had been active in Inter-Allied war efforts, including the Frenchman Jean Monnet (eventual founder of the European Community), the Anglo-Scot Sir Eric Drummond (Secretary General of the League in its first decade) and his American colleague, Raymond Fosdick, established the design and working practices of the League of Nations Secretariat, 'the only permanent element to this organisation' (Monnet 1978: 83). The Secretariat was at first a remarkably modest operation, given its huge remit: in December 1919, when the Secretariat was moved from London to Paris (in autumn 1920, it would move again, from Paris to Geneva) the entire business of the Council (nine states) and Assembly (forty-seven states) depended on a Secretariat staff of twenty (Monnet 1978: 86). An 'Administrative and Minorities Section' (normally referred to as the Minorities Section) was directed by the Norwegian diplomat, Erik Colban, initially with a staff of two 'officials' (civil servants): one responsible for the minorities treaties, and a second for 'administrative commissions', that is, territories such as the Saar and Upper Silesia, and the city of Danzig (now Gdansk) where two states shared jurisdiction with international supervision. In 1924, by which time fifteen states had signed minority agreements, the Section's director plus three officials, a secretary and two stenographers, handled all matters relating to the minorities treaties.[5]

As the archives of the Minorities Section indicate, this bureaucratic unit was involved in a wide and varied range of activities related to state-minority relations and to the international community's engagement in situations of potential or actual conflict. Memoranda document regular meetings between Section officials and diplomats of treaty-bound states, as well as between Section officials and representatives, community leaders or advocates of minorities; the files reveal extensive written correspondence as well. Apart from their work in Geneva, the Director of the Minorities Section, Erik Colban, normally accompanied by one of his staff, would visit the capitals of treaty-bound states to discuss minority issues with both government officials and minority representatives. Such visits could take up to six months of each year (Codding 1966). 'Experts' on the language or culture of a minority were sometimes consulted, though they also offered unsolicited reports and advice. European (especially British) travellers submitted reports of refugee camps they had visited, or of the general conditions in which refugees lived; these were duly filed, as were newspaper cuttings on, for instance, revolutionary assassinations and state reprisals, or inter-state disputes, culled from the region's national

---

[5] States with minority agreements in 1924 were: Albania, Austria, Bulgaria, Czechoslovakia, Estonia, Finland (in respect of the Aaland Islands), Greece, Hungary, Latvia, Lithuania, Poland, Romania, Turkey, Yugoslavia and Germany (in respect of Upper Silesia).

presses, particularly those newspapers addressed to the European public and thus published in French or German. The Minorities Section advised, kept tabs on and administratively supported several 'mixed commissions' involved in supervising state-organised population movements: the Greco-Bulgarian Reciprocal and Voluntary Emigration (a protocol of the 1919 Treaty of Neuilly) and the Greek-Turkish compulsory exchange of populations (agreed in the 1923 Treaty of Lausanne). In the course of these myriad activities, the Minorities Section developed an impressive knowledge of the minority situations under their supervision, as well as considerable power within the League institution as advisers, mediators and gatekeepers.

Among these activities, probably the most important – at any rate, the most extensively studied – concerned so-called minority petitions. The mechanism by which the League would 'supervise' each individual treaty-bound state's satisfactory fulfilment of its treaty obligations was initially codified by a committee led by the Italian delegate to the League Council, Mr Tittoni, presented in the 1920 'Tittoni Report'. The essential principle of 'the minority procedure' was this: although only a Member of the League Council (by definition, a state) could make a formal protest ('seize the Council' and 'raise an infraction') against an accused state, *anyone* – an individual, a state, an organisation, a group speaking as or on behalf of a minority – could communicate information to the League regarding an alleged violation of the treaty. The letters submitted were, in League parlance, 'petitions'.

Introducing the option to petition and allowing citizens a potential voice *against* their own or another state, the Tittoni Committee transgressed established, well-nigh sacred norms of statecraft in which only states could participate in inter-state relations. The anthropologist Lucy Mair, familiar with the League minority regime through her work with the Oxford classicist and internationalist Professor Gilbert Murray, captures the enormity of the innovation:

> [With the minority petition] in certain countries a section of the population has a right of appeal – though this appeal is not invariably heard – not possessed of the majority of subjects of that State, to an authority outside and above its own government. This is the greatest abdication of sovereignty which has been made by an independent State. (Mair 1928: 28)

The novelty of this mechanism, and its profound, though still vaguely grasped, implications for state/inter-state/citizen relations, caused consternation and confusion in equal measure. Matters of fierce debate were the nature of the petition and the minority procedure it poten-tially prompted. Was the procedure legal or political? What should it be? The Tittoni Committee articulated a 'statist' view, defining the pro-cedure as 'political', rather than 'legal'. It regarded the petition 'as infor-mation only', 'a report, pure and simple'. Authors of petitions could not be considered as plaintiffs or claimants undertaking a legal challenge; as the Council decreed from the start, and upheld over the first decade, 'minorities had no legal personality and were not parties to a suit but could only act as agents of information' (Dandurand 13 June 1929, cited in Stone 1931: 78, fn. 3). While the informational status of the petition rendered the identity of the person submitting it immaterial, this did not stop treaty-bound states from attempting to restrict who should, and who should not, be deemed valid petitioners or from objecting vociferously when petitions were forwarded to them. Many petitioners, for their part, addressed their petitions to the League of Nations Secretary General as appeals to universal justice, demanding adjudica-tion by an international court. And not a few internationalists argued that the minority protection system would have teeth only if it were generalised, and minority violations placed under the remit of the Permanent Court of International Justice.

The procedure was thus the object of strenuous contestation within League contexts throughout the entire decade of the 1920s. Sensitive to the challenge to their sovereignty that minority treaties entailed, treaty-bound states struggled to keep the minority procedure as res-trictive as possible, with narrow interpretation of treaty obligations and minority rights, demands that petitions fulfil stringent require-ments for precision, civility and rationality of wording and attempts to limit the right of petition to 'loyal' minorities only. Conversely, revisionist states (e.g., Bulgaria, Hungary and Germany), along with certain transnational organisations and individuals (including the Women's International League of Peace and Freedom, the Congresses of European Nationalities and Professor Gilbert Murray) argued for a broader interpretation of minority protections. They demanded, moreover, a universal system of minority rights and protections for *all* state members of the League, a Permanent Minorities Commission and similar monitoring bodies at the state level. Although the nar-rower approach won out, in favour of treaty-bound states and the notion of state sovereignty generally, the League Council, in a series of procedural revisions negotiated over the course of the decade, agreed certain concessions to minorities, as well as greater public accountability on the work of the Minorities Section in relation to petitions (League of Nations 1929). Moreover, in exceptional cases, minority treaty infractions were ultimately brought before and judged by the Permanent Court of International Justice.

RECEIVING PETITIONS

A notable feature of the new governmentality was the unprecedented power and influence, and often the recognised authority, of the international civil servant in terms of the actual day-to-day workings of minority protection. In many ways, this authority was of a piece with the changing role of administrators within political institutions at this historical moment, an element of the changing constellation of modern power theorised by Max Weber (Gerth and Wright Mills 1946). Administrators helped to consolidate state power – as their predecessors in the Hapsburg and Ottoman bureaucracies had, before them, maintained imperial power (with varying degrees of success) – while simultaneously becoming its exemplary agents. The League civil servant and his practices also illustrate well Michel Foucault's concept of power/knowledge, where power depended on knowledge (in this case, on the Minorities Section officials' growing 'expertise') yet the gathering and formulation of that knowledge was reliant on – produced through – specific structures and strategies of power (Foucault 1991). Characteristically, the nature and extent of international civil servants' power was not directly acknowledged by those working within the League system. In terms of the explicit justifications of the formal system, the Minorities Section officials' jurisdiction was held to be extremely and precisely limited. All petitions addressed to the Secretary General were to go to the Minorities Section and be examined by its officials for 'receivability'. In principle, this examination was meant merely to ensure that petitions conformed *in their form* to the criteria; it did not involve an evaluation of the petition's *substance*. As my research shows, in fact, Minorities Section officials did more than simply guarantee acceptable form; they also played a very substantial role in guiding the procedure, as well as determining the fate of specific individual petitions (see Cowan 2003).

In order to be forwarded to the relevant government for comment, a petition had to meet five conditions of 'receivability'. The conditions, published in the national presses of all League members, stipulated that petitions:

1. must have in view the protection of minorities in accordance with the Treaties;
2. in particular, they must not be submitted in the form of a request for a severance of political relations between the minority in question and the State of which it forms a part;
3. must not emanate from an anonymous or unauthenticated source;
4. must abstain from violent language;
5. must contain information or refer to facts which have not recently been the subject of a petition submitted to the ordinary procedure.

Setting conditions for petitions is normal practice today, as in the past. Applications to the European Court of Human Rights, for instance, are required to meet criteria of 'admissibility'. In the case of the League minority treaties, the rationale behind the conditions was to prevent a flooding of the Council by individual petitions, as well as to prevent petitions from being used for 'propaganda'. My investigations into the bureaucratic treatment of petitions pertaining to alleged minorities treaty violations in the southern Balkans, especially with respect to the region of Macedonia, have revealed that Section officials approached their task of examining for 'receivability' with great creativity, negotiating deftly between states and petitioners in pursuing their own, increasingly confident, sense of legality and justice (Cowan 2003).

In the remainder of this chapter, I want to explore a chance remark, a note of exasperation smuggled into a Minorities Section official's memorandum on one petition, and the line of speculation it has spurred for me on the ways some petitioners may have used the minority petition procedure. In a nutshell, the remark points to a practice whereby petitioners submitted, over and over again, without substantial revision and often without even minor revision, petitions that they would almost certainly have known were bound to 'fail', while disregarding advice that would enable them to 'succeed'. This puzzling practice, by no means confined to a single instance or organisation, has prompted me to wonder whether petitioners – and, importantly, those who encouraged and supported petitioners, and used the petition process that petitioners had set in motion – necessarily always *wanted* those petitions to 'succeed'. Assuming that petitioners were not intentionally self-defeating, how can we make sense of their actions? What, for them, actually constituted 'failure' and 'success'? Returning to the claim of 'failure' with which this chapter began, I wish to turn it on its head and ask, provocatively: might failure have been a means to succeed? This leads me to questions that Marie Dembour identified in her invitation to the Sussex workshop upon which this volume is based, when she drew on Hazel Genn's (1999) work on ordinary people's views about and relations to the UK justice system and suggested they were relevant for our explorations of paths to *international justice*. They are similarly transposable to the League context. Thus, we may ask: what led people to use the League petition procedure? What did they expect from the League of Nations in general, and its minorities regime in particular? Who wrote petitions and why?

IMPENITENT COMPLAINANTS

Let us start by considering some relevant excerpts from the League bureaucrats' commentary on two petitions.[6] The first petition was submitted by the Sofia-based *L'Union des Organisations des Emigrés Macédoniens*.[7] This was a union of national organisations, each of which was itself composed of smaller local organisations established in various countries in the Balkans, Europe and North America by immigrants from Macedonia.[8] The Union submitted the petition on behalf of a group of associations under its aegis, *Les Associations Macédoniennes de Bienfaisance*, which claimed to represent 300,000 emigrés.[9] Dated 2 September 1924, it is comprised of the resolutions passed by an exceptional congress held by these associations, convened 17 August 1924. Section officials, occupied with this petition for a full two months between 14 September and 13 November 1924, have found it troublesome: it contains important – in their view, serious and plausible – allegations of treaty violations, yet it is marred by formal inadequacies, making it, as a whole document, non-receivable. The officials are exploring with the Secretary General various potential strategies, including whether it might be possible to forward *portions* of the

---

[6] French and English were both in use within the Secretariat and its documents, although French was the official language of all inter-state agreements. All translations from French to English are mine.

[7] The Union of Macedonian Emigrant Organisations. File R1659, 41/38716/11974.

[8] The Bulgarian national chapter alone was composed of eighty-seven societies and brotherhoods. See file R1659, 41/35314/11974.

[9] Macedonian Beneficial Associations. On 4 September 1924, two days after the Union, as umbrella organisation, had conveyed the MBA's petition to the League Secretariat, the MBA sent the same set of resolutions from their congress to the Secretary General. File R1659, 41/38715/11974.

petition, which in themselves meet the receivability requirements, to the accused government. In the extensive and detailed comments in the circulating file, involving the Director of the Section, two officials from the Minorities Section, one from the Political Section and the Secretary General, it emerges that this organisation has submitted previous petitions. In his comments of 24 October, the Secretary General, Sir Eric Drummond, notes that

> there is another important and very detailed petition on the same subject, which we have referred back to the petitioners, explaining the reasons for which it had at present to be rejected, but suggesting a shape in which it could be received. If that petition returns to us in a different form, it is an infinitely more adequate document than the one at present under consideration.

This being an internal memorandum where background knowledge was assumed, the Secretary General did not specify the date or reference of this 'very detailed petition'. We can nonetheless glean several things from his comment. First, the bureaucrats are noticing a certain amount of repetitiveness in the petitions being submitted and thus they are scrutinising them carefully for 'any new allegations', which would prevent the petition being turned down on the basis of the fifth condition. Second, the Secretary General's comments are evidence that, well before the procedural reforms of 1929 when the Council instructed the Minorities Section to inform petitioners when petitions were deemed non-receivable, including communicating those conditions of receivability (Jackson Preece 1998: 82, League of Nations 1929: 19, 21–2), the Section officials were already taking the initiative, at their own discretion, to guide petitioners toward revisions that would facilitate their petition's acceptance. The comment also records the officials' resourceful approach to ensuring that petitions containing significant information that, in the Section's view, states should address, were not always or necessarily barred by problems of 'form'.

The commentary on the second petition alludes to this ongoing dialogue among officials and petitioners. The Twelfth Congress of an organisation, also based in Sofia, called *Organisation des Exilés et des Refugiés de Thrace en Bulgarie*, in correspondence dated 17 November 1927, forwarded a letter to the Secretary General, accompanied by the resolutions passed by the congress.[10] Summarising (in French) the

---

[10] Organisation of Exiles and Refugees from Thrace in Bulgaria. File R1695, 41/63129/39349.

document at Colban's request, the Persian Minorities Section official Mr Abol-Hassan Kahn Hékime notes that it comes from 'one of the organisations of Bulgaro-Macedonian refugees living in Bulgaria'.[11] The document 'doesn't say anything new'; it has no concrete facts, Hékime remarks in exasperation. 'This document, like all which precede it, contains no information relating to recent events involving the character of a flagrant infraction of the minorities treaties. Far be it from me to suggest that things are going better, from the minorities' point of view, but the complainants are impenitent in choosing their method of presenting their grievances.' In light of all the previous, similar petitions, 'I do not see how this can be subjected to the procedure currently in force'. Rather than identifying particular examples (i.e., which might be investigated), he continues that their grievances are 'vague, imprecise and generalised'. Consequently, it is 'not even worth examining whether they meet the conditions of receivability'. The clear insinuation is that the petitioners here, like those in the first of my examples, have been advised – indeed, more than once – how they might rephrase their petitions so that they would meet the requirements for receivability. Yet they 'are impenitent' and have chosen not to. Instead, they continue (knowingly, stubbornly, Hékime implies) to submit petitions with the same form, the same kinds of wording, the same content, which repeatedly 'fail' to meet the conditions, and thus simply do not progress to the next stage of the procedure.

What exactly are we to make of this bureaucrat's irritation and where might it lead us? Should we read this as merely an expression of an institutional Orientalism – or in this case, a Balkanism of the sort that

---

[11] Strictly speaking, this was an organisation of 'Bulgarians', probably including both Greek and Turkish nationals, who had fled Thrace (adjacent to Macedonia, to the east), rather than Macedonia, and were now living as refugees in Bulgaria. However, the original political project had, in fact, pertained to the territories of both Macedonia and Thrace. Macedonia's borders had always been indistinct, historically changing and contested; as Duncan Perry notes, 'when the Ottomans conquered the Balkan Peninsula in the fifteenth century, Thrace was generally known as Macedonia, and the cities of Plovdiv (Philipopolis) and Adrianople (Odrin, Edirne) were its primary urban centers' (Perry 1988: 12). That Thrace – by the late nineteenth century seen as a distinct territorial entity – was equally an object of nationalist desire and mobilisation can be seen in the names of the first revolutionary organisations: the Bulgarian-Macedonian-Adrianople Revolutionary Organisation, and the Secret Macedonian-Adrianople Revolutionary Organisation. This remained the view of most participants in the revolutionary struggle for 'Macedonia'. Hékime is, moreover, correct in noticing that the plethora of refugee associations, whose headquarters were almost always in Sofia, had close formal and informal links. Indeed, in the view of his colleague, Pablo de Azcárate, a long-standing Minorities Section official and then Director, whatever organisation was fronting them, all of these petitions actually emanated from the Macedonian National Committee, the legal, civilian wing of VMRO, the Macedonian Revolutionary Organisation (Azcárate 1945: 50).

Todorova has identified (1997) – an index of the vast chasm separating international civil servants in sleepy Geneva from inhabitants of a Balkans in turmoil? Or, perhaps we are observing here the bureaucrat's familiar impatience with applicants and supplicants who seemingly refuse to follow the rules, along with a blinkered incomprehension that petitioners might dance to different tunes. Discursive constructions of the Balkan petitioner may play a role, yet there is another specific history behind this outburst. Only a few months earlier, and explicitly in defence of The Union of Macedonian Emigrant Organisations – authors of the first petition mentioned above, and numerous others – who are appealing fervently for justice for their suffering compatriots, Hékime had challenged what he saw as his colleagues' overzealous application of the fourth condition, of rejecting petitions 'purely and simply for a slight excess of language' (Cowan 2003: 284–6). Hékime's own passionate stance had inspired more lenient interpretations from his colleagues, complementing the already existing practice of guiding petitioners toward more acceptable wordings. Having conceded this much, Hékime's frustration is palpable. He knew he was dealing with an organisation well linked to the wider network of refugee organisations in Sofia. That wider network included active, experienced and sophisticated petitioners, some of whom had been given quite explicit advice for revising their petition. Moreover, he knew that information about the petition procedure, including the conditions of receivability, had been published numerous times in the Bulgarian press and would be known to the petitioners. On that basis, he evidently assumed that when these organisations sent in petitions that did not meet the receivability conditions and were thus bound to fail, they did so knowingly.

Taking this interpretation as at least plausible, what might explain the petitioners' apparently self-defeating practice? Petitioners' aims, as well as the use of petitions by other persons who sponsored, encouraged, supported or opposed those aims, can be understood, I would argue, only if one moves beyond the narrowly defined institutional encounter that involved solely the League Secretariat, the accused government and a particular group of petitioners.

PETITIONS AND THE NATIONALIST PRESS

Once one shifts to observing petition processes through a wider-angle lens, a much broader field of action comes into view. For petitions circulated well beyond the institutional boundaries of the League. Indeed, they routinely travelled across international borders. They were passed between compatriots of the national community, at home and in diaspora, and disseminated to a larger world public. Although petitions were conveyed from one organisation to another via the postal system, through telegrams (in abbreviated form) or hand carried by individuals visiting compatriots elsewhere, the major medium for communicating petitions was the press.

More than merely vindicating Benedict Anderson's claims for print capitalism as central in the building of national publics (1991 [1983]), the extremely lively publishing scene in Europe in the early twentieth century witnesses how important nationalists felt it was to appeal *beyond* the national community. Alongside state-owned or supported newspapers and special interest publications of various kinds, nationalist publishing operations flourished, producing 'propaganda' – a term that did not necessarily carry the derogatory overtones it has today – for their cause. In the eighteenth and nineteenth centuries, as national movements for peoples living under Ottoman and Hapsburg rule were mobilising to gain independence and establish territorial homelands, publishing operations were often funded and run by nationalist intellectuals and activists living in European cities 'outside' the imagined national homeland. Not only did publishing abroad allow freedom from the imperial authority's constraints; it allowed nationalist intellectuals easier access to the European publics that were arguably their most important audiences. By the early twentieth century, and especially after the 1919 Paris peace settlement, many 'nationalities' had achieved a national state. Even in these successful cases, advocates often saw their national project as 'unfinished'; other homeland-seeking movements – Armenians, Kurds, Jews, Macedonians – were granted nothing at all. Nationalist publishing thus continued during the interwar period, with the cities of Lausanne and Geneva, located in neutral Switzerland, as notable centres.

Nationalists' creation and deployment of print media – newspapers, bulletins, brochures, pamphlets, tracts as well as books – was probably nowhere more extensive and elaborate than in respect to the contested territories of Macedonia and Thrace. Although Serbian and Greek propaganda efforts were by no means feeble, Bulgarians were particularly energetic publicists. Underpinning the exceptional intensity of Bulgarian publishing vis-à-vis Macedonia and Thrace was Macedonia's tragic role in the Bulgarian national narrative. Bulgarian citizens as well as its statesmen saw the terms of the 1919 Paris peace treaties as shockingly punitive as well as deeply unjust. Bulgaria's role as a war-time ally of Germany, and thus a vanquished enemy state, overrode for the diplomats at Versailles its claims to territory on ethnological grounds (which were, anyway, contested by other states), and Bulgaria emerged a smaller state than Bulgarians had hoped. The boundaries of the Bulgarian national imaginary were, in fact, those of the San Stefano Treaty of March 1878, in which Bulgaria had benefited from the power of its patron, Russia, vis-à-vis the Ottoman Empire to set the terms of the peace after armed conflict between the two imperial powers. That treaty created Bulgaria as an autonomous principality within the Ottoman Empire; its borders approximated those of the medieval Bulgarian Empire, including the greater part of the Ottoman vilayets of Selanik (Thessaloniki), Monastir (Bitola) and Uskub (Skopje), the administrative units constituting the imagined entity of 'Macedonia'. These borders lasted barely four months. Alarmed at the advantages the San Stefano treaty gave to Russia, the other Great Powers protested its terms, and the chancellor of the new German Reich, Otto von Bismarck, brokered a new treaty in Berlin in June 1878. The Bulgarian Principality was massively diminished, losing most of Macedonia and Thrace. Ever since the Treaty of Berlin superseded that of San Stefano, the 'loss' of putatively 'Bulgarian' territories that legitimately 'belonged' to the nation became a leitmotif of Bulgarian national life (Barker 1950; Crampton 1983; Perry 1988). Bulgaria had tried, and failed, to recuperate these territories in the Balkan Wars, and saw its territories narrowed by the 1913 Treaty of Bucharest; Bulgarians spoke of this treaty, along with the peace settlement as articulated in the 1919 Treaty of Neuilly, as 'national catastrophes'. Within the Bulgarian national narrative, Macedonia became a metonym for all Bulgarian territory 'lost' in the struggle between Balkan states, themselves proxies for Great Power interests.

In the 1920s, Bulgarian national newspapers addressed themselves not only to Bulgarian citizens, but also to Bulgarians living abroad, including those inhabiting the 'unredeemed lands' of 'Greater Bulgaria' (now 'occupied' by Greece and the Yugoslav Kingdom). Recognising the urgency of gaining the sympathy of influential Europeans, some newspapers published in German and French. The Bulgarian government funded lavish publications on Bulgarian history, claiming to 'tell the truth' about Macedonia, in English, French and German; these were regularly distributed, via diplomatic legations, to friendly journalists, scholars and other interested parties. Such publications railed unceasingly against the iniquities of the Paris treaties. They stoked the fires of outrage among their readers by emphasising the suffering of Bulgarian compatriots in 'Bulgarian lands' under 'Serb' or 'Hellenic domination'. As we know, not least from the comments in memoranda of Minorities Section officials who regularly read them, Bulgarian publications in both Bulgarian and other European languages, such as the French-medium journals, *La Bulgarie* and *La Revue Bulgare*, carried reports concerning the Bulgarian minorities in Yugoslavia and Greece. Home to the new international institutions, Geneva newspapers also reported on the League business: the *Journal de Genève* ran a daily section on *'La Société des Nations'*, where minority issues figured prominently.

Specifically Macedonian publications also flourished during the inter-war period, publishing from many locations and for different audiences. In Sofia, *Sloboda ili Smrt (Liberty or Death)*, which was the official organ of the Macedonian Revolutionary Organisation (VMRO), coexisted with numerous other bulletins and broadsheets devoted to Macedonia, including *Makedonia*, *Avtonomna Makedonia (Autonomous Macedonia)*, *Nezavisima Makedonia (Independent Macedonia)*, *Ilinden*, and *Pirin* (later called *20th July*). Outside of Bulgaria, the Geneva-based weekly, *La Macédoine: Journal Politique Hebdomadaire (Organe du Mouvement Macédonien de Libération)*[12] was from 1924 the main organ expressing VMRO's positions. The Vienna-based *La Féderation Balkanique: Organe des Minorités Nationales et des Peuples Balkaniques Opprimés*, was estab-lished in 1924 when a leftwing faction split off from the organisation; it called itself 'VMRO United' and promoted a socialist agenda, including the Balkan Federation of its title. *La Jeune Macédoine*, oriented specifically to youth, was published in Paris. In North America, the Macedonian Political Organisation published, from offices in Indianapolis, *Macedonian Tribune*, or in its Bulgarian version, *Makedonska Tribuna*.[13]

Newspapers were a major site of information, argument and exchange for those who considered themselves Macedonian in some sense, or who were sympathetic to the Macedonian cause. In their pages, they pub-lished testimonials by prominent European and North American intel-lectuals and statesmen, editorial features, opinion pieces, letters, book reviews and, not least, petitions that had been submitted to the League

---

[12] Macedonia: Weekly Political Journal (Organ of the Macedonian Liberation Movement).
[13] The historian Joseph Roucek, author of *The American Bulgarians*, notes that, due to the demand from immigrant communities, twenty-eight Bulgarian-language newspapers had appeared in America by 1927 (cited in Michaelidis 2005: 165).

of Nations. The Geneva-based *La Macédoine*, for instance, on 7 February 1930 published one of the petitions submitted by the petitioners Anastassoff, Chaleff and Ilieff, examined in the next section. Over the next two years, they reported the submission of additional petitions, following their progress through League procedures and various confrontations between the Council Committees of Three and the Yugoslav state, encounters which lasted until June 1932. The Yugoslav government spokesman's commentary, examined in the next section, also alerts us to the ways that petitioners used newspapers to communicate with both supporters and adversaries before an audience of the world public.

PUBLISHED WORDS AND POLITICAL ACTS

A striking case of the Macedonian revolutionary movement's enterprising use of both the petition procedure and the press can be pieced together from documents arising from a related series of four petitions. Between January and March 1930, the Secretariat received four petitions, authored in various combinations by three prominent individuals: Dimitri Chaleff (former mayor of Skopje), Dimitri Ilieff (former judge and lawyer) and Gligor Anastassoff (lawyer and former Member of Parliament). In the first long and detailed petition 'In the Name of the Bulgarian Population of Macedonia under Yugoslav Domination', Chaleff and Ilieff declare that 'Bulgarian national minorities' living in what was officially called southern Serbia are 'subjected systematically to a violent denationalisation and assimilation', a denial of political rights, economic servitude and social misery. Among their complaints: Bulgarian churches, libraries and reading rooms are closed; Bulgarian journals are forbidden; Bulgarian cannot be spoken on the streets; singing folksongs is 'considered a crime', the endings of surnames are forcefully serbianised. Yugoslav authorities impose the Serbian 'Slava' to replace 'our own' nameday customs, and, to facilitate assimilation, even force young Macedonian women to marry Serbian gendarmes. Finally (giving some named examples) they claim that 'Macedonian intellectuals' are refused access to state services, and may be imprisoned or assassinated. The second and third petitions concern the late arrival in Geneva of Anastassoff, his passport having been delayed (referring to Yugoslav state harassment). Singly authored by Anastassoff, the second petition reiterates his association with Chaleff and Ilieff, as a legitimate representative of the Bulgarian population of Macedonia; the third, from Chaleff and Ilieff, confirms his association with them.

In the fourth, the three complain that the authorities called together a group of Macedonian intellectuals and, attempting to persuade them with threats, demanded that these intellectuals denounce the petitioners' claims. 'This', Anastassoff, Chaleff and Ilieff protest, 'is a threat against the right of petition to the League of Nations itself.'

The petitions managed to overcome the hurdle of receivability, and were forwarded to the government of the Kingdom of the Serbs, Croats and Slovenes (i.e., Yugoslavia) for comments.[14] In its reply, the accused government maintains: first, that 'no Bulgarian minority exists', thus the petitions 'bear no relation to the protection of minorities'; and second, that the petitions are worded using violent language and comprising 'insulting attacks (*attaques injurieuses*) against the Yugoslav government'.[15] Examples of phrases considered 'insulting' included: 'The Yugoslav government has resorted to measures considered everywhere else as a complete negation of current civilised and elementary notions of liberty'; and 'Macedonian intellectuals are murdered'. The government spokesman insists that 'this is clearly a malevolent propaganda against the Yugoslav Kingdom'. Thirdly, 'the questions here have been raised repeatedly' in previous petitions. His objections refer to receivability conditions 1, 3 and 5; the very existence of the government reply nonetheless indicates that the Minorities Section, supported by the Secretary General, deemed the petition 'receivable' despite these undoubtedly anticipated reactions.

Providing an extensive historical justification for his objections, the Yugoslav government spokesman points out that since 1923, when Yugoslavia increased its 'anti-terrorist actions', the National Committee (VMRO) has intensified its propaganda abroad, particularly during the years 1927–8. His argument emphasises the close interrelation between words and acts, between political rhetoric and revolutionary practice. In this period, he stresses, 'one could say that every petition was underlined by a terrorist attack', a fact that prompted severe measures in the government surveillance of national borders. He notes how, in the present case, associations supporting the Macedonian revolutionary cause used the press to commend and

[14] See Document C.242.1930.I which contains copies of the four petitions (also filed as 4/16962/166) as well as the government response. The Kingdom of the Serbs, Croats and Slovenes, sometimes referred to in League documents as 'the Serbian government' or 'the Serbian authorities', officially changed its name to Yugoslavia in 1927. Nonetheless, the documents mix both the old and the new name in describing the current government and authorities.

[15] On the significance of the condition prohibiting violent language in petitions, see Cowan 2003.

encourage the petitioners. Thus, Stanicheff of 'the Committee' sent a congratulatory telegram, which was published in the 24 January 1930 issue of the Sofia-based journal, *Makedonia*. The petitioners replied by letter, acknowledging the congratulations 'which encouraged them to fulfil their duty to the utmost'. That amicable correspondence, along with the petitioners' similarly warm response to a congratulatory telegram from 'Ilindeska', an organisation of former '*comitadjis*', was reported in issue no. 127 of the Geneva-based *La Macédoine*.[16] In the Yugoslav government's view, the enthusiastic support of the Macedonian National Committee and 'Ilindeska' stands as evidence of the petitioners' insurrectionary aims.

Further proof, according to the Yugoslav government, is provided by an article these same petitioners published in the official VMRO journal, *Sloboda ili Smrt (Liberty or Death)*, under the title 'After words, come acts'.[17] Allegedly, the petitioners have claimed that although Macedonian delegates have submitted petitions to the League of Nations, the League Council has remained silent, bowing to the pressure of the Little Alliance, linked with France. The Macedonian Revolutionary Organisation (VMRO) 'must take into consideration the manifestation of a mentality belonging to the era of Calligula or Nero, of Machiavelli or Bismarck'. Revolutionary organisations for minorities, the petitioners' reportedly insist, 'will not allow the flame to be extinguished', showing that the 'lost nationalities' are reviving themselves for their new life. 'VMRO', the petitioners are said to claim,

> has never been under the illusion that liberty will come herself, or come from outside, or will be offered generously or graciously . . . VMRO exists for this because it knows that neither one single petition, nor 101, are enough to open the eyes and ears of the proud and contented who do not want, on account of the minorities, to break their friendship with bastards like the Belgrade authorities and with other such oppressors. VMRO realises that it must speak with the songs of guns, the Gods of infernal machines, the cry of open revolution.

The Yugoslav spokesman emphasises again: words – that is, petitions – are incessantly followed by acts. He offers another example: the above

[16] *Comitadjis*, literally, 'committee members', was the term for armed revolutionaries for Macedonia; 'Ilindenska' refers to the Ilinden (St Elijah) Uprising against the Ottoman authorities in 1903, the highpoint of the Macedonian resistance.

[17] In French, '*Après les paroles viendront incessament les actes*'. To my knowledge, the publication existed only in Bulgarian; the government spokesman presumably was translating into French from the Bulgarian original.

article in *Liberty or Death* was published on 1 March; and 'the first act' occurred on 3 March in Pirot, followed by further terrorist incidents on 6 March in Kriva Palanka, and on 9 March in Stroumitza.

The Yugoslav government's report concludes with an indignant recounting of a political prank orchestrated by the petitioners in their Geneva base. Having submitted their petitions, the three men approached the bishop of the Russian Orthodox Church of Geneva, tricking him into saying a mass 'for all those killed in Macedonia since 1913' – these being martyrs for the cause of an autonomous Macedonia – then publishing the announcement of the requiem in the religious news section of the Geneva daily, *La Suisse*. Learning the histories behind the names he had blessed, the bishop was apoplectic; he would never have permitted his church to be used for political demonstrations, particularly against Yugoslavia, 'noble protector of Russian émigrés abroad'.

Such petitions formed part of the 'web of propagandas' that, the government spokesman lamented, 'was not taken into consideration by the League of Nations'. Therefore, 'while not formally contesting the receivability of the petitions' the Yugoslav government proposed to submit a memoir containing specific information 'to enlighten the Council about the situation'.

This account of Macedonian revolutionary rhetoric and action articulates the perspective of a nationalising state, disinclined to recognise the existence of – much less bestow rights upon – a 'Bulgarian minority' and intent on establishing the petitioners' association with VMRO. Yet the overall description of VMRO objectives is not in dispute. VMRO, like the Bulgarian state, never accepted the validity of the borders agreed at Versailles. Throughout the 1920s, civic organisations affiliated with one or another of VMRO's factions lobbied the League of Nations for an autonomous Macedonia (Azcárate 1945, Barker 1950). Simultaneously, VMRO aimed to demonstrate that the minorities treaties on behalf of 'Bulgarian minorities' were not only accoutrements of an unjust peace but remained unenforced due to France's unwillingness to allow any League sanctioning of the Yugoslav government. VMRO also put pressure on this population to boycott the Greco-Bulgarian Voluntary and Reciprocal Emigration (Ladas 1932: 104).[18] This protocol of the 1919

---

[18] Among the largely peasant population included under the League rubric of 'Bulgarian minorities' (*les minorités bulgares*), individuals' engagement in national questions ranged from passionate commitment to one or another nationalist project for Macedonia (be it annexation to a larger state, or some form of autonomy or independence) to utter indifference and a desire to be left alone.

Treaty of Neuilly, agreed between the Greek and Bulgarian governments, allowed 'Bulgarians of Greek nationality' to apply to emigrate to Bulgaria and acquire Bulgarian nationality (that is, citizenship), and vice versa. VMRO opposed this 'solution', since its political claims for a united Macedonia relied on the continuing residence of this population in Macedonian territory that the Organisation considered to be 'under Hellenic occupation'. In short, VMRO's success depended on the League's real – and perceived – failure. Appeals by the Macedonians, the historian Elisabeth Barker pointed out, 'even if heard, could never have been of profit to [VMRO]; if, through the League of Nations' intervention, the demands of the Macedonians of Yugoslavia and Greece had been satisfied, [VMRO] would have lost its reason for existence' (Barker 1950: 38). Whether motivated by organisational self-preservation, as Barker suggests, or a vision of social justice, VMRO had a profound political interest in drawing continuous attention to the international community's dismal, and very public, failure to render justice to the righteous and suffering Macedonians.

THE SUCCESS OF FAILURE

Putting together several kinds of evidence – the existence of a number of repetitive, virtually identical petitions in the files, a bureaucrat's irritated remark, petitions and correspondence published in the press, a government commentary on one set of petitions, related and corroborating historical documentary materials – I am arguing for a more subtle and differentiated reading of petitioners' strategies. Not all of them, I submit, would have aimed for their petition to 'succeed' within the terms of the minority procedure.

Let me be clear. League files contain numerous petitions from individuals which stem from their idiosyncratic predicaments: the undervaluing of a house and fields for which they were to be reimbursed, a desire to withdraw an application to emigrate that had previously been submitted, a complaint against the authorities or a fellow villager. There is no reason to think that these petitioners wanted anything other than a just and speedy resolution to their specific complaint. But organisations, rather than individuals, account for about three quarters of petitions in the 'Bulgarian minorities' files; their objectives could be much more complex and diffuse. Bulgarian and Macedonian civic associations based in Europe and North America, many of them closely associated with VMRO, submitted dozens of petitions.

Although some-times alleging specific acts of state violence (e.g., police brutality, unfair trials), many petitions eschewed details. They protested the suffering of the local population – whether labelled 'Macedonians', or the 'Bulgarian minorities' – linking this to the injustice of the peace treaties and the ruthlessness of the occupying authorities. They might refer to the closing of Bulgarian schools, forced expulsions of Bulgarians and the desperate conditions facing the refugees in Bulgaria. Civic associations also routinely wrote to the Secretary General, as to other international bodies, immediately following their annual or semi-annual congresses, attaching resolutions passed by the assembled membership. Painting a vivid portrait of barbarity and oppression in broad strokes, petitions and resolutions seldom listed names, dates and locations of violations that the League could investigate.

Composing, presenting, defending, negotiating and voting on resolutions at annual congresses, then recording and sending them to the League of Nations in the form of a petition: these diligent practices must have been filled, in the early days, with hope and expectation. As time passed, the intransigence of treaty-bound states reluctant to carry out minority protections would have become evident to the petitioners. Similarly, they would have noticed the unwillingness of the European powers to alter the terms of the peace treaties. Although organisations speaking on behalf of minorities, their internationalist allies and the newspaper editors and writers who supported their cause continued to demand that the League enforce the minority treaties, their faith in such a possibility must have become strained. The typically guarded way that the League Secretariat dealt with petitioners would have reinforced this sense of an ineffectual League. If Minorities Section officials occasionally wrote directly to petitioners to offer guidance designed to ensure a petition's receivability, more frequently they merely sent a formal acknowledgment of receipt that gave no indication of what was – or was not – happening behind the doors of the Secretariat.

Ironically, the sweeping rhetoric of state oppression and minority suffering that rendered such petitions ineffective within the League is precisely what was demanded outside of it. In public spaces dominated by discourses of social reform, passionate prose signalled conviction, sincerity and commitment to The Truth. Perhaps petitioners were 'impenitent', above all, in privileging the fiery language of militancy for documents that were intended to shuttle between the two domains. When circulated, published, or even just referred to, in contexts beyond the League, petitions – not least when they 'failed' – played a crucial role in a wider project of consciousness raising. They identified Macedonia and her people as victims, constructing them as a community suffering at the hands of states, in full view of an indifferent League.

As expressions of outrage at Macedonian victimisation and calls for support, petitions appealed to real or potential community members, as well as to concerned outsiders. Constructing the community of suffering, too, was both an internal process and one that depended, for its political force, on its recognition by non-members, particularly the world public. Hence, the intense efforts by Macedonian organisations to enlist the support of European and North American intellectuals, scores of whom published analyses of, or personal testimonials for, the project of Macedonian autonomy in newspapers, gave lectures or spoke on behalf of the Macedonian project at public forums all over the world (see Anastasoff 1945, Višinski 1991). Cultivating a widespread public perception of international injustice was a key strategy for advocates of Macedonia as they struggled, through various legal and illegal means, to create the conditions for the Versailles treaties to be altered, abandoned or superseded.

Failure as a tactic brings to mind other cases in our own, contemporary moment. Think of the paramilitaries and associated mafia-style small businesses in the former Yugoslavia who ensured that peace talks always broke down, since the conflict was much too profitable to be allowed to end. From Northern Ireland to Sierra Leone, Chechnya to Somalia, Peru to the Gaza Strip, various actors for various reasons have sabotaged the 'resolution' of a particular conflict (see, e.g., Ignatieff 1998, Laitin 1998). One must tread carefully here. Much recent attention in political science and international relations has focused on the allegedly novel character of post-Cold-War civil conflicts, captured in Mary Kaldor's (1999) distinction between 'old' versus 'new' wars. Research in this vein portrays 'old' civil wars as 'ideological, political, collective and even noble' and new ones as 'characteristically criminal, depoliticised, private and predatory' (Kalyvas 2001: 100). In a review of this literature, Stathis Kalyvas (2001) disputes the neat dichotomies of 'old versus new', 'justice-seeking versus loot-seeking', 'greed versus grievance' models as based on a mischaracterisation of both past and present conflicts. Insurgencies against the state, now no less than before, typically draw upon both collective and individual aspirations; deep desires for political change can coexist with coercive commandeering of resources. The more insidious danger of these debates, though, is the way they naturalise the ostensibly superior morality of existing governing arrangements: as if agents of the state never had their hands in the till, behaved criminally or themselves profited from unresolved conflict (Aretxaga 2003)! When political and religious movements use failure tactically, demanding justice while striving to ensure that such justice is always 'inadequate', this cannot necessarily be reduced to pecuniary (or other wicked and selfish) motives. It may equally constitute a bid to reframe the discourse and the power relations which place such movements at a permanent disadvantage.

THE FAILURE OF 'FAILURE'

Assertions of the League of Nation's 'failure' are perplexing not only because they are so sweeping, but because they do not even ask the simple question: failure for whom? Immediately, it is clear that the League of Nations and the minorities regime are being judged, first, from the perspective of those committed to maintaining the new postwar political order, and second, from the *imagined* (rather than carefully ascertained) perspective of minorities who, it is assumed, had *as their sole or primary aim* the protection of their rights within the terms of the framework of the new order.

Yet those whom the minorities treaties were meant to protect held widely varying views about them (see, e.g., Robinson et al. 1943). In archival papers and published accounts, one easily finds disagreements within 'a minority' – a category, we should not forget, largely constituted by the treaties – not only on strategy and tactics, but on what the minority's objectives should be. Individuals favoured everything from assimilation to secession, and all points in between. My account brings to light another duality remarked upon in the historical evidence, but seldom analysed: the double strategy of some organisations of penning a plethora of pleas for justice, while simultaneously discrediting and undermining the procedure. This requires us to reconsider what various groups using the minority procedure wanted to achieve, and to query more carefully what constituted 'success'.

The Macedonian-case example underpins several broader arguments. The first is theoretical; I have tried to show that the examination of 'paths to international justice' needs to look well beyond institutionally defined procedures and interactions, and to take account of wider social and political fields in which petitions (or in today's context, allegations of human rights violations) circulate. Submitting a petition or a formal allegation instigates not simply an institutional process, but a potentially much wider social and political conversation, one which often uses the media and which has several important, though different, key audiences. Petitioners are involved in a political performance, which may be embedded in a web of other performances, including the kinds of guerrilla theatre enacted at the Russian Orthodox Church in Geneva in 1930. These may elicit counter-performances, exemplified in the sardonic, uncompromising 'observations' of the Yugoslav government to the petitions of Chaleff, Ilieff and Anastassoff. The logic of any particular group's use of petitions will reside in a larger, perpetually evolving, strategy of political action. VMRO's objective was to construct a public perception that the Versailles peace had been unjust, and that the minorities treaties did not work. Among its own actual and potential supporters, many of whom were readers of the Macedonian press, the organisation emphasised a further message: that the community of nations constituting the League of Nations had no intention of altering the political status quo, and that violent revolution was the only means to effect change.

My second argument is historical. I am intrigued by the forgetting of continuities between the League of Nations and the United Nations within hegemonic narratives of rights and international justice. Mark Mazower (2004: 380) discerns two kinds of explanations for the emergence of a human rights regime: the 'Eleanor Roosevelt version' of noble and visionary individuals shaming resistant states, and the 'Adolf Hitler version' of world revulsion to Nazi evil. Whichever version one chooses, good triumphs: universal human rights are deemed to construct justice afresh, untainted by the League's tawdry legacy.[19] In fact, the post-1948 United Nations human rights system built on, rather than simply repudiated, League precedents, however much their logics differ. The minority petition procedure is a case in point: by establishing a space where state subjects or citizens might speak about their own state to a body of other states, it altered the character of that sphere from strictly inter-state to something more properly 'international'.

This was never going to be a conversation that could be contained within the boundaries of the League institution; the procedure, and

[19] Mazower identifies Glendon (2001) as exemplifying the former and Power (2003) the latter approach. For accounts that, by contrast, portray the emergence of human rights as a protracted, often faltering and politically ambiguous process, see Cowan, Dembour and Wilson 2001, Simpson 2001, Ishay 2004 and Mazower 2004.

the responses it generated, circulating in multiple social and discursive sites, effectively initiated the spadework for a different conception of the political and moral nexus between citizen, state and the international (see also Berman 1993). The now multi-sited conversation about minorities fed into one of the central public debates of modernity – indeed, still ongoing – concerning the nature of citizenship, the citizen's relation to the state and the world, and the international community's responsibilities toward both state citizens and the stateless. It matters less that the minorities petition procedure worked, or did not work, in relation to particular petitions or particular national cases than the very fact that a procedure had been invented which cared to listen to the voices of ordinary subjects, and not simply state agents. Restrictive though it was, it raised expectations – often disappointed – that equal civil and political rights for members of racial, linguistic and religious minorities existed and would be defended. Without the public's complicated experience of the League supervision of the minorities treaties, not merely of its tragic failure to defend them but of its more fundamental success in establishing that the rights of individuals mattered – even those of members of minorities – and should be defended by the international community in the first place, it is difficult to see from whence the impetus for a universal human rights regime might have come.

REFERENCES

Anastasoff, Christ. 1945. *The Case for an Autonomous Macedonia (A Symposium)*. St. Louis: The Central Committee of the Macedonian Political Organization of the United States and Canada.

Anderson, Benedict. 1991 [1983]. *Imagined Communities: Reflections on the Origin and Spread of Nationalism* (revised edition). London and New York: Verso.

Aretxaga, Begoña. 2003. Maddening States. In *Annual Review of Anthropology* 32: 393–410.

Azcárate, Pablo de. 1945. *League of Nations and National Minorities: An Experiment*. Washington, DC: Carnegie Institute for International Peace.

Barker, Elisabeth. 1950. *Macedonia: Its Place in Balkan Power Politics*. London and New York: Royal Institute of International Affairs.

Berman, Nathaniel. 1993. 'But the Alternative is Despair': Nationalism and the Modernist Renewal of International Law. In *Harvard Law Review* 106(8): 1,792–903.

Buwalda, Ambassador Petrus. 1994. Protection of the Rights of Minorities – Back to the League of Nations? In *Legacies of the Collapse of Marxism* (ed.) J. Moore. Fairfax: George Mason University Press, 133–48.

Claude, Inis. 1955. *National Minorities: an International Problem*. Cambridge, MA: Harvard University Press.

Codding, George. 1966. Interview with Pablo de Azcárate. Personal papers files. The League of Nations Archives, The United Nations Library, Palais des Nations, Geneva.

Cornwall, Mark. 1996. Minority Rights and Wrongs in Eastern Europe in the Twentieth Century. In *The Historian* 50: 16–20.

Cowan, Jane K. 2003. Who's Afraid of Violent Language? Honour, Sovereignty and Claims-Making in the League of Nations. In *Anthropological Theory* 3(3): 271–92.

Cowan, Jane K., Marie-Bénédicte Dembour and Richard A. Wilson (eds.). 2001. *Culture and Rights: Anthropological Perspectives*. Cambridge: Cambridge University Press.

Crampton, Richard J. 1983. *Bulgaria 1878–1918: a History*. Boulder and New York: East European Monographs.

Donnelly, Jack. 1993. *International Human Rights*. Boulder: Westview.

Dreyfus, Hubert L. and Paul Rabinow. 1982. *Michel Foucault: Beyond Structuralism and Hermeneutics*. Brighton: Harvester Press.

Fink, Carole. 1995. The League of Nations and the Minorities Question. In *World Affairs* 157(4): 197–205.

Finney, Patrick B. 1995. 'An Evil for All Concerned': Great Britain and Minority Protection after 1919. In *Journal of Contemporary History* 30: 533–51.

Foucault, Michel. 1991. Governmentality. In *The Foucault Effect: Studies in Governmentality* (eds.) G. Burchill, C. Gordon and P. Miller. Chicago: University of Chicago Press.

Genn, Hazel. 1999. *Paths to Justice: What People Do and Think about Going to Law*. London: Hart.

Gerth, H. H. and C. Wright Mills. 1946. *From Max Weber: Essays in Sociology*. New York: Oxford University Press.

Glendon, Mary Ann. 2001. *A World Made New: Eleanor Roosevelt and the Universal Declaration of Human Rights*. New York: Random House.

Henkin, Louis. 1990. *The Age of Rights*. New York: Columbia University Press.

Herman, Joost. 1996. The League of Nations and its Minority Protection Programme in Eastern Europe: Revolutionary, Unequalled and Underestimated. *The League of Nations 1920–1946: Organization and Accomplishments. A Retrospective of the First Organization for the Establishment of World Peace*. New York and Geneva: United Nations.

Ignatieff, Michael. 1998. *The Warrior's Honor: Ethnic War and the Modern Conscience*. London: Chatto and Windus.

Ishay, Micheline. 2004. *The History of Human Rights: from Ancient Times to the Globalization Era*. Berkeley: University of California Press.

Jackson Preece, Jennifer. 1998. *National Minorities and the European Nation-States System*. Oxford: Oxford University Press.

Kaldor, Mary. 1999. *New and Old Wars: Organized Violence in a Global Era*. Cambridge: Polity Press.

Kalyvas, Stathis. 2001. 'New' and 'Old' Civil Wars: A Valid Distinction? In *World Politics* 54: 99–118.

Kymlicka, Will. 1995. *Multicultural Citizenship: a Liberal Theory of Minority Rights*. Oxford: Clarendon Press.

Ladas, Stephen P. 1932. *The Exchange of Minorities: Bulgaria, Greece and Turkey*. New York: Macmillan.

Laitin, David D. 1998. *Identity in Formation: The Russian-Speaking Populations of the Near-Abroad*. Ithaca: Cornell University Press.

League of Nations. 1929. *Protection of Linguistic, Racial or Religious Minorities by the League of Nations: Resolutions and Extracts from the Minutes of the Council, Resolutions and Reports Adopted by the Assembly, relating to the Procedure to be followed in Questions concerning the Protection of Minorities* (Document C.24.M.18.1929.1). Geneva: Series of League of Nations Publications.

Maier, Charles S. 1992. Unsafe Haven. In *The New Republic*. 21 October.

Mair, Lucy. 1928. *The Protection of Minorities: the Working and Scope of the Minorities Treaties under the League of Nations*. London: Christophers.

Mazower, Mark. 1997. Minorities and the League of Nations in Interwar Europe. In *Daedalus* 126(2): 47–63.

2004. The Strange Triumph of Human Rights, 1933–1950. In *The Historical Journal* 47(2): 379–98.

Michaelidis, Gregory. 2005. Salvation Abroad: Macedonian Migration to North America and the Making of Modern Macedonia, 1870–1970. Dissertation in partial fulfilment for the Degree of Doctor of Philosophy, Department of History, University of Maryland (UMI Number 3178605). Ann Arbor: UMI Microforms.

Monnet, Jean. 1978. *Memoirs*. London: Collins.

Perry, Duncan. 1988. *The Politics of Terror: the Macedonian Liberation Movements 1893–1903*. Durham and London: Duke University Press.

Power, Samantha. 2002. *A Problem from Hell: America and the Age of Genocide*. New York: Basic Books.

Robinson, Jacob, Oscar Karbach, Max M. Laserson, Nehemiah Robinson and Marc Vichniak. 1943. *Were the Minorities Treaties a Failure?* New York: Institute of Jewish Affairs of the American Jewish Congress and the World Jewish Congress.

Simpson, A. W. Brian. 2001. *Human Rights and the End of Empire: Britain and the Genesis of the European Convention*. Oxford: Oxford University Press.

Steiner, Henry J. and Philip Alston. 2000. *International Human Rights in Context: Law, Politics, Morals*. Oxford: Oxford University Press.

Stone, Julius. 1931. The Legal Nature of the Minorities Petition. In *The British Year Book of International Law* 12: 76–94.

Todorova, Maria. 1997. *Imagining the Balkans*. New York and Oxford: Oxford University Press.

Višinski, Boris. 1991. *La Macédoine Vue Par L'Europe, 1925–1929*. Skopje : Editions Revue Macédonienne, Ministère de l'Information de la République de Macédoine.

CHAPTER 3

LAW, CIVIL SOCIETY AND CONTESTED JUSTICE AT THE INTERNATIONAL CRIMINAL TRIBUNAL FOR RWANDA

Emily Haslam

The International Criminal Tribunal for Rwanda (ICTR), like its sister institution at the Hague, the International Criminal Tribunal for Yugoslavia (ICTY), has struggled throughout the period of its operation to satisfy the justice demands of two of its key constituents: survivors – in particular victim-witnesses – and defendants and their lawyers (FIDH 2002; Buisman, Gumpert and Hallers 2005; Peskin 2005; Sluiter 2005).[1] For, whilst the Tribunal has decided a number of cases of vital importance to the development of international criminal law, its operation has raised controversial issues for these groups. This chapter reflects upon the significance of this contestation in international criminal law.

Some commentators, particularly so-called 'insiders' to the Tribunal, have sought to minimise differences that have emerged between the Tribunal and its constituencies, attributing them to initial difficulties in the operation of the ICTR or to false expectations having been generated about the role and purpose of the court. Typical in this respect is the approach of United Nations Assistant Secretary-General for Legal Affairs, Zacklin, writing in his personal capacity, that

> The ICTY and ICTR have also been the victims of general misunderstanding on the part of the populations for whom they function as courts. Criminal courts exist for the purpose of establishing individual accountability – not to uncover the fates and locate the remains of loved ones.

[1] My thanks go to Yutaka Arai, Davina Cooper, Marie Dembour, Rod Edmunds, Tobias Kelly, Wade Mansell, Gerry Simpson and the anonymous reviewers for Cambridge University Press.

Nor is it their purpose to provide an official history. To the extent that a historical record is integral to individual trials, it might be said that this is incidental to the work of the ICTY, but it is not its primary purpose. Even less so is the awarding of material compensation to victims. (Zacklin 2004: 544)

In writing of the Yugoslav Tribunal, Zacklin notes that while the misunderstandings are 'certainly not the responsibility of the ICTY, they are no less real and provoke genuine anger and consternation among victims' groups' (2004: 544). In this way, whilst the authenticity of survivors' concerns is acknowledged, they are seen as stemming from misconception rather than indicating a need on the part of the Tribunals to re-think their approach towards 'the populations for whom they function as courts' (Zacklin 2004: 544). Similarly, another insider notes that 'the image of the ICTR has been harmed by unjustified criticism by the media, NGOs and other interest groups' (Moghalu 2002: 22).

This chapter challenges such dismissals of civil society discontent, which no doubt stem in large part from the fact that the traditional sources of international law take no cognisance of non-state actors and, in relation to the activities of courts and tribunals, acknowledge formal legal judgment only. This chapter argues that this civil society contestation is legally meaningful and urges a radical re-think of the relationship between civil society and international criminal law. It draws upon Mary Kaldor's description of civil society in a post-modern sense, which is as 'an arena of pluralism and contestation, a source of civility as well as incivility' (Kaldor 2003: 9). The term civil society is used here as shorthand to describe an arena of contestation about international law that is located outside the traditional state-derived framework of international law and takes place amongst actors who have no formal legitimacy to adjudicate or to develop international law.

It is contended that attempts to minimise civil society contestation are descriptively and normatively flawed. This is because they fail to capture the reality of international criminal justice practice. From an historical perspective, it is clear that civil society activism has resulted in changes at the ICTR and contributed to broader shifts in international criminal law which would not otherwise have taken place. As this chapter demonstrates, the ICTR has found – to its cost on a number of occasions – that it cannot afford to overlook the justice demands emanating from civil society. The fact that the Tribunal cannot operate in a meaningful way without the consent of civil society requires it to be responsive to civil society claims. This chapter argues in favour of a more explicit recognition of the agency of civil society in effecting legal change, even if such agency, or its effects, may sometimes be hard to discern and is replete with conflicting and discordant voices.

Moreover, that these developments are to be welcomed is linked to the normative desirability of civil society contestation. This chapter proceeds from the assumption that there is an inevitable gap between international criminal law and international criminal justice. As has been widely observed, law only ever incompletely captures 'justice' (Douzinas 2002; Derrida 2003). In her analysis of Derrida's approach towards justice, Borradori (2003: 168) notes that:

> Insofar as law is organized around the demand for universality – rules and imperatives – it operates in the domain of what is possible, often predictable, and certainly calculable. Justice presents us instead with a series of impossible demands: judging what is absolutely singular, relating to the other in her full alterity, and coming to decisions in the face of the infinite perfectibility of any decision.

Although this gap between justice and law is inherent in law and legal regulation (Douzinas 2002: 368), the dislocation may be especially marked in the particularly complex context of transitional justice, which requires a range of conflicting interests to be mediated amongst participants at the individual and collective levels. Another reason why there is a divergence between law and justice is that even progressive norms embody relations of power (Stammers 1999; Rajagopal 2003). As this chapter will demonstrate, what have been described elsewhere as 'elitist blind spots' (Rajagopal 2003: 406) have also permeated the practice of the Tribunal. This chapter argues that civil society challenges to those 'blind spots' have resulted in overall positive changes to the practice of international criminal law at the Tribunal and beyond.

If progress towards justice requires contestation, paradoxically at another level it also requires the consent of civil society. Over and above the establishment of guilt, transitional justice is aimed at collective transformations (Osiel 2000). Even Security Council Resolution (SCR) 955 establishing the Tribunal is focused not just at the establishment of individual guilt but also at reconciliation. To the extent that such collective transformations are directed at actors beyond the accused, the engagement of civil society is a logical prerequisite since civil society is both an agent and recipient of the processes by which the collective purposes of international criminal law are mobilised by the individual trial.

It is therefore critical to acknowledge that in practice international criminal justice is not bestowed upon grateful objects, but is and should be negotiated amongst a wider range of actors than the traditional sources of international law indicate. International criminal law is the richer for this engagement. In the resulting contestation lies the continuous re-negotiation of international criminal law. This constitutes progress towards (albeit ultimately unachievable) justice. At the same time this contestation is an important indicator of consent which is also necessary for the achievement of the collective aims of international criminal law. This chapter calls for a more explicit recognition of the activities of civil society between consent and contestation in international criminal law.

CIVIL SOCIETY AND THE INTERNATIONAL CRIMINAL TRIBUNAL FOR RWANDA: THE FORMAL POSITION

The ICTR was established as an organ of the United Nations by SCR 955 on 8 November 1994, arguably as an act of 'political contrition' (Zacklin 2004: 542), with a mandate to prosecute 'persons responsible for genocide and other serious violations of international humanitarian law committed in the territory of Rwanda and Rwandan citizens responsible for genocide and other such violations committed in the territory of neighbouring states, between 1 January 1994 and 31 December 1994' (SCR 955, para. 1). Although the Rwandan Government had requested the UN to establish a tribunal, it voted against SCR 955 because it objected to the location of the Tribunal outside Rwanda, its temporal jurisdiction, and the fact that the Tribunal was not empowered to order the death penalty. Although it did accept the need to cooperate with the Tribunal, the Rwandan Government's objections have continued throughout the Tribunal's operation and have been augmented by other complaints: the slowness of the Tribunal's work; the Tribunal's inefficiency; and allegations of corruption amongst Tribunal staff (Des Forges and Longman 2004: 55). Relations between the Rwandan Government and the Tribunal have not been easy, and Rwandan domestic opinion is said to be appreciably influenced by the Government's criticism of the Tribunal (Habimana 2004: 84).

The activism of international civil society played a major role in ensuring the establishment of both *ad hoc* Tribunals (Hazan 2004; De Cesari 2005: 113). Despite this, the drafters of the Statutes and Rules of Procedure and Evidence (RPE) of the ICTR and ICTY followed the typical approach of international law towards civil society. The Tribunals' formal provisions proceed from a world view in which members of civil society are subordinate, albeit useful actors, interacting with the Tribunals within, as described in another context (Gready 2004: 27), the framework of a 'consensual' rather than contested relationship.

In addition to article 17 of the Statute of the Rwandan Tribunal (providing that the Prosecutor can initiate investigations based on information obtained from NGOs), rule 74 of the RPE provides for non-governmental *amicus curiae* intervention in the following way:

> A Chamber may, if it considers it desirable for the proper determination of the case, invite or grant leave to any State, organisation or person to appear before it and make submissions on any issue specified by the Chamber.

Through the admission of *amicus curiae* briefs a broader range of voices should be admitted into the courtroom widening the knowledge available to the court (Shelton 1994; Mohammed 1999; Razzaque 2001). However, admission as *amicus curiae* is circumscribed in a variety of orthodox legalistic ways. Rule 74 makes the Chamber's decision discretionary. It also introduces a vague and potentially restrictive consideration that intervention must be desirable for the proper determination of the case. In the *Butare Case* the ICTR summarised the circumstances in which leave had been granted in previous decisions.[2] These were where an applicant 'has strong interests in or views on the subject matter before the court'; where it was 'desirable . . . to enlighten the Tribunal on events that took place in Rwanda in 1994', and where it 'may be useful to gather additional legal views . . . with respect to the legal principles involved, not with respect to the particular circumstances of this or any other case'. In the *Butare Case* the chamber also found that submissions by a third party should be in the 'interest of justice' in so far as they should aid the court in the performance of its mission.[3] Even if a brief is admitted, its impact upon the Tribunal is not always easy to determine. Only some *amicus curiae* are referred to in judgments, although even those that are not referred to or admitted may be significant in raising awareness of a particular issue. Perhaps the most well-known example of this is the *amicus curiae* brief submitted in the *Akayesu Case* by the NGO

---

[2] *Decision on the Motion of Tharacisse Muvunyi For Leave to Make Submissions As Amicus Curiae in the Butare Trial*, 8 June 2001, ICTR-98-42-T at para. 11.

[3] *Decision on the Motion of Tharacisse Muvunyi For Leave to Make Submissions As Amicus Curiae in the Butare Trial*, 8 June 2001, ICTR-98-42-T at para. 13.

Coalition for Women's Human Rights in Conflict Situations. Whilst the Tribunal did not formally make a decision in respect of the submission, which called for the ICTR to prosecute crimes of sexual violence, the Prosecutor amended the indictment to include such charges.[4] Further, it is argued in this chapter that formal intervention alone, whether successful or not, insufficiently describes the impact of civil society on the practice of the Tribunal and the development of the law. The practice shows that where formal procedures do not facilitate participation, civil society may well resort to informal 'procedures' to raise issues and challenge the status quo. It is these informal procedures, far more than formal mechanisms such as *amicus curiae*, which are responsible for promoting dialogue, challenge and contested engagement both within civil society and between it and the Tribunal, constructively advancing international criminal law and justice.

Drawing upon formal and informal civil society activity, this chapter focuses on the contestation that has arisen between the Tribunal and survivors' groups and the Tribunal and defence activists. This chapter is neither an insider account nor is it based on field research within those groups.[5] It reflects upon the role of non-state actors traditionally silenced by, and without status in, prevailing legality, with a view to demonstrating the normative desirability and descriptive reality of non-state participation in international criminal processes. This chapter examines activism amongst survivor and defence communities because the Tribunal's treatment of, and reception by, these communities is essential to assessing the extent to which it may be said to have approximated 'justice'. A few words of caution are called for here. First, these actors are part of (but clearly not totally representative of) civil society. Notably, these activists represent very different constituencies. However, they have in common the articulation of alternative concepts of justice that would not otherwise have come before the Tribunal. Second, the justice demands examined here are neither exhaustive nor uncontested. Nor are each group's claims irrefutable. The significance of these justice claims lies less in their objective truth than in their bringing to the fore that which is singular in 'justice' and its implications for the application of law. In this way contestation drawing in

---

[4] Subsequent Coalition *amicus* attempts appear less successful. The Court rejected its application for leave to argue for an amendment to the indictment in the *Cyangugu Group Case* to include sexual offences and the Coalition's appeal on this point. See further on the Coalition's activity at http://www.womensrightscoalition.org/index_en.html.

[5] See Stover and Weinstein (2004) and Stover (2005) for such research.

these perspectives advances international criminal law in directions, to echo the earlier words of Borradori, which come closer to realising the 'impossible demands' of international criminal justice.

THE ICTR AND SURVIVORS

Victim-witnesses, survivors and international criminal law

Despite frequent claims that a principal function of international criminal law is its vindication of the rights of survivors, the approach of international criminal law towards them has been instrumental, not least because it has tended to assimilate the needs and interests of survivors with those of the prosecution (Jorda and de Hemptinne 2002: 1394). Nuremberg and Tokyo provided only a limited platform for victim-witnesses and they did not provide compensation. The principal international criminal law instruments (the Genocide Convention, the Geneva Conventions and their Protocols) say little about the rights of victims directly, thereby reflecting, in addition to the hitherto almost exclusive dependence of international criminal law upon the mechanisms of indirect enforcement, the relegation of victims' rights to the domestic sphere. Similarly, the ICTR's approach to survivors was not auspicious, at least in terms of its formal provisions. According to its Statute and RPE the Tribunal cannot compensate, although it can order restitution of property: compensation is left to national courts or to another competent body.

Despite this, the ICTR relies heavily upon victim-witness participation because its predominantly adversarial procedures (alien for many of the witnesses testifying before it) depend in large part upon live oral evidence. Whilst testimony is given in the first instance for the purpose of conviction or acquittal, the Tribunal's reliance upon the delivery of testimony in the form of live oral evidence reflects not only the initial hegemony of Anglo-American lawyers in the drafting of the Rules of Procedure and Evidence,[6] but also a widespread assumption, which underpins most of the literature on transitional justice and which is pervasive in international policy, that testifying in legal *fora* is curative. This assumption is problematic for there is often an inescapable tension in international criminal hearings between the formal requirements

---

[6] The length of ICTY and ICTR proceedings had become a cause of concern by 1999, with the result that an Expert Group was set up to recommend procedural improvements. These included reducing the number of witnesses and the length of oral testimony. Controversial procedural reforms followed which provided greater, although still limited, resort to written evidence (Wald 2001: 535–51).

associated with testifying and the therapeutic requirements of healing (Dembour and Haslam 2004; Stover 2005). By assimilating all too readily the interests of victim-witnesses to those of the prosecution (Jorda and de Hemptinne 2002: 1390–1), whilst simultaneously claiming to provide 'justice' for them, the danger is that the Tribunal may create false expectations. One particular concern is that such expectations may play a significant role in ensuring witnesses' consent to testifying in the first place.

Contested 'justice': the issues

Even before the first trial began, it became apparent that many survivors of the genocide and victim-witnesses had a different understanding of 'justice' to that of the Tribunal. This became manifested in the troubled relations between the Tribunal and survivor groups, which on occasion led to public demonstrations against the ICTR.[7] Groups such as the umbrella organisation IBUKA (ibuka means 'remember' in Kinyarwanda), the principal survivors' organisation in Rwanda, and AVEGA (Association des Veuves du Génocide Agahozo), which acts for widows of genocide, voiced a number of concerns about the ICTR. These included: the location of the Tribunal outside Rwanda; the slowness of international justice; and until 2003, when a separate Prosecutor was appointed for the ICTR, the fact of a shared prosecutor with the ICTY. These specific concerns were not the only focus of civil society contestation about the operation of international law and its institutions. There were also important voices expressing broader concerns that included, first, a sense of grievance and disillusionment over the inaction of the United Nations during the genocide, and, second, disputing whether the proper remit of the Tribunal should embrace compensation. The failure of the United Nations, more specifically the Security Council, to prevent the genocide (Carlsson 2005; Dallaire, Kishan and Nishan 2005)[8] challenges the legitimacy of the Tribunal established by Security Council Resolution and has been a familiar leitmotiv throughout IBUKA's interventions. Thus:

> The failure of Tribunal to live up to its mandate re-enforces our shaky faith in the UN which, as you know is founded on those fateful days of

---

[7] For example, criticising the performance of the ICTR, BBC (1997); on the release of Barayagwiza, BBC (1999); on ICTR's track record, Hirondelle (2004).

[8] In *The Prosecutor v. Kayishema and Ruzindana*, 1 June 2001, Case No. ICTR-95-1-A, para. 59 the ICTR Appeals Chamber considered the role of the United Nations during the genocide was irrelevant in this respect.

April 1994 when we were abandoned to our killers. . . . Waiting for justice is a terrible ordeal at times more painful than the pain inflicted by the crimes.[9]

Moreover, according to the Rwandan author, Aynido:

The retributive understanding of crime and justice, upon which the ICTR is founded, is discordant with the world view of many African communities. To emphasize retribution is the surest way to poison the seeds of reconciliation. If anything, retribution turns offenders into heroes, re-victimizes the victims and fertilizes the cycle of violence. (Quoted in Habimana 2004: 87)

Once the Tribunal became operational survivors' groups drew attention to the negative courtroom experiences of victim-witnesses, especially those testifying to sexual offences; the failures of the witness protection scheme;[10] and the failure of the Tribunal to provide compensation.

Contested 'justice': the campaigns

The Tribunal's public response to criticism at times has appeared defensive, such as its reaction to reports from NGOs, the International Crisis Group and Amnesty International, which had corroborated some of the concerns voiced by survivor groups.[11] Despite this, survivor groups persisted in their challenges to the Tribunal's treatment of victim-witnesses. One such high profile challenge was prompted when, during the *Butare* trial, the unfortunate (but incorrect) impression was created that the judges laughed at witness TA, a survivor of rape, whilst she was giving evidence. This incident very quickly became a cause célèbre with AVEGA, amongst others, calling for sanctions to be implemented against the judges involved, calls which were renewed during an International Conference on Survivors jointly organised by IBUKA in November 2001 (Gruvellior 2001). In these external fora civil society

[9] Open letter to the UN Secretary-General seeking the removal of Louise Arbour, 9 April 1997 at http://129.194.252.80/catfiles/0828.pdf.

[10] The safety of defence witnesses is also a cause for concern (Agence France Presse 2005). Notably, Sluiter (2005: 975) criticises the 'apparent lack of concern for detained witnesses' considering it 'indicative of a witness protection orientation that is mainly driven by self-interest, i.e. obtaining the witness's presence in the courtroom, and not by genuine concern for witnesses' fears, motives and overall position'.

[11] See for example its response to a critical report from Amnesty International that '[i]t is fashionable in some quarters to denigrate and distort the effort of the International Criminal Tribunal for Rwanda, to wilfully suppress the achievements it has recorded in the most challenging conditions . . .' (ICTR 1998a). See further the Statement by the Registrar on the Report of the International Crisis Group (ICTR 2001).

participants challenged alleged judicial behaviour that ran counter to the demands of justice and the delivery of a fair trial in ways that were unlikely to find adequate consideration in the Tribunal's own proceedings.

The validity of some justice claims voiced by survivor groups was acknowledged even if Tribunal staff felt that they could do little about them. In 2000 the Judges at the ICTR announced that the Tribunal was unable to compensate (Breton-Le Goff 2002: 18). Judge Pillay wrote to the United Nations Secretary-General acknowledging the importance of compensation in reconciliation processes suggesting the establishment of a special fund (FIDH 2002: 11). To the extent that Judges felt constrained by the Statute of the ICTR, it may have been, as Breton-Le Goff suggests, that they were hoping for NGO mobilisation around this issue (Breton-Le Goff 2002: 19). Formal intervention around issues of compensation has been even less successful. In two cases the NGO African Concern unsuccessfully sought leave to address the ICTR on its power *inter alia* to order restitution. In both the *Musema Case*[12] in March 1999 and the *Bagosora Case* in 2004,[13] leave was denied. African Concern argued that in the absence of restitution, victims' interests were not effectively represented by either the defence or prosecution because restitution was vital to the promotion of justice and reconciliation in Rwanda. Their applications were, however, rejected as irrelevant. It had not been alleged in the indictments that the accused had taken property unlawfully and since no such finding had been made, the application was held to be premature. Hence the provisions on restitution contained in RPE 88 did not come into play. It follows that the discussion on the 'general problem of the unlawful taking of property in Rwanda' was 'unrelated to the specific facts at issue.'[14] Hence the *amicus curiae* interventions were not considered necessary for the determination of either case.

The question of compensation has been particularly problematic in relation to survivors who have developed HIV/AIDS transmitted as a result of rape during the genocide,[15] a crisis which has been brought to

---

[12] *The Prosecutor v. Alfred Musema, Decision on An Application By African Concern For Leave to Appear as Amicus Curiae*, 17 March 1999, ICTR-96-13-T.

[13] *The Prosecutor v. Bagosora, Kabiligi, Ntabakuze and Nsengiyumva, Decision on Amicus Curiae Request by African Concern*, 23 March 2004, ICTR-98-41-T. The reasoning is similar in this and the *Musema Case*. The text refers mainly to the *Bagosora Case*.   [14] At para. 10.

[15] Between 66.6% and 80% of women survivors are estimated to be suffering from HIV/AIDS (Nduwimana 2004:10).

the attention of the international community largely through the activities of civil society (Nduwimana 2004: 16).[16] Nduwimana (2004: 34–5), critical of what she takes to be the Tribunal's unnecessarily restrictive approach towards compensation generally, reports (2004: 31–2) three unofficial reasons provided by the Tribunal for its failure to provide anti-retroviral treatment (ARVs) to victim-witnesses: its mandate, credibility with the defence and lack of evidence connecting sexual violence to HIV/AIDS status. To these three she adds a further concern: the Tribunal's inability to provide continuing care once its work ends (2004: 32). The Tribunal's failure to treat victim-witnesses suffering from HIV/AIDS stood in stark contrast to its provision of ARVs to defendants in Tribunal custody. Eventually the Tribunal changed its policy in 2004 (Nduwimana 2004: 34), demonstrating a welcome and tangible outcome flowing from civil society challenges mounted in a space beyond the formal panoply of the Tribunal and traditionally accredited law-making actors.

When the Tribunal eventually attempted some institutional re-organisation to take on board some of the survivors' concerns and develop its relations with civil society, problems arose, not least when these developments appeared to conflict with the interests of other (civil society) actors. The tension between the discordant or opposing demands of different civil society actors is itself a challenging dimension of the increased recognition and acceptance of the normative and justice contribution that these actors make. Inevitably this may sometimes result in compromise. For example, in 2000 the Tribunal established a victim-oriented *Support Programme for Witnesses and Potential Witnesses* to be put into operation by five Rwandan NGOs including AVEGA, focusing in particular on those who had suffered from sexual violence (Breton-Le Goff 2002: 9; Nduwimana 2004: 24). At the inception of the programme the Registrar claimed '[t]he idea of restitutive justice is thus the future direction of international criminal justice' (ICTR 2000). Its initial conception was expansive and included financial measures to mitigate post-trial poverty, help with re-housing and medical aid (Breton-Le Goff 2002: 9). That the Tribunal was engaging in such work was, however, controversial. The Association of Defence Lawyers disputed the powers of the ICTR to establish such a programme

---

[16] Nduwimana (2004: 16) notes that in 1999 AVEGA-AGAHOZO was the first to estimate the number of rape victims infected with HIV during the genocide, after which a number of other reports followed, for example, by Save the Children, Amnesty International and African Rights.

and its impact on the Tribunal's impartiality and neutrality, as did Counsel in the *Akayesu* appeal (Breton-Le Goff 2002: 18; FIDH 2002: 10–11; Nduwimana 2004: 25). In the face of such criticism, the Registrar tried to justify the project on the basis of Article 21 of the ICTR Statute and Rule 34 RPE which, Nduwimana argues (2004: 30), are not dependent upon the criminal liability of an accused. On receipt of legal advice from the UN Head Quarters in 2002, the programme was re-designed, with the result that the social elements were removed (Breton-Le Goff 2002: 17; Nduwimana 2004: 32). Notably, from then on the Tribunal only provided assistance to testifying victims (Nduwimana 2004: 32). Significantly, the programme was also criticised from a survivor perspective (International Crisis Group 2001: 32) quoting Nahahire from IBUKA:

> There is a risk of confusion. The distinction must be made between assistance and reparation. Assistance is a voluntary, commendable act. Reparations are entirely different: one gives what is owed. We do not look to the Tribunal for assistance. Rather, it should help us recover our debts by including us in the judgements.

These reforms to the witness support programme were insufficient to satisfy the demands of survivor groups. In January 2002, IBUKA and AVEGA decided to suspend cooperation with the ICTR, leading to the adjournment of proceedings. Their reasons included: allegations that defence investigators had been involved in the genocide; deficiencies in witness protection; hostile cross-examination; absence of victim participation in the Tribunal's procedures; and the lack of compensation and medical care at the ICTR (FIDH 2002: 6). As a result, the ICTR Registrar met various civil society organisations in Rwanda, with a view to addressing the concerns of survivors, although IBUKA and AVEGA boycotted these meetings. In the event the joint commission that the Registrar had promised to set up to examine these concerns was not established because disputes arose between the Tribunal and the Rwandan government over the scope of the Commission's activity. In its report on the relations between the Tribunal and survivors' groups, *Victims in the Balance: Challenges Ahead for the International Criminal Tribunal for Rwanda*, the NGO, the International Federation for Human Rights (FIDH) recommended that the ICTR establish a 'systematic dialogue' with survivor associations and 'clear rules of collaboration' and that the ICTR 'recognise their importance' (FIDH 2002: 22). Since then the Tribunal has announced its 'intention to revive, pursue and develop a better and harmonious working relationship' with IBUKA and AVEGA, recognising that improved relations will help to achieve its mandate and to implement its completion strategy (ICTR 2003). As part of its outreach programme, established in 1998, the ICTR has encouraged civil society visitors (Hirondelle News Agency 2005e), and established a documentation centre in Kigali in September 2000. Notably, however, some ICTR officials did not initially consider that outreach was a proper function of the court (Peskin 2005: 953). Whilst Moghalu has claimed that the image of the Tribunal amongst Rwandans is 'increasingly positive' (Moghalu 2002: 28), others have questioned the impact of the Tribunal amongst Rwandans (Des Forges and Longman 2004), and have noted that the outreach programme has relied more upon information exchange than engagement (Peskin 2005: 954–5). Although it still does not compensate, since 2004 the Tribunal has provided medical support to victim-witnesses, including ARVs under a restructured programme within the Registry (UK Parliament 2004; Hirondelle News Agency 2005a) reportedly spending 200,000 US dollars on HIV/AIDs medication in 2004 (Hirondelle News Agency 2005a). The dialogue and challenges around compensation and assistance are instructive on a broader level too. This activity has revealed inconsistent and competing standpoints within civil society (and between civil society and ICTR insiders) as to the extent to which international criminal practice should allow judicial bodies to administer aspects of restorative justice. In response the Tribunal was explicitly moved to review its practice and, equally significantly, make a formal pronouncement indicating its future intention to promote its involvement and dialogue with civil society actors. It is more than a matter of coincidence that the International Criminal Court provides both for victim participation and compensation.

ICTR AND THE DEFENCE

Fair trial and international criminal law

As the creators of the Tribunal recognised, the guarantee of a fair trial is fundamental to its success and legitimacy. However, the ICTR's Statute does not refer expressly to the defence, nor do the Statute and RPE contain provisions protecting the independence of defence counsel (Ogetto 2006: 504). Instead the drafters of the Tribunal's statutes and RPEs appear to have equated justice for the accused with the incorporation of due process rights. These rights are undoubtedly fundamental and their application in hybrid proceedings, such as the ad-hoc Tribunals, which deal with difficult and traumatic events, is controversial and complex (Cogan 2002: 114–15). Despite extensive litigation around these issues, however, defence counsel, and in some cases defendants themselves, have resorted to extra-legal forms of intervention in order to voice concerns that had either already been unsuccessfully litigated at the Tribunal or were unlikely to have come before the Tribunal in the first place even if they potentially impacted upon a fair trial.

Contested 'justice': the issues

Defence counsel have claimed to be institutionally marginalised at the Tribunal standing 'wholly outside the body politic' (Morrison 2001: 14). For example, defence counsel were not part of the official discussions when the RPE were revised (ICDAA 2000: 2.1). It was not until 2003 that defence lawyers were permitted to take part in the Tribunal's plenary sessions (Hirondelle News Agency 2003).[17] They are institutionally isolated from the other officers:

> An ad hoc court is by nature mission-oriented, and missionaries (judges, prosecutors, and administrators) tend to form a sense of camaraderie and community. By contrast, defence at the tribunals has been task-oriented: attorneys generally represent only one defendant and often commute from their home countries to the Hague and Arusha. The inevitable result is that the culture of international criminal law excludes the defence. (Anonymous 2001: 1995)

Defence counsel have objected to the control exercised by the Registry over their services, and the political context within which the Tribunal operates, including its general framing of jurisdiction, the exercise of prosecutorial discretion and the completion policy. All this, defence counsel have claimed, adversely affects their capacity to defend their clients effectively as well as their contribution to the development of the institution more broadly. Adopting similar strategies to victim-witness and survivor groups, counsel have sought to have their concerns addressed through extra-legal intervention as much as through the submission of *amicus curiae* and courtroom advocacy.

---

[17] ADAD was not consulted about amendments to the Professional Code of Conduct for Defence Counsel. See its *Request To Freely Intervene as Amicus Curiae In Support of the Joint Defence Motion for the Reinstatement of Jean Degli* at para. 39.

Contested 'justice': the campaigns

Civil society, being essentially victim focused, has tended, with some notable exceptions, to neglect defence issues in international criminal law (Cogan 2002: 112). Defence counsel have responded to their perceived institutional marginalisation by establishing professional civil society organisations to protect their own interests and to increase awareness of the defence point of view in international criminal law. At the ICTR the Association des Avocats de la Défense auprès du Tribunal pour le Rwanda (ADAD), established in 1997, claims to represent defence counsel. Its aim is to 'promote and defend the rights of the Defence, protect the professional interests of the lawyers and those of the members of the Defence teams and generally, what ensues therefrom'.[18] However, not all defence counsel at the ICTR are members of the ADAD. In contrast to the ICTY, where membership of the Association of Defence Counsel of the ICTY (ADC-ICTY) is compulsory (Ellis 2003: 969), membership of the ADAD is voluntary and is not a prerequisite for practice at the ICTR. The failure of the ICTR to accord official recognition to the ADAD places it in a weaker position in relation to the Tribunal than its counterpart ADC-ICTY. This can be seen in the 'outdated'[19] disciplinary regime of the ICTR, a situation which the ADAD claims impacts adversely upon its ability to conduct an effective defence and which it has resisted through the submission of amicus curiae in the Military I[20] and the Seromba Cases.[21] It is reported that the ADAD is considering the establishment of a Bar Association to further strengthen its position at the ICTR (Hirondelle News Agency 2005d).

Even if in a less enviable position than the ADC-ICTY, the ADAD has been active in seeking to protect the interests of its members and to ensure the Tribunal takes on board the wider interests of the defence,

---

[18] ADAD, *Request To Freely Intervene as Amicus Curiae In Support of the Joint Defence Motion for the Reinstatement of Jean Degli*, Article 2.

[19] ADAD, *Request To Freely Intervene as Amicus Curiae In Support of the Joint Defence Motion for the Reinstatement of Jean Degli*, at para. 76.

[20] ADAD, *Request To Freely Intervene as Amicus Curiae In Support of the Joint Defence Motion for the Reinstatement of Jean Degli*, at para. 20 in which the ADAD argued that the Registry's response to allegations of fraud on the part of defence counsel Degli was procedurally flawed and did not sufficiently take account of the need for a fair trial. Notably, the Chamber rejected the Registrar's contention that leave should be refused because of ADAD's unofficial status and granted ADAD leave to appear although it came to reject the application for Degli's reinstatement (Ogetto 2006: 511–12).

[21] As part of protest action by ICTR detainees, counsel had been instructed by his client not to appear. After unsuccessfully petitioning the Chamber to allow him to withdraw, Counsel left the courtroom and was duly sanctioned. ADAD's application for leave to appear as *amicus curiae* on a motion to vacate sanctions against him was rejected as was the motion itself (Ogetto 2006: 510–11).

both through courtroom advocacy and extra-legal lobbying. Early on in the life of the Tribunal, defence counsel challenged the way in which the Registry organised the representation of indigent defendants under the Directive on the Assignment of Defence Counsel for the ICTR (Wilson 2002). ICTR jurisprudence, which supported the Registrar's insistence that the defendant did not have an absolute right to counsel of his choice, imposed additional requirements on the selection of counsel: tribunal resources, geographical distribution and balance of the world's principal legal systems (Wilson 2002: 164–6). The ADAD and another defence association, the International Criminal Defence Attorney's Association (ICDAA) submitted an *amicus curiae* brief in the *Akayesu Case* arguing for the right of an indigent accused to select his own defence. However, although the Court did not decide whether the ADAD and ICDAA brief was admissible, it denied that the right of an accused to free legal assistance equated to a right on the part of the accused to choose his or her own counsel (Ellis 2003: 965). The ICDAA also lobbied against the moratorium imposed by the Registrar on the assignment of Canadian and French counsel, who had been disproportionately represented at the Tribunal. The ban was lifted later in 1999 (ICDAA 1999), although not the criteria requiring geographical distribution and balance of legal systems (Buisman, Gumpert and Hallers 2005: 16). Criticism that the ICTR has unnecessarily restricted the defendant's right to choose counsel has continued (Buisman, Gumpert and Hallers 2005: 15).

Defence counsel have argued that the principle of equality of arms has been breached. They claim that they have only restricted access to necessary basic resources, such as office facilities and legal documents (ICDAA 2000: 2.1). They also argue that the Registry, which oversees defence services at the ICTR, does not only have the efficient running of the Tribunal at heart, but also the interests of other actors such as victims and witnesses, whose concerns diverge from those of the defence (Wilson 2002: 176–7). Notably, however, a number of decisions of the Tribunal have rejected the equation of the principle of equality of arms with equality of resources (Wilson 2002: 187).

Issues of pay and conditions have been a source of concern for defence counsel, including the exclusion of legal assistants and defence investigators from trial (ICTR 2004; Buisman, Gumpert and Hallers 2005: 78). Issues around witness protection and allegations of misconduct on the part of defence counsel have also caused consternation. On a number of occasions ADAD sought to raise these problems, writing to the United Nations Secretary-General in 1998 and to the ICTR Registrar in September 2000 (Ogetto 2006: 506). Matters came to a head when on 19 March 2002 ADAD threatened to strike. Amongst the ADAD's concerns was the joint Commission which the Registrar had suggested establishing in its response to complaints from survivor groups, a body which the ADAD had described as an 'affront to the expected independence and impartiality of the tribunal' (Ogetto 2006: 507, 514). In the event a strike did not take place. Nor was the commission established. In a strongly worded statement from which the Registrar sought to distance the Tribunal, the ADAD praised the ICTR for abandoning the proposal as a 'bold and unprecedented move to reject the manipulative demands from Kigali' (Ogetto 2006: 514). However, whilst this strike did not go ahead, defence counsel, and not just members of the ADAD, conducted a two-day strike on 28 and 29 January 2004. This led to the adjournment of the *Military I* trial. On 30 January counsel returned to work when the Registrar agreed to discuss their concerns and abandon searches of defence counsel perceived to be oppressive. Whilst defence counsel's right to strike (in these circumstances) has been disputed (Buisman, Gumpert and Hallers 2005: 79), it is clear that the Tribunal cannot operate without their cooperation and consent.

If some of their concerns have been met by the Tribunal, defence counsel have been less successful in challenging the broader political context of the Tribunal's operation. Two concerns in particular pit defence counsel and the defence directly against the justice claims of survivors: namely the transfer of trials to Rwanda and the prosecution of members of the Rwandan Patriotic Front (RPF). As part of the ICTR's completion strategy (the completion of investigations by 2004, trials by 2008 and appeals by 2010),[22] negotiations took place between the Tribunal and the Rwandan Government to transfer trials from Arusha to Rwanda. In an application to submit an *amicus curiae* brief in the *Seromba* and *Nzabirinda Cases* the ADAD objected to the Prosecution's request to hold these trials in Rwanda.[23] This application was undecided when the Prosecutor withdrew the motion. However, the ADAD continued to object extra-legally to the transfer of trials to Rwanda. In February 2005, ADAD President, Hamuli Rety, even attempted to enlist the support of UN High Commissioner for Human

---

[22] As per SCR 1503.

[23] *The Prosecutor v. Nzabirinda, Decision on the Prosecution's Request to Withdraw Motion for Trial in Rwanda*, ICTR-01-77-1.

Rights and former Chief Prosecutor, Louise Arbour (Hirondelle 2005b), a move which led the Rwandan representative to the ICTR to accuse defence lawyers of conducting 'political propaganda aimed at misleading the public' (Hirondelle 2005c).

On a number of occasions detainees have taken measures in their own hands to protest at the Tribunal's operation and to show solidarity in the face of what they perceived to be the unfair treatment of particular defendants.[24] Detainees also made known their objections to transfer. In September 2004, detainees boycotted ICTR proceedings for a short period, refusing counsel a mandate to represent them, with forty-three suspects going on hunger strike as a means of protest (Financial Times Information 2004). Later in February 2005, forty-six of the fifty-seven detainees at the Tribunal made known their objections to the transfer of trials and convicted persons to Rwanda in a letter to ICTR President Møse, in which they stated their conviction 'that this scheme is intended to send us to certain death in the most frightful conditions' (Hirondelle News Agency 2005c). Notwithstanding, the transfer of trials to Rwanda is embedded in the ICTR completion strategy.

Another source of dispute has been the prosecution policy, particularly in relation to members of the RPF. Since the failure to prosecute is not judicially reviewable (Reydams 2005: 983), the scope for raising this question within the courtroom is limited. This has not silenced civil society in pressing its concerns. In 2004, amidst demands by the Rwandan government that she resign, Carla Del Ponte announced her intention to conduct 'special investigations' into members of the RPF. She was subsequently replaced as Chief Prosecutor. Given the pressures of the completion strategy, it appears unlikely that any member of the RPF will be indicted for crimes at the Tribunal. For Reydams, this state of affairs represents a 'regrettable return to the Nuremberg paradigm', being a paradigm which 'stands for victor's justice, prohibition of the *tu quoque* defence, and clear separation between victims and perpetrators' (Reydams 2005: 977). The Tribunal's failure to prosecute these crimes is of even greater concern because it may have the worrying effect of

---

[24] Twenty-five detainees went on hunger strike to express solidarity with Akayesu (ICTR 1998b). Twenty-two went on strike in 2000 to express solidarity with Barayagwiza. Barayagwiza's release had been ordered by the Appeals Chamber on grounds of his inordinately long pre-trial detention. This led to widespread protests from survivors and the Rwandan government. During hearings in which the Appeals Chamber reconsidered its ruling, the Rwandan Attorney General by means of *amicus curiae* raised the prospect of further non-cooperation with the Tribunal. The Appeals Chamber reversed its decision to release Barayagwiza on 31 March 2000 (Cogan 2002: 134–5), to the dismay of the ADAD which had called for the Tribunal to resist Rwandan government pressure (Ogetto 2006: 513).

silencing a group of victim-witnesses and survivors who are not readily recognised in domestic transitional justice processes (Rombouts and Vandeginste 2005: 335).

CIVIL SOCIETY PARTICIPATION IN INTERNATIONAL CRIMINAL JUSTICE PROCESSES AND THE PROBLEM OF INSTRUMENTALISATION

This chapter argues that civil society challenges to, and participation in, international criminal justice processes is both traceable and normatively desirable. But that is not to say that informal intervention is free from considerations of power. Power and standing of particular civil society organisations may be increased by the enhanced legitimacy that engagement with a legal institution such as the ICTR might bring to the detriment of that of other non-state actors. IBUKA's strong links with the Rwandan Government have led some to question its credentials in representing the interests of all victims (FIDH 2002: 15). FIDH reported that whilst some smaller victims' associations desired to end the 2002 boycott, they did not publicly disagree with IBUKA and AVEGA (FIDH 2002: 14). The ICTR has also been criticised for paying most attention to civil society groups that enjoy close links with the Rwandan Government (Peskin 2005: 961). The irony is that informal contestation, which this chapter welcomes precisely because it admits justice claims that would not otherwise have found an entry point into the legal process, is likely also to exclude other voices. These problems should not be underestimated. However, this chapter suggests that they relate less to questions of the status and nature of the interveners than to another more fundamental problem in international criminal law: how can the law and its processes ensure genuine (in the sense of non-instrumentalised) representation of individuals whose role in the proceedings has come about not only as a result of harm suffered or perpetrated, but because the suffering experienced, or allegedly inflicted, is related in some way to a wider collective? Even FIDH, which claims to have – and, no doubt, does have – the interests of survivors at heart, accepts the premise that international prosecution is an ultimate good and witnesses bear an 'historic duty' for the sake of 'justice':

> The role of victims' associations is obviously to guarantee the interests of victims, but also to remind them of their historic duty to testify in order for truth to be established and justice done. (FIDH 2002: 15)

From FIDH's overwhelming concern for the uninterrupted continuance of international criminal justice processes, it follows that

> The associations are clearly entitled to choose the means they deem appropriate to publicise allegations by witnesses and other parties. But if such means obstruct the work of the ICTR and those accused of serious crimes are freed, they are by no means acting in the interests of victims, who are calling for justice and an end to impunity. The situation could even lead to further reprisals against those who risked testifying. (FIDH 2002: 15)

Thus even if international criminal law exhibits a more responsive attitude towards survivors, it is difficult, if not impossible, to see how it could adopt an approach towards survivors and victim-witnesses that is not ultimately instrumental.[25] Similarly, even whilst criminal accountability is grounded on the responsibility of the individual, prosecution, non-prosecution and the parameters within which a defence can be conducted may also be framed by reference to a defendant's relationship with the collective. Thus there may be a tension between the achievement of justice at the individual and collective levels. Civil society activists may not be wholly representative (nor may they claim to be). They may not pursue united or consistent challenges and campaigns. Equally, their justice demands should not be accepted without question. However, they have the potential to illuminate those areas where the collective might otherwise obscure the individual and thereby to bring to the fore what is 'particular' in justice. It is upon this, rather than focusing on status, that questions of legitimacy might usefully focus.

CONCLUSION: CIVIL SOCIETY, JUSTICE AND INTERNATIONAL CRIMINAL LAW

The nature and type of crimes that took place during the genocide in Rwanda make it unlikely that legal justice could ever fully satisfy the demands of survivors and alleged perpetrators either individually or collectively, especially where those demands conflict with each other. Legal justice after atrocity might then represent 'the least awful alternative' (Bass 2000: 304). Whilst defence and survivor activists at the Tribunal do not operate from a shared understanding of international criminal justice, they have in common the fact that they have given

---

[25] For a similar argument in relation to defence witnesses see Sluiter (2005: 975) and above note 10.

voice to alternative understandings of justice to that which was emanating from the ICTR. Although they represent very different constituencies, survivor and defence campaigners have effected significant
changes to the way in which 'justice' is seen and done at the Tribunal
and beyond. They have thereby ensured that the Tribunal takes on
board more closely interests which, although essential to its operation
and effectiveness, it seemed initially set to overlook. If contestation
is vital to the development of the Tribunal, these experiences also
show that consent on the part of civil society to governance by the
Tribunals is just as fundamental to their operation as consent by the
Tribunals to civil society activity, something which the formal legal
position belies.

Admittedly it is difficult to chart the effect of civil society intervention, especially where it did not yield immediate results for particular
individuals before the ICTR. But difficulty is not sufficient reason to
overlook vibrant and vigorous interactions whether they are between
civil society and international Tribunals or the different constituent
elements within such Tribunals. However imperceptibly, these campaigns, challenges and contestations are responsible for shaping international law and its relationship with justice. Beyond the ICTR there
are changes in international criminal law and procedure that indicate
civil society's on-going influence. For example, the International
Criminal Court provides both for victim participation and compensation, as well as for the institution of the defence by providing for an
independent defence organisation. Thus a full account of legal change
needs to go beyond examining formal judgments if it is to represent
faithfully the continuous accommodation between visions of justice –
even where this negotiation takes place outside the courtroom – which
finds its ultimate expression in substantive legal norms and practices.

A variety of sites of activism on the part of civil society can be
observed, inside and outside the courtroom, sometimes in conjunction
with other civil society or state actors. Whilst the *amicus curiae* procedure has the potential to allow a range of interests and views into the
courtroom wider than those of the defence and prosecution, the procedure is legalistic and opaque in its terms and operation. This makes its
effectiveness in accommodating civil society justice claims difficult to
assess. In practice it does not appear to have fully facilitated the participation of civil society. Cases in which there is *amicus curiae* involvement are relatively few, even if the effect of intervention in some
instances has been significant. This chapter has also indicated instances

where informal challenges have operated alongside an *amicus curiae* that the Tribunal ignored, rejected or did not have cause to determine. Moreover, it is clear that civil society influence also operates informally beyond the realm of international criminal procedure. Thus the Tribunal as an institution has been faced with claims that extend beyond those traditionally found in courtroom litigation. In this respect it has acted both to mediate between defence and survivor group claims on the one hand and to respond to claims made directly upon it on the other. That the Tribunal has been responsive to at least some of these external claims evidences the essential mutability of the practice of 'international criminal justice' and that these 'blind spots' existed in the first place indicates the Tribunal's ambivalent institutional position in relation to legal hegemony: as an institution it has the potential both to confront and to validate established legality.

Civil society plays an essential role in international criminal justice. The challenge for lawyers is to provide a legal framework which acknowledges the twin requirements of civil society consent and con-testation in international criminal law.

REFERENCES

Agence France Presse. 2005. Lawyer for key Rwandan genocide suspect ques-tions very basis of trial. 12 April (lexis nexis).

Anonymous. 2001. Developments in the Law – International Criminal Law: III. Fair Trials and the Role of the International Criminal Defence. In *Harvard Law Review* 114: 1982–2006.

Bass, Gary J. 2000. *Stay the Hand of Vengeance: the Politics of War Crimes Tribunals*. Princeton: Princeton University Press.

BBC. 1997. Demonstration against international prosecutors in capital. 27 May (lexis nexis).

BBC. 1999. Rwanda: Hundreds attend demo in Kigali to protest release of genocide suspect. 16 November (lexis nexis).

Borradori, Giovanna. 2003. *Philosophy In A Time of Terror: Dialogues With Jürgen Habermas and Jacques Derrida*. Chicago and London: University of Chicago Press.

Breton-Le Goff, Gaelle. 2002. *Analysis of Trends in Sexual Violence Prosecutions in Indictments by the International Criminal Tribunal for Rwanda. Report On behalf of the NGO Coalition for Women's Human Rights in Conflict Situations* available at www.womensrightscoalition.org/index_en.htm.

Buisman, Caroline, Ben Gumpert and Martine Hallers. 2005. Trial and Error – How Effective is Legal Representation in International Criminal Proceedings? In *International Criminal Law Review* 5: 1–82.

Carlsson, Ingvar. 2005. *The UN Inadequacies.* In *Journal of International Criminal Justice* 3: 837–46.

Cogan, Jacob K. 2002. International Criminal Court and Fair Trials: Difficulties and Prospects. In *Yale Journal of International Law* 27: 111–40.

Dallaire, Romeo, Manocha Kishan and Degnarain Nishan. 2005. The Major Powers on Trial. In *Journal of International Criminal Justice* 3: 861–78.

De Cesari, Patrizia. 2005. NGOs and the Activities of the Ad Hoc Criminal Tribunals for former Yugoslavia and Rwanda. In *Civil Society, International Courts and Compliance Bodies* (ed.) T. Treves, M. F. di Raltalma, A. Tanzi, A. Fodella, C. Pitea and C. Ragni. The Hague: TMC Asser Press.

De Feyter, Koen, Stephan Parmentier, Marc Bossuyt and Paul Lemmens. 2005. *Out of the Ashes: Reparation for Victims of Gross and Systematic Human Rights Violations.* Antwerp and Oxford: Intersentia.

Dembour, Marie-Bénédicte and Emily Haslam. 2004. Silencing Hearings? Victim-Witnesses at War Crime Trials. In *European Journal of International Law* 15: 151–77.

Derrida, Jacques. 2003. Autoimmunity: Real and Symbolic Suicides: A Dialogue with Jacques Derrida. In *Philosophy in a Time of Terror: Dialogues with Jürgen Habermas and Jacques Derrida* (ed.) G. Borradori. Chicago and London: University of Chicago Press.

Des Forges, Alison and Timothy Longman. 2004. Legal Responses to Genocide in Rwanda. In *My Neighbour, My Enemy: Justice and Community in the Aftermath of Mass Atrocity* (eds.). E. Stower and H. M. Weinstein. Cambridge: Cambridge University Press.

Douzinas, Costas. 2002. *The End of Human Rights: Critical Legal Thought at the Turn of the Century.* Oxford: Hart Publishing.

Ellis, Mark S. 2003. The ICTY at Ten: a Critical Assessment of the Major Rulings of the International Criminal Tribunal over the Past Decade: the Evolution of Defence Counsel Appearing before the International Criminal Tribunal for the Former Yugoslavia. In *New England Law Review* 37: 949–73.

FIDH. 2002. Victims in the Balance. Challenges ahead for the International Criminal Tribunal for Rwanda available at www.iccnow.org/documents/FIDHrwVictimsBalanceNov2003.pdf?PHPSESSID=7649b68c6d87016fa2d15c4133b190e0.

Financial Times Information. 2004. Rwandan Genocide Detainees Go On Hunger Strike. 21 September (lexis nexis)

Gready, Paul. 2004. *Fighting for Human Rights.* London: Routledge.

Gruvellior, T. 2001. Getting things into perspective. In *International Justice Tribunal Reseau Intermedia.* 13 December (lexis nexis).

Habimana, Aloys. 2004. Judicial Responses to Mass Violence: Is the International Criminal Tribunal for Rwanda making a Difference towards

Reconciliation in Rwanda? In *International War Crimes Trials: Making a Difference?* (eds.) S. R. Ratner and J. L. Bischoff. Texas: University of Texas.

Hazan, Pierre. 2004. *Justice in a Time of War: the True Story Behind the International Criminal Tribunal for the Former Yugoslavia*. Texas: A and M University Press.

Hirondelle News Agency. 2003. Defence Lawyers Association Unveil New Committee. 22 April (lexis nexis)

2004. *Rwanda:* Thousands Demonstrate Against UN Tribunal. 29 February (lexis nexis).

2005a. Women and gender, ICTR Medical Support Programme Targets 2,300 Witnesses. 28 January (lexis nexis).

2005b. Defence Lawyers turn to UN Rights Body for Help. 10 February (lexis nexis).

2005c. Rwanda, Prisoners again Raise Voices over Potential Transfer to Rwanda. 23 February 2005 (lexis nexis).

2005d. Legal and Judicial Affairs: Defence Lawyers at the ICTR Intend to Create Bar . 28 February (lexis nexis).

2005e. Rwanda: After Visit, Rights Group Remains Critical of UN Court. 15 November (lexis nexis).

ICDAA. 1999. Annual Report at www.hri.ca/partners/aiad-icdaa/reports/E-Anual99.htm.

2000. Annual Report at www.hri.ca/partners/aiad-icdaa/reports/aren.htm.

ICTR. 1998a. Statement on Amnesty International's Report, 'International Criminal Tribunal for Rwanda: Trials and Tribulations'. ICTR INFO-9-2-117 at www.ictr.org/ENGLISH/PRESSREL/1998/117.htm.

1998b. ICTR Detainees End Hunger Strike. ICTR/INFO-9-2-145 at http://65.18.216.88/ENGLISH/PRESSREL/1998/146.htm.

2000. ICTR Launches Victim Support Initiative in Rwanda. ICTR/INFO-9-2-242.EN at www.ictr.org/ENGLISH/PRESSREL/2000/242.htm.

2001. Statement by the Registrar on the Report of the International Crisis Group. ICTR/INFO/0-3-01.EN at www.ictr.org/ENGLISH/PRESSREL/2001/9-3-01.htm.

2002. ICTR President Calls for Compensation for Victims. ICTR/INFO-9-2-326.EN at www.ictr.org/ENGLISH/PRESSREL/2002/326e.htm.

2003. ICTR Initiates Major Moves to Strengthen Relationship with Rwandan Genocide Survivor Groups. ICTR/INFO-9-2-352.EN at www.ictr.org/ENGLISH/PRESSREL/2003/352.htm.

2004. *Registry's Response to the Allegations of Serious and Repeated Violations of Rights of the Defence*. ICTR/INFO-9-3-15.EN.

International Crisis Group. 2001. *International Criminal Tribunal for Rwanda: Justice Delayed*. ICG African Report No. 30 June 2001 at www.grandslacs.net/doc/2257.pdf.

Jorda, Claude. 2004. The Major Hurdles and Accomplishments of the ICTY:

What the ICC Can Learn From Them. In *Journal of International Criminal Justice* 2: 572–84.

Jorda, Claude and Jérome de Hemptinne. 2002. The Status and Role of the Victim. In *The Rome Statute of the International Criminal Court: A Commentary Volume II* (eds.) A. Cassese, P. Gaeta and J. R. W. D. Jones. Oxford: Oxford University Press.

Kaldor, Mary. 2003. *Global Civil Society: An Answer to War.* Oxford: Polity Press.

Moghalu, Kingsley C. 2002. Image and Reality of War Crimes Justice: External Perception of the International Criminal Tribunal for Rwanda. In *Fletcher Forum of World Affairs* 26: 21–42.

Mohammed, Abdelsalam A. 1999. Individual and NGO Participation in Human Rights Litigation before the African Court of Human and Peoples' Rights: Lessons from the European and Inter-American Court of Human Rights. In *Michigan State University – DCL Journal of International Law* 8: 377–96.

Morrison, Howard. 2001. The Quest for Justice. In *Counsel* June: 14–17.

Nduwimana, Françoise. 2004. *The Right to Survive Sexual Violence, Women and HIV/AIDS* at www.dd-rd.ca/English/comdoc/publications/women/hivAIDSviolEn1.htm.

Ogetto, Kennedy. 2006. The Defence Lawyers' Association at the ICTR (ADAD). In *Defence in International Criminal Proceedings: Cases, Materials and Commentary* (eds.) M. Bohlander, R. Boed and R. Wilson. Ardsley: Transnational.

Osiel, Mark. 2000. *Mass Atrocity, Collective Memory and the Law.* New Brunswick: Transaction.

Peskin, Victor. 2005. Courting Rwanda: The Promises and Pitfalls of the ICTR Outreach Programme. In *Journal of International Criminal Justice* 3: 950–61.

Rajagopal, Balakrishnan. 2003. International Law and Social Movements: Challenges of Theorizing Resistance. In *Columbia Journal of Transnational Law* 41: 397–433.

Razzaque, Jona. 2001. Changing Role of Friends of the Court in the International Courts and Tribunals. In *Non-State Actors and International Law* 1(3): 169–200.

Reydams, Luc. 2005. The ICTR Ten Years On: Back to the Nuremberg Paradigm? In *Journal of International Criminal Justice* 3: 977–88.

Rombouts, H. and S. Vandeginste. 2005. Reparation for Victims in Rwanda: Caught Between Theory and Practice. In *Out of The Ashes: Reparation for Victims of Gross and Systematic Human Rights Violations* (eds.) K. De Feyter, S. Parmentier, M. Bossuyt and P. Lemmens. Antwerp and Oxford: Intersentia.

Shelton, Dinah. 1994. The Participation of Nongovernmental Organisations in International Judicial Proceedings. In *American Journal of International Law* 88: 611.

Sluiter, Göran. 2005. The ICTR and the Protection of Witnesses. In *Journal of International Criminal Justice* 3: 962–76.

Stammers, Neil. 1999. Social Movements and the Social Construction of Human Rights. In *Human Rights Quarterly* 21: 980.

Stover, Eric. 2005. *The Witnesses: War Crimes and the Promise of Justice in The Hague*. Philadelphia: University of Pennsylvania Press.

Stover, Eric and Harvey M. Weinstein. 2004. *My Neighbour, My Enemy: Justice and Community in the Aftermath of Mass Atrocity*. Cambridge: Cambridge University Press.

UK Parliament. 2004. *Baroness Amos Response to Questions* at http://www.publications.parliament/uk/pa/1d199900/1dhansrd/pdvn/1ds04/text/40616w.

Wald, Patricia. 2001. To 'Establish Incredible Events by Credible Evidence': The Use of Affidavit Testimony in Yugoslavia War Crimes Tribunal Proceedings. In *Harvard International Law Journal* 24: 535.

Wilson, Richard. 2002. Assigned Defence Counsel in Domestic and International War Crimes Tribunals: the Need for a Structural Approach. In *International Criminal Law Review* 2: 145–94.

Zacklin, Ralph. 2004. The Failings of Ad Hoc International Tribunals. In *Journal of International Criminal Justice* 2: 541–5.

CHAPTER 4

TRANSPARENT BROADCAST? THE RECEPTION OF MILOŠEVIĆ'S TRIAL IN SERBIA

Jelena Tošić

'*Good morning, it's time for catharsis*', goes the motto of Serbia's radio station B92, which formed part of the main opposition media in the 1990s and continues to address the issue of war crimes today.[1] For some years, B92's TV channel also broadcasted, virtually live, the trials taking place at the International Criminal Tribunal for the Former Yugoslavia (ICTY) at the Hague. Can such 'transparent' broadcasting be said to facilitate the confrontation of war crimes? In order to assess the impact of international justice 'at home', this chapter explores the unique constellation of effects brought about by the direct accessibility of international justice which B92's broadcasting of the trials established in Serbia.

Undoubtedly, one of the main issues in the prominent discourse about transition in Serbia concerns the role of, and cooperation with, the ICTY. The Tribunal was established by the United Nations in 1993, in the midst of the war raging in former Yugoslavia. Its mission was to determine individual criminal responsibility for – among other crimes – genocide and crimes against humanity.[2] The UN Security Council saw one of the Tribunal's roles as contributing to lasting peace and security

[1] I would like to thank especially Marie-Bénédicte Dembour for her interest in my work and for inviting me to the workshop 'Paths to International Justice'. I am grateful to her, Tobias Kelly, Richard Wilson and Jane Cowan for constructive critical comments on drafts of this chapter. Big thanks to Julene Knox for correcting my English. The core of the research presented here was undertaken during my appointment at the Commission for Social Anthropology at the Austrian Academy of Sciences, which also funded my participation at the workshop.

[2] Alongside grave breaches of the Geneva Convention of 1949 and violations of the laws or customs of war. See Articles 2 to 5 and 7 of the Statute of the International Criminal Tribunal for the former Yugoslavia.

in the region as well as national reconciliation.[3] This chapter assesses the extent of this contribution by reference to the impact the ICTY has had on national politics and society. It does so through an analysis of the way Slobodan Milošević's trial, broadcast live on the B92 TV channel, was watched by people, covered by journalists and generally debated at a time when Milošević's sudden death in March 2006 and the lack of a proper judicial outcome for the 'trial of the century' could not have been predicted. This chapter thus deals with a specific period and the impact of the live broadcast of the Milošević trial upon local perceptions of international justice, war crimes and human rights in general. But it also illuminates a wider understanding of social and political responses to and construction of the Hague trials.

Establishing a war tribunal can be considered to constitute in itself a step towards political transparency (Sanders and West 2003: 2). In the case of the ICTY, the fact that the judicial proceedings were watched on TV more or less as they were taking place produced a different kind of transparency. In this chapter, I shall analyse its 'double-edgedness' (Coutin, Maurer and Yngvesson 2002: 837) by examining the way the Milošević trial was received in Serbia in 2002 and 2003, when I was conducting fieldwork in the country. By 'showing everything' the daily broadcast of the trial not only revealed the 'facts' of war crimes through key witnesses but it also made visible complex aspects of the trial process, arising for example from inconsistent testimonies. This had the potential to result in the public shifting its attention from taking stock of the facts of crimes to watching with excitement the 'dramatic battle' between the protagonists on the judicial scene. Media transparency therefore does not necessarily assist in establishing the desired image of international justice – one of a competent and responsible tribunal assessing the truth regarding the responsibility for war crimes and there-fore contributing to reconciliation. Instead, it can create an atmosphere where the viewer, watching an amusing televised 'courtroom drama', sides with either the accused or the prosecution. Sanders and West (2003) have noted the proximity of transparency and conspiracy. Here it is arguable that the public's daily exposure to Milošević's line of argu-ment before and against the ICTY was instrumental in the revival of conspiracy theories in Serbia.

Not surprisingly the broadcast of ICTY trials entered not only popular consciousness but also national politics. Local politicians,

---

[3] Security Council Resolution 1534/2004.

journalists, members of the intelligentsia and representatives of civil society all felt they needed to take a stand. I shall discuss their interpretation effort, focusing on the ways in which representatives of local media and civil society dealt with the transparency of the trial procedure at the ICTY and its potential for causing new ideological demarcations and restructurings. Debates on both the character and function of the ICTY and the media coverage clearly constitute a field for constructing ideological and political labelling of 'others'. Significant in this respect is a split which has emerged among those who used to be united in their opposition to Milošević. This will lead me to question the strategy, pursued by some purportedly progressive sections of local civil society, of portraying the Tribunal as the 'cornerstone of democracy'. I shall argue that this strategy may be counterproductive and even fuel the considerable nationalist potential in Serbia. Before doing this, however, I shall briefly sketch the official stance of Serbia towards the ICTY so as to provide a context in which to explore the non-legal and more social aspects of the impact of international justice on local developments.

SERBIA AND THE ICTY: BETWEEN REALPOLITIK AND A DEMAND FOR JUSTICE

The extradition in June 2001 of Slobodan Milošević, President of Serbia from 1989 to 1997 and President of Yugoslavia from 1997 to 2000 and considered the mastermind of the Yugoslav wars which gripped the region from 1991 to 1999, highlighted the extent to which the ICTY, an institution of international justice, was affecting local political developments. It certainly marked the recrudescence of the internal political conflict which had started to besiege the coalition (Democratic Opposition of Serbia, DOS) then leading the country.[4] The Tribunal's tremendous impact can also be seen, to this day, in the fact that both the start of possible EU-accession negotiations and foreign donations and loans have been made conditional on cooperation with the Tribunal, specifically in terms of extradition of indictees.[5]

---

[4] An alliance of eighteen political parties whose candidate (Vojislav Koštunica) had won the federal presidential elections in September 2000. A DOS government ruled Serbia until December 2003.

[5] At time of writing the most-wanted Serbian indictees accused of genocide in Bosnia, Radovan Karadžić and General Ratko Mladić, are still on the loose. The arrest of the Croatian general Ante Gotovina (8 December 2005) is likely to increase significantly the international pressure on Belgrade and Republika Srpska to extradite Karadžić and Mladić.

Compared with its presence in recent public debates, during the Milošević era the ICTY (established in 1993) was hardly an issue. Certainly one crucial reason for this was the Milošević regime's unambiguous rejection of cooperation with the ICTY. The basis for this refusal was the same argument that the 'star-accused' later used to delegitimise this institution of international justice – the ICTY is a political instrument and the crowning glory of a 'global anti-Serbian plot' (see next section). Another reason for the initial low level of public and political interest in the ICTY was the fact that for a long time the Tribunal primarily focused on minor perpetrators.[6] A further crucial factor for the low impact of the ICTY at a local level in Serbia was its inevitable embeddedness within a changing and controversial international political and diplomatic context. Especially during the Dayton negotiations in 1995, the stance of the United States and its European allies towards the ICTY was strongly influenced by political considerations (Williams and Scharf 2002: 116). Having established Slobodan Milošević as the Dayton 'peace factor', significant elements of the international community were not willing to address his responsibility for war crimes at that time, although relevant indictments of high-ranking persons for war crimes in Bosnia had already been made public.[7] It was not until the Kosovo crisis in 1999 that Milošević was indicted by the ICTY.

Not even the fall of the Milošević regime in 2000 brought about a substantial change in the official position towards the Tribunal; that is, the international community embraced the 'democratic' turn in Serbia and tolerated the statement by the new president Vojislav Koštunica that cooperation with the ICTY was 'clearly not one of his priorities'.[8] In the spring of 2001, however, this international support showed its other – not merely rhetorical – side: the United States offered further financial aid contingent upon the arrest of the former president. From this point onwards, positioning towards the ICTY started to impact substantially on the local political landscape in Serbia. A direct consequence of this economic condition was the conflict between the two leading political figures at that time – President Vojislav Koštunica and Prime Minister Zoran Djindjić.

---

[6] As a rule, during the first five years the Tribunal put on trial minor perpetrators (guards, foot soldiers and paramilitaries such as Duško Tadić, Dražen Erdemović, Hazim Delić, Esad Landzo), and only a minority of defendants of higher rank (such as Slavko Dokmanović, the mayor of Vukovar) (Williams and Scharf 2002).

[7] The ICTY indicted Radovan Karadžić and Ratko Mladić for war crimes committed in Bosnia in July 1995.

[8] In spite of this stance the European Union lifted the sanctions on Yugoslavia.

The conflict regarding the issue of cooperation with the ICTY rumbled on first through the imprisonment in Belgrade and then through to the extradition of Slobodan Milošević to the Hague on 28 June 2001. Koštunica accused Premier Djindjić – as the architect of Milošević's transfer to the Hague – of breaking the law and illegally extraditing the former president, and he threatened to withdraw from DOS. Apart from triggering substantial domestic instability (and almost the disintegration of the Democratic Opposition), the trans-fer of Milošević exactly one day prior to an important Donors' Conference also shows the considerable economic significance of cooperating with the Tribunal. After the extradition of the former president – characterised by Prime Minister Zoran Djindjić as 'Serbia's most valuable export commodity' (cited in Hagan 2003: 210) – Serbia and Montenegro instantly received an aid package worth more than $1.25 billion. Slobodan Milošević's arrival at the Hague was a turning point both for the Tribunal and for Serbia. Trying a former head of state for genocide (on the grounds of command responsibility) for the first time in history contributed substantially to the international legitimacy of the ICTY. On the other hand, after the extradition of Slobodan Milošević and the beginning of his trial – by means of its daily presence on TV screens in Serbia – the ICTY started to provoke fervent debates on the war crimes of the 1990s.

The extradition of the most prominent accused, Slobodan Milošević, can thus be seen to have resulted primarily from Zoran Djindjić's efforts. On 12 March 2003 Djindjić was assassinated. Presumably it was his decision to cooperate with the ICTY and to enable further extraditions (of members of the military, police and the political elite) that cost this reform-oriented politician his life (Helsinki Committee for Human Rights in Serbia 2004: 28). After the assassination, which further strengthened conservative right-wing forces and caused a flare up of nationalism in Serbia, political unwillingness to cooperate with the Tribunal met with much less resistance. From the point of view of some in human rights NGO circles, cooperation with the Tribunal after the death of Djindjić can be seen to have come to a halt. Although several further accused[9] left for the Hague (either 'voluntarily' or following arrest by the police), Koštunica's policy was by and large one of non-cooperation.

[9] Jovica Stanišić, Frenki Simatović, Veselin Šljivančanin, etc., have been arrested by the Serbian police (for a detailed list of detainees of the UN detention unit in Sheveningen, see Helsinki Committee for Human Rights in Serbia 2004: 50–1).

Apart from the ambivalent but predominantly non-cooperative stance towards the Tribunal adopted by Koštunica and his political party (Democratic Party of Serbia), currently the strongest and most explicit opponents of the Tribunal are the Serbian Socialist Party and the Serbian Radical Party whose (former) leaders (Slobodan Milošević and Vojislav Šešelj) have been on trial before the ICTY. This stance is backed up by a segment of the intellectual elite, the so-called 'patriotic block',[10] which is often referred to as the 'anti-Hague lobby' by the representatives of local human rights NGOs (Helsinki Committee for Human Rights in Serbia 2005: 23). The argument shared by these actors is that of the illegitimacy of the ICTY, which they consider to be a political rather than a legal institution created to impose collective guilt upon the Serbs. One further argument of the 'patriotic block' – strongly opposed by a section of the human rights NGO scene – is the claim that an ICTY conviction of Milošević for genocide would have substantially influenced the outcome of Bosnia-Herzegovina's charge against Yugoslavia before the International Court of Justice and would subsequently have led to expensive reparations.

The current official attitude of the government towards the ICTY (apart from that held by radical opponents) is simple and pragmatic: cooperation is an obligation and crucial for the country's future. Here the critique of the NGOs comes into play. NGO activists working on human rights often criticise this attitude among politicians, claiming that merely cooperating with the Tribunal without acknowledging and enforcing its role in establishing truth and justice will not lead to a sense of condemnation of war crimes by the population, especially given the high level of mistrust regarding the ICTY among the population.[11] The resulting cooperation is merely political and a financial necessity instead of addressing the issue of 'Serbian society's morality'.

> The Hague Tribunal's potential for placing on the table the issue of the Serbian society's morality . . . was not put to use. Serbia cooperated with the Tribunal only under outside pressure, while the cooperation itself was commercialised: indictees were exchanged for financial support. Such an

---

[10] Members of the University, the Serbian Academy of Sciences, Serbian literary circles, etc., who are expressing their views in media such as *Ogledalo*, *Srpska Reč* and *Geopolitika*.
[11] An opinion poll conducted by the Centre for Political Studies and Public Opinion Research at the Institute for Social Sciences in Belgrade shows that the overwhelming majority of the population in Serbia and Montenegro perceives the ICTY with a significant level of mistrust. The rate of mistrust has continually increased since 2000, reaching a peak in 2002 (78%), decreasing insignificantly during 2003 (75%), reaching another peak in May 2004 (77%), and finally decreasing in December of the same year (70%) (http://www.cpijm.org.yu/scharts/Izvestaj1.pdf).

attitude aroused cynicism that actually stood in the way of raising the question of the recent past. (Helsinki Committee for Human Rights in Serbia 2004: 26)

According to several human rights NGOs, instead of enforcing confrontation with the recent past, local elites have instead promoted a 'normalisation of the crime'.[12] Furthermore, local elites engage in a 'reinterpretation of history' implying a 'relativisation' and 'de-ethnification' of war crimes, by demanding that the truth regarding all crimes and victims, irrespective of their ethnic background, be established (see below). While it is not surprising that representatives of civil society hold the members of the 'anti-Hague lobby' responsible for the 'normalisation of the crime', it is significant that the 'Serbian anti-war alternative' is also held to account. Important targets of this critique are representatives of the local independent media (see below). According to the report on human rights in 2003 by the Helsinki Committee for Human Rights in Serbia, the process of facing the recent past should necessarily be grounded in a national policy backed by a nationwide consensus and should be the precondition for democratisation. The unwillingness of Serbian society – and above all its elite – to carry out such a project becomes most visible in the attitude towards the ICTY, and more particularly the trial of Slobodan Milošević (Helsinki Committee for Human Rights in Serbia 2004: 8).

WATCHING THE 'TRIAL OF THE CENTURY'

The courtroom is an international stage, and here he can play his part in the face of the media. He is aware of their impact. . . . Milošević needs an audience. . . . As long as he is in the centre of attention he has the opportunity to present his version of history, which is his main goal in this trial. It is not about proving real facts, but – as it has always been – about reinterpreting history. (Drakulić 2004: 126–7)

The old insurance company building in the Hague which now houses the ICTY strikes Pierre Hazan – a journalist who covered the ICTY trials for *Libération* and *Le Temps* – as a 'theatre of truth' (Hazan 2004). He observes that the trial chambers have become television studios from which the proceedings in the courtrooms are broadcast almost

---

[12] The 'normalisation of the crime' is apparent in the fact that four indictees were allowed to participate as candidates at the parliamentary elections in December 2004 (Helsinki Committee for Human Rights in Serbia 2004: 28).

live. The content of the unfolding trials was and is public because any person with access to television could, or with access to the internet still can, follow the proceedings at the ICTY. Due to this media transparency, which is in a way a 'hallmark' of the ICTY, the impact of the broadcasts cannot be left to chance.

> The lighting, the decoration of the courtroom, even the choice of colours have been savvily chosen for media impact. . . . The rules are strict. The cameras focus first on the judges, then on the accused or on the lawyers. The photographer is forbidden to film public demonstrations, a judge or lawyer whispering in the ear of another, or a close-up of any document. By constructing the image of a Tribunal marked by solemnity, emphasis is placed on the conscience and responsibility with which the international community has undertaken this work of memory and justice. (Hazan 2004: 5)

The opponents of the Tribunal were also very well aware of the importance of the trial broadcast. Although regarding it as illegal, Milošević also viewed the Tribunal as a space in which 'truth telling' could not only unfold freely but in addition be directly accessible to the public. Thus, Milošević used the global media transparency of the process of international justice to influence the formation of opinion in Serbia. Always elegantly dressed – in a dark suit and, mostly, a red tie – he visibly enjoyed being arrogant towards witnesses and the court. He seldom lost his temper and often spoke directly into the camera. In spite of the frequent disruptions by the judges, Milošević used every opportunity to address the public from the Hague 'stage' and to tell the 'true' history of Yugoslavia and its downfall. Moreover Milošević used the trial and its live broadcast in order to style himself as a guilt-free victim and as the 'defender of the Serbian people'. Milošević claimed moral superiority vis-à-vis the Tribunal, of which he was a captive and by which, according to him, he was a priori found guilty. He identified his allies in the 'trial of the century' as no less than truth and justice. Milošević concluded his opening defence statement as follows:

> In the true history of this era, this ad hoc justice of yours will be placed or used as an illustration of monstrous events at the changing from one century to another. Gentlemen, you cannot imagine what a privilege it is, even in these conditions that you have imposed on me, to have truth and justice as my allies. I am sure you cannot even conceive this.[13]

---

[13] Avaialble at: www.un.org/icty/transe54/040901IT.htm:32299.

In his 'narrative about the real events', which resembled a history lecture or a political speech rather than a defence statement, Milošević felt free to elaborate widely on the armed conflicts of the 1990s, which he always set in the historical context of the twentieth century (especially of World War II). His main statement was clear and he did not tire of repeating it: the illegal Tribunal – which he saw as a political and not a legal institution – was the culmination of the anti-Serbian plot by global forces, mainly the USA, Germany and the Vatican. This 'global plot', according to Milošević, had one exclusive goal: the destruction of Yugoslavia as the last 'other' – the last bastion of an alternative development to neo-liberal capitalism and the last locus of a harmonic, multi-ethnic coexistence.

> After the break-up of the Eastern Bloc, some kind of Cold War has continued in this context in order to prevent in any way the survival of a society, which could serve as an example of a successful alternative to this current simple introduction, or imposition, of the capitalist model. . . . In any case, Yugoslavia was not to outlive the Warsaw Treaty, because the Eastern European countries would have an uncomfortable example of independent development and an alternative to unquestioning acceptance of the values of the West, thus posing an obstacle to the new world order as introduced or imposed by the United States as the only remaining superpower in the world, namely the transformation of the world into a corporation society under the leadership of the World Bank and the United States, where robbery would be the main motive.[14]

Following Milošević's line of argument, the Tribunal became the last proof of his world-plot theory, which throughout the 1990s served as the most effective instrument for the legitimisation of his authoritarian rule. Thus, the media transparency of the trial process in this case became a potential medium for reviving local conspiracy theories. In his narrative, Milošević's extradition to and indictment by a representative of international justice became not only the climax of his battle against the 'new world order'; in fact, Milošević also interpreted the ad-hoc Tribunal as a sign of the decay of global justice and the system of the United Nations, confirming and legitimising the imperialism of the great powers, thus allowing itself to become an instrument for achieving their ends.

Through live coverage the ICTY became a contested space for the establishment of truth in a global context, which was present at the

---

[14] Available at: www.un.org/icty/transe54/040831ED.htm:32208-32209.

local level on a daily basis. One could even say that a new TV genre was created: live coverage from the courtroom, combined with interviews and analysis, bore the name 'Proces TV'[15] and was broadcast on B92 every morning. In spite of the fact that the television ratings[16] after the first months of the trial broadcast had dropped and later fluctuated according to the prominence of particular witnesses, this unique privilege of observing the contested versions of Serbia's 'own' history on a global stage created a substantial amount of public interest. The audience was varied. As one local journalist wrote, 'people who are biting their nails when the prosecution speaks, who jump up on their chairs and kiss their children when they see their hero on the screen'; 'temporarily' unemployed, middle-aged refugees, whose children work at the flea-market; regular customers in countless pubs where the trial broadcast is screened; or, once-very-young anti-Milošević demonstrators and now somewhat-less-young ministry employees or NGO activists in their lunch break: all were, in spite of their different interests, motives and divergent political positions, the potential audience of the Hague performance.

However, the live broadcast of the trial often seemed to miss its target and even seemed to produce the opposite effect to that expected by representatives of local civil society. Victims of human rights abuses, who appeared as witnesses before the Tribunal, were not perceived as people whose lives had been marked by grave harm, personal loss and the quest for justice. In the context of resurgent nationalism in Serbia, they were often perceived as fake and even primed witnesses. Rather than the intended 'catharsis'[17] through confrontation with the crimes, and, thus, the mobilisation of empathy and responsibility, the broadcasting of the

---

[15] This programme primarily broadcast the Milošević trial and ceased to exist after the sudden death of Milošević.

[16] Available figures regarding the issue of how often the trial broadcast was watched by the citizens (by the Belgrade Centre for Human Rights and Strategic Marketing Research; www.bgcentar.org.yu/index.php?p=236) – the Milošević trial comprising the largest part of the broadcast – show that only 33% of the population in 2003 and 34% in 2004 did not follow the trials at all. The percentage of citizens who occasionally followed the trials significantly increased from 20% in 2003 to 28% in 2004. The percentage of citizens who fairly regularly watched the trials stayed constant (11% in 2003 and 10% in 2004). Most often the trials were watched by pensioners and persons with higher education.

[17] In the context of war crimes the term 'catharsis' refers to an analogy with the psychodynamic model of psychotherapy implying that truth-telling decreases suffering and contributes to reconciliation (Weinstein and Stover 2004: 12), which although highly criticised (ibid.) is relevant and widely used in Serbia. For instance, the description of the concept of the radio broadcast on radio B92 named 'Catharsis' refers to an overarching project of confrontation with the truth and responsibility for the 'heavy burden of evil' carried over from the last decade (www.b92.net/trr/radio/katarza.html).

trial was coupled, if not exclusively with patriotism and nationalism, then certainly with a kind of sensationalism. Instead of enhancing concern for and opinion about the question of war crimes, the trial coverage seemed to focus the viewers' attention on 'thrilling' witnesses, the hiatuses of the indictment, the scoring of the prosecution and the defence team, or the 'exposure' of particular witnesses by Milošević. The impression I built from the interviews I conducted is that people spoke about the Tribunal as they would about an exciting football match or a thriller. Who was the hidden witness? What did Stipe Mesić say? Would Bill Clinton appear on the witness stand? Did the prosecution present the 'smoking gun'?

Behind these frequently grotesque and inappropriate ways of perceiving the trial – which overshadow the ultimate issue of the crimes committed – many of my interview partners sensed a counterproductive rise in the popularity of the former president.[18] That is, the viewers' attention was primarily focused on Milošević, who, assured by his claim of defending Serbia against the world, had the potential to become a hero and a martyr. One of my interview partners, a young Belgrade historian, analysed this effect of the ICTY trial on the formation of public opinion in the following way:

> Milošević is perceived as a kind of a hero. He has become a martyr. He has become someone who we are supposed to like. In this way, my mother, for instance, who hated Milošević more than anyone else, is transformed into a person who watches the trial broadcast with the same pleasure as Spanish telenovelas; she is transformed into someone who encourages him with 'bravo' shouts, although she hated him for ten years . . . And this is counterproductive, which one can recognise in the fact that when Slobodan encouraged his voters from the Hague to vote for Šešelj, those people said 'We are listening to Slobo' and Šešelj got 600,000 votes. (Personal interview)

If the coverage of the trial may have produced a sense of solidarity or even identification with the accused on the part of Milošević's former opponents, the consequences of Milošević's messages from the Hague to his former voters were far more momentous. Although not directly from the Tribunal 'stage' but instead through a message sent via a courier, Milošević supported the candidacy of the ultra-nationalist

---

18 Although his popularity must not be overestimated, the trial returned Milošević to the public eye. At the time of my fieldwork Milošević held fifth place in opinion polls surveying politicians' popularity, which is remarkable for a toppled dictator accused before a UN international Tribunal for war crimes.

Vojislav Šešelj at the presidential elections in 2002. Through this explicit appeal to his voters, Milošević managed – precisely because of his imprisonment in the Hague and not in spite of it – to influence considerably local political development from his prison cell. Thus, in regard to the presidential elections in 2002, for Milošević the ICTY figured not only as a stage for profiling and reinterpreting the past but also as a space for agency. In this case the rising popularity of Milošević, which was a substantial effect of the trial and its live coverage, became a means of mobilising the considerable nationalist voter potential in Serbia.

An associate of the Institute for European Studies in Belgrade interprets this move by Milošević as affirmation of his identity-construction strategy, which was based on his imprisonment in the Hague. Milošević sought to transform his identity as the accused and a prisoner into that of a hero, who, although behind bars, still had the power not only to influence development in his country, but also to write history.

> The form of Milošević's decision, a hand-written letter, proves his self-perception as an imprisoned antique hero and revolutionary, who is making fateful decisions that he sends, as did for example Lenin or Tito, in the form of a letter, which he probably thinks should one day be exhibited in a museum. Through this self-perception, which is totally bizarre and unrealistic, he strikes us as a friendly guy. (NIN 2694, 15 August 2002)[19]

Appadurai (1996) identifies the effect of the global media as the crucial trait of globalisation (apart from migration). In his wake, one can interpret the Tribunal, and in particular its 'immediate absorption into the public discourse', as a resource for the construction of imaginaries regarding the self and the world (Appadurai 2000: 3). Through its daily presence, which overshadows both the spatial distance and the discrepancy in objective power between the local and the global, in this case, the 'stage of global justice' – although broadcast only locally on a daily basis – potentially creates the effect of 'the whole world watching' and the viewer's impression of participating in the 'correction' of history and the quest for 'telling the whole story'. According to a Belgrade journalist covering the trials at the ICTY, the pronounced public interest in the Milošević trial was grounded in the citizens' unsatisfied need for 'the West to be told what it had done to them'. According to this interpretation, Milošević was perceived as the advocate or the 'megaphone'

---

[19] Available at: www.nin.co.yu/2002-08/15/24574.html.

of those who saw themselves primarily as victims who experienced harm, culminating in the controversial NATO bombing of 1999.

> Milošević constantly attacks NATO for having bombed the country, and the people are very fond of this. Due to the daily live broadcast of the trial they have the impression that someone is telling the truth about what was done to them directly to the world for the first time, and, moreover, that the whole world is watching. The current government has not satisfied this Serbian need for 'telling the West' and Milošević got a chance to do exactly that in the Hague and the people liked that a lot. (Personal interview)

As a result of this reading of the Milošević trial, the collective, nationalist identity of the people as 'victims and martyrs', as well as the conspiracy theory – which was officially abandoned after the fall of Milošević – was again present in everyday discourse by means of the potential for identification of viewers with Milošević's line of argument.[20] Paradoxically in this case, the media presence and transparency of an institution of international justice (which explicitly claims that its aim is not to detect *collective* but *individual* guilt[21]) had the potential to lead to a strengthening of nationalistic collective identification in the local context. This process somehow reproduced the inconsistent intention of the accused – to falsify the alleged accusation of collective guilt by defending a whole nation.

However, the transparency of the trial not only gave Milošević the opportunity to address and influence the public directly, but it also gave his audience at home access in their living room to the chronology and the dynamics of the trial. An important aspect of the latter was the gradual weakening of Milošević's line of argument. Even within the first, Kosovo phase of the trial,[22] which was 'totally overshadowed by his omnipresent commemoration' (Hazan 2004: 8), and which ended 'in a

---

[20] According to an opinion poll carried out by the Belgrade Centre for Human Rights and Strategic Marketing Research (www.bgcentar.org.yu/index.php?p=236) as many as 74% of Serbian citizens interpreted the main purpose of the ICTY along the lines of conspiracy theories, strikingly resembling the main lines of Slobodan Milošević's argument before the ICTY. 32% held that the purpose of the ICTY is 'to blame the Serbs for all war suffering and thus make Serbia dependent on the International Community', 30% held that its purpose is to 'justify NATO aggression in 1999 by blaming the Serbs and Serbia' and 12% held that its purpose is 'to establish a new world order with the USA as its leader'.

[21] In her talk at the London School of Economics, Carla Del Ponte said: 'The other important function of prosecution is to emphasise individual criminal responsibility, and to break down the idea of collective guilt and demonisation of whole groups' (Del Ponte 2003).

[22] The trial against Slobodan Milošević before the ICTY consisted of three segments: the war crimes in the region of Kosovo marked the first part of the trial, followed by occurrences in Croatia and Bosnia.

feeling of ambivalence' (ibid.), one could see how his strategy of 'exposing' witnesses without actually going into the facts about crimes against civilians in Kosovo was gradually losing ground. In particular, testimonies by insiders, such as those by the hidden witness K-41[23] or Captain Dragan Karleuša,[24] revealed Milošević's strategy of glossing over the facts regarding war crimes committed by Serbian military forces. These developments – although continuously distorted and denied by nationalistic circles in Serbia – were accordingly echoed in the trial coverage by independent local media and in the public perception of the Milošević trial. Regarding the testimony of K-41, for example, the weekly magazine *Vreme* noted that while the public had so far primarily been influenced by Milošević's alleged exposure of witnesses, 'the former soldier, the witness K-41, has produced a completely opposite effect – to the majority his narrative came across as convincing and has, like only a few testimonies so far, produced so many comments asking – were we really doing all these things during the war?'.[25] According to local journalists, the Croatia phase of the trial further exposed the inadequacies of Milošević's line of argument to the public. Due to the testimonies of further inside witnesses,[26] Milošević's strategy of denying any responsibility for the conflicts in Croatia gradually became increasingly unconvincing. While analysing the progress of the Milošević trial, one Belgrade journalist highlighted the crucial difference between the Kosovo and Croatia stages of the trial as follows:

> Watching the Croatian phase of the trial is as if you are watching a different trial. While Milošević is claiming that he had nothing to do with the war in Croatia – which no one here ever believed anyway – the generals and politicians he appointed are filing through the witness stand in front of his eyes and are denouncing him. (Personal interview)

However on air the Milošević trial – its complexity, chronology and dynamics – produced different and often opposing reactions. The actual impact of the transparency, that is, the daily accessibility of the unfolding developments in the courtroom through live coverage, was

[23] A former soldier who testified about executions of Albanian civilians near Prizren.
[24] Karleuša convincingly testified about the process of hiding evidence of war atrocities committed in Kosovo by the Serbian army in relation to the transportation of the bodies of eighty-six dead Albanians to Serbia and their burial near Belgrade.
[25] Avaialble at: www.vreme.com/cms/view.php?id=321843.
[26] One of the crucial testimonies in the Croatia phase of the trial was that of Milan Babić, a member of the government of the Republic of the Serb Krajina (originally the hidden witness C-061).

96

continuously being coloured by the interpretations of local elites. In the following section I will focus on a debate between elements of the former Milošević opposition carried out within the pages of a renowned Belgrade weekly that evolved around the issue of the demands placed on local coverage of ICTY trials.

THE POINT OF DIVERGENCE: ICTY COVERAGE BETWEEN 'OBJECTIVITY' AND 'THE DEVIL'S ALLIANCE'

The discourse on truth and responsibility regarding war crimes and human rights abuses has not only permeated everyday life through the media, but it has also revealed a deep division in society – especially among the former Milošević opposition. A prime example in this context is the polemic carried out in *Vreme*[27] from 1 August to 11 November 2002. The participants were (among others) journalists reporting from the ICTY and local human rights activists; mostly like-minded people who had made up the nucleus of anti-war opposition during the wars in Croatia and Bosnia (Helsinki Committee for Human Rights in Serbia 2003b: 295). The polemic in the distinguished weekly was triggered by an interview the director of the Helsinki Committee in Serbia gave to the Croatian weekly *Feral Tribune*. In this interview, Sonja Biserko pointed out that the Serbian media tend to generalise, relativise and de-ethnify war crimes and take a negative stand on the ICTY. She further stated the radical and provocative claim that the 'new truth marketed via media, notably via so-called independent media, spearheaded by B92 or *Vreme* is as totalitarian as was the nationalism which recently fuelled the war machinery' (Helsinki 2003b: 294).

The 'point of divergence' (*tačka razlaza*), as it was labelled in the publication of the *Vreme* polemic by the Helsinki Committee for Human Rights in Serbia (2003a), evolved around the issue of the objectivity of the coverage of the Milošević trial by local media as well as around the question of collective guilt, particularly responsibility and the '(de)ethnification' of war crimes. The following question – the essence of the polemic – was raised: does the Serbian elite use independent media (B92 and *Vreme*) in order to relativise and de-ethnify the crimes? Two positions quickly became evident. The first (among

---

[27] The independent weekly magazine *Vreme* was established in Belgrade in 1990 and was among the most distinguished oppositional print media in Serbia during the Milošević regime and also in the present.

Vreme and its defendants) held that the coverage was objective and that the crimes ought to be de-ethnified, as their ethnification would have implied the 'collective guilt of the whole people'. The opposite opinion (held by representatives of human rights NGOs, among others) was that *Vreme* was relativising the crimes, since ethnic cleansing could not be de-ethnified, and ethnification does not imply the 'collective guilt of the whole people' but rather a moral responsibility (Helsinki Committee for Human Rights in Serbia 2003a: 6).

The focus of the debate soon shifted from issues of the nature of the crimes, and guilt versus responsibility, to debating the character and ideological positioning of the participants in the debate. According to a local human rights activist the 'so-called barking' independent media portrayed the Milošević trial 'as a match between equally honourable and impartial teams, without hiding that they are Milošević fans' (Helsinki Committee for Human Rights in Serbia 2003a: 36). The allegedly biased coverage of the trial would thus show that local journalists had entered a 'devil's alliance' with the star-accused and become (or even had always been) nationalists. The journalists' reply to these extreme accusations was diverse in its scope and intensity. It ranged from empathy with the frustration of human rights representatives at the progress of the Milošević trial, to the labelling of them as the 'post-modern informbiro',[28] which sees nationalism everywhere in order to legitimise its existence, that is, to gain further funding from the West (ibid. 43–4). Despite its extreme heterogeneity the journalists' reply included one common claim regarding their professional ethics: namely, the journalists, whose work and whose professional mission – to report objectively on the trials at the ICTY – was the target of critique by human rights NGOs, felt attacked without justification. Although one could be sure of Milošević's guilt, one could not, according to the journalists, base the coverage of the ICTY on the claim (by human rights activists) that a conviction is a priori given and that the Tribunal would have only to confirm it. As one *Vreme* journalist put it: 'It is my wish that this court manages to establish the truth and to punish the perpetrators, but it is not my role to be the advocate of the prosecution' (personal interview). According to the journalists, such a partisan stance enforces the already negative perception held by citizens of the ICTY and human rights values instead of establishing the work of the Tribunal as legitimate and 'truth finding'.

[28] The 'Yugoslav version' of the Kominform (Communist Information Bureau), which severely sanctioned the pro-Russian stance after Tito's conflict with Stalin (1948–55).

A B92 journalist who reports from the Hague courtroom on a regular basis described her perception of the debate and her own professional task. While, according to her, surveys showed that the citizens recognised that war crimes had been committed and that the people who were responsible for those had to be put on trial and punished, the point of divergence in the context of the polemic instead lay in the perception of the progress of the Milošević trial in the Hague. Some aspects of the trial greatly disappointed her high expectations as an expert and advocate of the Tribunal and of international justice in general:

> We diverged, I think, in our assessments of and expectations regarding this Tribunal. If this is supposed to be a UN Tribunal and the trial of the century, as it was labelled, and if it is being claimed that this Tribunal represents and is supposed to represent the most luminous example of international justice, then those people, including myself, who have high expectations of this Tribunal, those who feel that the prosecution has to be convincing, should not be accused. The prosecution has seventy members of staff, a team of translators, huge financial means and a lot of field data. And secondly, if this Tribunal really deals with war crimes in the territory of former Yugoslavia, it has to, at least ostensibly, be interested in all crimes – for the sake of objectivity. This was, I think, the point of argument. Because what one saw in the first months of the Milošević trial was really not impressive. (Personal interview)

Precisely the demand for objectivity proves to be one of the crucial points of the debate. The contested issue of objectivity relates to both the scrutiny of the Tribunal's approach to war crimes in former Yugoslavia (by local journalists) and the critique (by human rights activists) of the way local journalists were covering the trials. That is, the journalists stressed the importance of the Tribunal's role in prosecuting all crimes, and they were concerned that indications of a biased approach would further worsen the image of the ICTY among the citizens in Serbia and thus decrease their readiness to face the recent past. The most common issue in this context was the suspension of the investigation into possible war crimes during the NATO bombing campaign against Serbia and Montenegro.[29] Further problematic issues were choice and chronology: respectively, indictments

---

[29] After her initial willingness to investigate NATO war crimes on 2 June 2000, Chief Prosecutor Carla Del Ponte 'bluntly [put] a stop to any idea of an investigation into the air campaign of the Atlantic Alliance' (Hazan 2004: 133). Despite the strong critique based on reports of the NATO bombings by Human Rights Watch, the International Red Cross and Serbia and Montenegro, an investigation was never resumed.

(not) pursued by the Tribunal and the delay in investigations that were conducted.[30]

When local journalists addressed the crucial importance of the Tribunal's objectivity, human rights activists interpreted it as proof of the journalists' 'more sophisticated' but nevertheless nationalistic stance (Helsinki Committee for Human Rights in Serbia 2004: 24). According to the Helsinki Committee for Human Rights in Serbia (2004) the journalists – although having been 'the Serbian alternative morally and financially supported by the world for their anti-war stance over the past decade' (ibid.) – now pursued the same goal as representatives of Serbian nationalism. This goal consisted of the intent to relativise war crimes, particularly the responsibility for the crimes. This intention was evident in the claim ascribed to journalists that 'Serbs are responsible for some crimes, but the others committed crimes as well' (ibid.). Without producing evidence for this alleged relativising intention on the part of local journalists, human rights activists simplistically equated two basically different stances towards war crimes: the emphasis on the need for the ICTY to live up to the self-asserted goal of investigating all war crimes committed during the war in former Yugoslavia (which is crucial for a positive perception of the ICTY by the local population), on the one hand, and a nationalistic refusal of responsibility for the crimes and a strategy for relativising them by means of 'counting them up', on the other. Moreover, the accusation by some human rights activists insinuated that the journalists' stress on the importance of the Tribunal's objectivity tacitly implied that they claim all conflicting parties in former Yugoslavia should bear equal responsibility for war crimes.

Another important aspect of the debate regarding the issue of objectivity was the dispute over the coverage of the Milošević trial. A highly illustrative example in this regard is the journalists reporting on the prosecution's insecurity (in particular the lack of credibility of several witnesses) in the course of the Kosovo phase of the Milošević trial, and their concern about a further decline in public acceptance of the ICTY. Namely, local and international observers noted that during the cross-examination by Milošević, some witnesses repeatedly refused to

[30] Due to the Tribunal having missed the opportunity to indict former Croatian president Franjo Tudjman before his death, it is unlikely that the systematic plan of ethnic cleansing of Serbs in Croatia will be fully revealed (Williams and Scharf 2002: 123). Likewise, despite the constant requests by officials in Serbia and Montenegro for an ICTY investigation into the Kosovo Liberation Army (KLA) atrocities against non-Albanians in Kosovo, the first trial against KLA members did not begin until November 2004.

acknowledge the presence of the Kosovo Liberation Army (KLA) in their villages in spite of evidence to the contrary (Hazan 2004: 166). While commenting on these developments in the course of the Milošević trial even the most pronounced advocate of the Tribunal on the local political scene, Prime Minister Zoran Djindjić, referred to the Milošević trial as a 'circus' and deplored that 'the Tribunal permits Milošević to deploy demagoguery and to direct the trial' (cited in Hazan 2004: 167).

Human rights activists interpreted the local coverage of these problematic aspects of the course of the Milošević trial merely as proof of the nationalistic and pro-Milošević stance of journalists. Without viewing the Milošević trial from a legal standpoint, and thus without acknowledging the problem of the lack of credibility of witnesses and its potential to impact negatively on the acceptance of the ICTY by the viewers of the daily broadcast, one human rights activist in the course of the polemic accused local journalists of affirming this 'petty obscene farce' and ironically referred to their work as 'courageously and independently reporting how Milošević – as so many times before – had proven that Albanian witnesses are lying' (Helsinki Committee for Human Rights in Serbia 2003a: 36). In response to the accusation of taking sides with Milošević, journalists stressed that their professional task should not consist of rooting for either Milošević or the prosecution, but rather of approaching the Milošević trial in a 'fact-oriented and down-to-earth manner' (Hazan 2004: 47). In the course of the polemic one of the journalists noted:

> In the last couple of months a number of Albanian witnesses in the Hague courtroom in fact avoided telling the truth about important details of the Kosovo war drama. While cross-examining, Milošević took advantage of this mercilessly and without measure, which – speaking in terms of a trial – is not a 'petty obscene farce', but rather one of the basic rights of the defence . . . . The journalists are merely the bearers of the information from the Hague. They are not responsible for the shortcomings of the prosecution, the cynicism of the accused and the lack of credibility of the witnesses. (Hazan 2004: 47–8)

The problematic issue of the credibility of witnesses in the course of war crimes trials cannot, however, be adequately approached without considering the political and psychological context of testifying. In this case of Albanian peasants from Kosovo, cross-examined by Milošević – who was not interested in their suffering and loss, but only in the KLA presence in their villages – the context seems rather obvious. It consists of directly facing and verbally struggling with the eloquent former 'master of the Balkans' (Hazan 2004: 166), while being aware of the live broadcast of the trial and its impact in both Serbia and Kosovo.

However, the journalists of the independent media – who allegedly joined the 'devil's alliance' and sided with Milošević – not only included the issue of witness credibility in their coverage of the trial, but they also provided their readers with the relevant political context and an affirmation of the crucial aspect of the testimonies of Albanian witnesses that was often overshadowed by Milošević's cross-examination – the experience of having been witnesses and victims of war crimes. Analysing the issue of witness credibility, one of the journalists and participants of the *Vreme* polemic highlighted precisely this key point that inconsistent testimonies must be seen within the political context and must not be considered proof that victims of war crimes are not telling the truth about their severe losses and the harm they experienced.

> The fact that Albanian witnesses have possibly been thoroughly instructed or threatened that they must not testify about the activities of the KLA doesn't have to lead to a complete devaluation of their testimony in the Hague in the eyes of the judges. Let us assume that the poor A.Z., who lost sixteen family members in the Kosovo war, was really scared and that he deeply regretted that he – while being cross-examined by Milošević – 'revealed' that his village fed and clothed 300 KLA fighters, although he originally denied the KLA presence in the village . . . This does not mean that he lied about the martyrdom of the residents of the village of Vilice . . . Albanian witnesses may not be fearless moral figures, but in no way does that mean that they are lying when they are telling about their suffering. This also does not mean that they are not leaving a by-far stronger impression on the court than on the Serbian public, which – when the suffering of Albanians is the issue – is far more cold-hearted than the western one. This again attests to Serbian society and its political sensibility.[31]

While seeking to fulfil its role in a post-authoritarian society by strongly opposing the persistent refusal of the resurgent nationalistic element in Serbia to face the issue of war crimes, a part of the human rights sector seems to have gone too far. Homogenising the local media landscape by accusing independent media of having sided with the 'anti-Hague block' seems to have had rather counterproductive effects on the public

---

[31] Available at: www.nin.co.yu/2002-02/28/22176.html.

perception of the ICTY and human rights in general. Moreover, this stance potentially further empowers the stigmatisation of human rights values and activism by ultra-nationalist circles in Serbia.

DEMOCRACY'S 'HOLY COW': THE COUNTERPRODUCTIVE EFFECTS OF EQUATING ICTY CRITIQUE WITH NATIONALISM

Human rights activists often talked about the need for the 'de-Nazification' (Helsinki Committee for Human Rights 2005: 17) of the local population. They also tended to demonise any critical stance toward the ICTY and interpret it essentially as a sign of Serbian nationalism. Paradoxically, Milošević fans who, every day, enthusiastically observed on their TV screen Milošević 'telling the truth' at the Hague, could benefit from the uncompromising and extreme position adopted by human rights activists, for it meant they were not alone in increasingly regarding this institution of international justice as an irritation.

The accusation that independent journalists were the 'real nationalists and Milošević defenders' is, for example, explicitly rejected by younger citizens who see themselves as advocates of democracy and human rights values. In this spirit one of my interviewees – a law student and participant of a human rights school[32] – criticised the radical approach by human rights activists for not acknowledging the long-term struggle against the Milošević regime within which the independent media played a crucial role: 'There was the claim that *Vreme* and B92 were as totalitarian as state TV during Milošević's rule. . . . One simply must not mark the only two media who were fighting for democracy as totalitarian' (personal interview). Postulating the unquestioning acceptance of the Tribunal almost as the cornerstone of 'being democratic', the radicalism of several human rights activists gives the impression of the curtailing of freedom of opinion even among NGO activists who see themselves as advocates of the Tribunal. In the course of my fieldwork I attended a conference[33] where one NGO activist working on reconciliation expressed her discontent with the postulated 'inviolability' and 'canonisation' of the ICTY as follows:

> Nowadays nobody is allowed to touch the Tribunal, because it is like touching a sanctum, the holy cow, so to speak. If one wants to legitimate

---

[32] Human rights schools are regularly organised by several local NGOs. In my fieldwork I documented human rights schools organised by the Belgrade Centre for Human Rights.

[33] Conference 'Which model of truth and reconciliation applies to former Yugoslavia?' (11–12 October 2002, organised by the Victimology Society in Serbia).

oneself as a democrat, it seems that one has to completely accept or at least not criticise the Tribunal. I simply don't want to be censured by anybody regarding my stance towards the Tribunal. I really approached the Tribunal with an open heart and I sometimes felt quite disappointed. Believe me, the public is forced to believe that the Tribunal is the holy cow.

In addition to this idealising stance towards the Tribunal turning out to be an irritation even for advocates of human rights and reconciliation, the stance taken by some human rights activists much less ambiguously encourages nationalist arguments and positions against the ICTY and human rights values and activism in general. In this way, the existing negative perceptions of the human rights sector in everyday discourse are being strengthened substantially. The nationalist stance is still strongly characterised by the old-world conspiracy theories of the Milošević era, which label human rights activists merely as 'lackeys of the West' and a threat to Serbian identity. A frightening example of how extreme-right reactions can be provoked by the discourse of 'de-Nazification' is the following statement by the representative of 'Obraz' – an extreme-nationalist Serbian movement:

> It is also a human right to be protected from all manipulations by the contemporary, self-proclaimed guardians of human rights. Nowadays one can speak of a totalitarian religion of human rights, of a cult of human rights, which becomes a taboo and which no one is allowed to touch. (Personal interview)

Although this member of the extreme-right movement felt in no way represented by Milošević,[34] his argument against the Tribunal was in line with that of the 'star-accused' – i.e. that the ICTY is an illegitimate institution, whose praxis is obviously characterised by double standards. Daily coverage from the Tribunal's courtroom and the 'ineffective efforts at improvement' by human rights activists, 'although at the first sight one would tend to think the opposite, [would have] a sobering effect on the citizens' (personal interview). The citizens – including those who tended to affirm the Tribunal – would, according to the Obraz representative, realise that 'individuals are not put on trial in the Hague, but rather the whole Serbian nation' (personal interview). Interestingly, this statement of 'collective guilt' being imputed to the ICTY by the Obraz member is, however, not being condemned. Rather

---

[34] In this extreme-right context, Slobodan Milošević was perceived as belonging to the left and not as a nationalist.

this extreme-right movement creatively reinterpreted and transformed the claim of collective guilt and instrumentalised it for its own purposes and goals – the nationalistic mobilisation of local population. By means of posters, graffiti and public panel discussions, the campaign 'Svaki Srbin Radovan' ('Every Serb is Radovan') was made public. According to the Obraz representative, this campaign had precisely the goal of reviving the 'choked national consciousness' through a collective identification with the 'Serbian hero par excellence' haunted by the ICTY. Radovan Karadžić, the self-proclaimed president of the Republika Srpska,[35] and one of the most-wanted indictees for the genocide in Bosnia, here serves as the symbol for the quest and successful struggle for national and territorial unity in light of 'adverse historical conditions'. As the Obraz representative said:

> We, as prime representatives of authentic Serbian nationalism, hold that as a matter of fact every Serb is Radovan. Radovan Karadžić is crucial for us both in the sense of the threat he is exposed to by the Tribunal and in the sense of the quality he has shown in his struggle. He is the only one who managed, in spite of adverse conditions, to establish a Serbian national state. (Personal interview)

Interpreting the role of the ICTY and its local advocates within the human rights scene as one of imposing collective guilt upon Serbia obviously serves the goals of this extreme-nationalist movement well. A person who is indicted for war crimes by the ICTY is not only proclaimed a 'hero', but, moreover, is presented as a general role model.

CONCLUSION: MILESTONES ON THE TRICKY PATH OF JUSTICE

In spite of the criticism related to the legal praxis and political embeddedness of the Tribunal, the ICTY represents an important step towards the identification of individual responsibility regarding war crimes committed during the war in former Yugoslavia. One of the key arguments of this chapter is that it is a false approach to argumentatively either accept or dismiss the ICTY, but rather that it is important to analyse its impact in terms of the relevant local discourses and in particular the interpretation efforts of local elites regarding the live broadcasting of the trials. If one were to ask to whom this chapter ascribes responsibility for the lack of confrontation of war crimes among the

---

[35] One of the two recognised entities of Bosnia and Herzegovina (by the Dayton Accords 21 December 1995).

Serbian population, the answer would have to point in large part to the local politicians, the media and the NGO-representatives, and not merely the ICTY itself. The criticism by local independent journalists of the course of individual cases before the ICTY must not, however, be equated with and misinterpreted as a basic nationalist rejection of this institution of international justice.

The transparency of the trials at the ICTY by means of the live broadcast, and its complex and controversial effects nevertheless represent important steps on the path towards detecting and facing responsibility for war crimes in former Yugoslavia. The transparency of the process of international justice in this case, although highly disputed, is in a way a novel resource for dealing with the past, including not least the visible ambiguity of the progress of international justice. The real-time immediacy of crucial testimonies, evidence, verdicts and guilty pleas – such as that by the former president of Republika Srpska Biljana Plavšić[36] – also communicates the profound presence and the pressing issue of the recent past and calls for appropriate political and symbolic deeds. The media transparency of the course of international justice can even override the legal relevance of pieces of evidence in the context of particular trials. As in the case of the Srebrenica video[37] – which was displayed in the course of the live coverage of the Milošević trial, but which was later ruled out as evidence against the accused – the visibility of crime stepped out of the legal context in which it originated. It had a profound effect on local processes of confronting the past. After it had been shown in the Hague courtroom, the video was broadcast on all TV stations in Serbia. Subsequently, several members of the paramilitary unit ('documented' in the video murdering Bosnian Muslims) were referred to by President Boris Tadić as 'murderers, who are among us' and were arrested by the police. In spite of controversial reactions both in Serbia and Bosnia the President of Serbia attended the Srebrenica commemoration and bowed in front of up to 8,000 victims of the Srebrenica genocide committed by Serbian military and paramilitary forces in July 1995.

REFERENCES

Appadurai, Arjun. 1996. *Modernity at Large: Cultural Dimensions of Globalization*. Minneapolis and London: University of Minnesota Press.

[36] On 16 December 2002, Plavšić pleaded guilty to crimes against humanity in Bosnia.
[37] The video showed members of a Serbian paramilitary unit (the Scorpions) torturing and killing six Bosnian Muslims from Srebrenica. The video was shown at Milošević's trial in June 2005.

2000. Grassroots Globalization and Research Imagination. In *Public Culture* 12 (1): 1–19.

Coutin, Susan B., Bill Maurer and Barbara Yngvesson. 2002. In the Mirror: the Legitimation Work of Globalization. In *Law and Social Inquiry* 27 (4): 801–43.

Del Ponte, Carla 2003. *The Role of International Criminal Prosecutions in Reconstructing Divided Communities* (Public lecture at the London School of Economics) available at www.lse.ac.uk/Depts/global/DelPonte.htm.last accessed on 17 January 2007.

Drakulić, Slavenka 2004. *Keiner war dabei: Kriegsverbrechen auf dem Balkan vor Gericht* [They Would Never Hurt a Fly: War Criminals on Trial in the Hague]. Vienna: Paul Zsolnay Verlag.

Hagan, John 2003. *Justice in the Balkans: Prosecuting War Crimes in the Hague Tribunal.* Chicago and London: University of Chicago Press.

Hazan, Pierre 2004. *Justice in a Time of War: The True Story Behind the International Criminal Tribunal for the Former Yugoslavia.* College Station: Texas A and M University Press.

Helsinki Committee for Human Rights in Serbia. 2003a. *Tačka razlaza: Povodom polemike vodjene na stranicama lista 'Vreme' od 1. avgusta do 21. novembra 2002* [The Point of Divergence: Regarding the Polemic in the Pages of the Weekly Magazine 'Vreme' between 1 August and 21 November 2002]. Belgrade: Helsinki Committee for Human Rights in Serbia.

2003b. *Human Rights in the Shadow of Nationalism: Serbia 2002.* Belgrade: Helsinki Committee for Human Rights in Serbia.

2004. *Human Rights and Accountability: Serbia 2003.* Belgrade: Helsinki Committee for Human Rights in Serbia.

2005. *Human Rights and Collective Identity: Serbia 2004.* Belgrade: Helsinki Committee for Human Rights in Serbia.

Sanders, Todd and Harry G. West 2003. Power Revealed and Concealed in the New World Order. In *Transparency and Conspiracy: Ethnographies of Suspicion in the New World Order* (eds.) Harry G. West and Todd Sanders. Durham and London: Duke University Press.

Weinstein, Harvey M. and Eric Stover 2004: Introduction. Conflict, justice and Reclamation. In *My Neighbour, My Enemy: Justice and Community in the Aftermath of Mass Atrocity* (eds.) Eric Stover and Harvey M. Weinstein. Cambridge: Cambridge University Press.

Williams, Paul R. and Michael P. Scharf. 2002. *Peace with Justice? War Crimes and Accountability in the Former Yugoslavia.* Lanham, New York and Oxford: Rowman and Littlefeld Publishers.

PART 2

. . . TO INTERNATIONAL . . .

CHAPTER 5

THE LIMITS OF INTERNATIONAL JUSTICE AT THE EUROPEAN COURT OF HUMAN RIGHTS: BETWEEN LEGAL COSMOPOLITANISM AND 'A SOCIETY OF STATES'

Başak Çalı

The European Court of Human Rights (ECtHR) is a key transnational site, where the relationship between national and international justice is played out.[1] As the adjudicator of human rights in Europe, the ECtHR is concerned with what the appropriate division of labour between international and national levels of competency and authority should be and to what extent and under what kinds of circumstances the Court should override the decisions of sovereign states as an agent of international justice.[2] These are difficult questions which raise issues as to the grounds upon which the ECtHR is *better placed* than the national legal and political authorities to deliver a human rights focused account of justice.[3] In this chapter I will argue that the ECtHR does not have a clear answer to these questions due to the conflicting commitments it exhibits towards legal cosmopolitanism and a 'society of states approach' to drawing the boundaries between international and national spheres of justice. The relationship between international and domestic spheres is constantly made and remade in the jurisprudence of the ECtHR in ways that reflect not only considerations of the facts of the case, but also these conflicting commitments. I further aim to show

---

[1] I thank the editors for their detailed constructive criticisms on earlier drafts. This piece has benefited in many ways from conversations with Juan Amaya-Castro.
[2] Partly Dissenting Opinion of Judge de Meyer in Z v. Finland (Application No. 22009/93) 25 February 1997, 1997-I, (1997) 25 EHRR 371.
[3] The concept of justice can focus on many different things, ranging from criminal law to tort law. Human rights focused justice is concerned with standards that define the fundamental human rights of individuals and corresponding duties that public authorities should have to provide for the object of the right or remedy for the violation of the right.

that the use of the doctrine of margin of appreciation by the ECtHR is merely a way of stating a conclusion rather than a way of reaching one based on the appropriate division of labour between domestic and international justice. I aim to demonstrate this argument by using the case of *Şahin v. Turkey* as an analytical tool, where the Court invoked the doctrine of margin of appreciation to state its conclusion on the merits of the case.[4] The existence of a margin of appreciation doctrine means that the Court regards the task of securing human rights, 'in the first place',[5] as the role of states.[6] The ECtHR performs a secondary and subsidiary role in human rights protection.[7] I aim to show, however, that this doctrine explains neither the point and purpose of the subsidiary character of transnational adjudication nor the appropriate degree of deference to sovereign state authority.

The case of *Şahin v. Turkey* came before the Fourth Section of the ECtHR in 2004 and before the Grand Chamber in 2005. It concerned a Turkish university student at Istanbul University who wore a *türban*.[8] She was refused entry to lectures and exams for wearing a *türban* following a circular from the Vice Chancellor of Istanbul University which banned students with beards or headscarves from campus.[9] Leyla Şahin received an official warning for non-observance of the university's regulations regarding dress and a one-term suspension after she attended an illegal protest against the dress code. These penalties were lifted following a general amnesty issued by the Grand National Assembly. Şahin subsequently moved to Vienna and continued her education there. She submitted to the Court that her rights to freedom of religion, freedom of expression, freedom from discrimination and right not to be denied education had been violated by the university regulation on wearing headscarves on campus. The Court in its Chamber judgment decided that there was no violation of freedom of religion and no separate issues arose under any of the other protections. The Grand Chamber discussed the freedom of religion and the right not to be denied education at length and also found, with one

---

[4] *Leyla Şahin v. Turkey* (Application No. 44774/98) 29 June 2004 (from now on Chamber Judgment) and Grand Chamber Judgment of 10 November 2005 (from now on Grand Chamber Judgment), available at www.coe. echr.int/echr.

[5] *Handyside v. United Kingdom* (Application No. 2476) 7 December 1976, Series A No. 24 (1976) 1 EHRR 737 para. 48.   [6] Sweeney (2005).

[7] *Handyside v. United Kingdom* (Application No. 2476) 7 December 1976, Series A No. 24 (1976) 1 EHRR 737 para. 49.

[8] *Türban* is a particular style of wearing a headscarf covering the hair and neck. I shall use the terms '*türban*', '*headscarf*' and '*Islamic headscarf*' interchangeably in this paper.

[9] Circular of the Vice Chancellor of 23 February 1998.

dissenting opinion, that there had been no violation of any Convention rights.

The case was concluded on the basis of the doctrine of margin of appreciation.[10] The Court gave a long list of reasons towards a justification of why the Turkish state enjoyed a margin of appreciation. These included the lack of common ground in Europe on the regulation of the manifestation of religious symbols at education institutions,[11] the strong commitment that the Turkish state exhibited to its fundamental constitutional principles of secularism and equality, which were 'consistent with the values underpinning the Convention'[12] and having due regard to what is at stake in the case: 'to preserve public order and to secure civil peace and true religious pluralism, which is vital to the survival of a democratic society'.[13]

The political and legal stakes were high in this case, both from the perspective of the ECtHR and of existing alignments between different branches of the Turkish state. This was the first judgment to be delivered on the wearing of headscarves at *higher* education institutions by students within the context of freedom of religion.[14] The case also tapped, however, into broader questions of state regulation of religious symbols and attire, particularly with respect to the manifestation of Islamic beliefs, if framed as a European judgment about a European question (Knights 2005; Burgorgue-Larsen and Dubout 2006). With the exception of Turkey, Albania, Azerbaijan and Bosnia-Herzegovina, Islam is a minority religion in Europe subject to stigmatisation, marginalisation and stereotyping (Asad 2003). The political expectations from this seminal judgment were diverse within Europe. They were interwoven with themes of inclusion, islamophobia and gender as common concerns of the European polity on the one hand and different types of legal regulation of religious manifestation within autonomous sovereign entities on the other.

The Turkish state also exhibited divisions between the current government, the opposition party and the judiciary on the issue. There have not been any explicit laws banning forms of religious attire for

---

[10] Chamber Judgment, para. 114 and Grand Chamber Judgment para.122.

[11] Grand Chamber Judgment para. 55–65.

[12] Chamber Judgment para. 110; Grand Chamber Judgment para. 114.

[13] Grand Chamber Judgment para. 110.

[14] Two earlier cases, where two applicants raised their refusal of graduation pictures with the *türban*, were declared inadmissible by the European Commission on Human Rights. *Karaduman v. Turkey* (Application No. 16279/90) 3 May 1993 (1993) and *Bulut v. Turkey* (Application No. 18783/91) (1993).

university students in Turkey. There were, however, two Constitutional Court judgments offering an interpretation *in abstracto* favouring a ban on headscarves and *türban* at higher education institutions in 1989 and 1991. The Constitutional Court provided an interpretation of republicanism and secularism as fundamental principles of the Turkish state. It highlighted the duty of Turkish higher education institutions to educate modern and republican youth, the duty of the state to counter the coercive nature of the traditional family and social environments in forcing girls to cover and the symbolic value of the headscarf for anti-republican and anti-secular political ideologies. The spirit of these judgments was followed by higher education institutions by way of issuing circulars on dress code. The individual lecturers in everyday life, however, have not followed the practice of banning students from lecture halls in a consistent manner.[15] Legal and political communities were also divided with respect to the interpretation of the legal status of the Constitutional Court judgments in Turkish domestic law and whether university administrations were able to use their regulative authority to restrict rights and freedoms in the absence of explicit laws (Altıparmak and Karahanoğulları 2004).

The judgment is the first in the history of the Court where the Prime Minister,[16] the President of the Parliament,[17] the Minister of Foreign Affairs[18] and members of Parliament[19] of the ruling *Adalet ve Kalkinma Partisi* (Justice and Development Party) from the defending state strongly protested that the Court did not find a violation of the Convention. It may also have been the first case where the ECtHR defended the finding of no violation to state authorities. The President of the Court, Judge Wildhaber, paid a visit to Turkey in the aftermath of the Grand Chamber judgment and asked that the respect that the ECtHR demonstrated for the Turkish Courts should not be condemned, but praised.[20] The

---

[15] This is why the applicant was able to wear the *türban* while she was studying in Bursa, a city near Istanbul, and also during the earlier part of her education at Istanbul University.

[16] 'Başbakan: Türban konusunda mahkemelerin söz söyleme yetkisi yok (Courts do not have the authority to judge the *türban*, the Prime Minister says)' *Aydınlık*, 20 November 2005.

[17] 'Gül: Bu Türkiye'nin kendi sorunudur [This is a problem of our own]' *Hürriyet*, 11 November 2005.

[18] 'Türban olmasın da ne olsun, ben bunu soruyorum [If not the *türban*, then what?]' Press Release of the President of the Grand National Assembly of 15 November 2005, www.tbmm.gov.tr, accessed 10 February 2006. 'Arınç: AIHM Bizi bağlamaz [ECtHR does not bind us]' *Sabah*, 14 November 2005.

[19] 'Bu beyaz Avrupa'nin karari'(This is the judgment of white Europeans says Parlimentarians)' *Hürriyet*, 11 November 2005.

[20] 'Wildhaber: Herkesi memnun edemeyiz [Wildhaber: We cannot make everyone happy]' *Radikal*, 9 January 2006.

divergent expectations of the Court were complex and multifaceted inside Turkey and elsewhere in Europe.

How does the ECtHR deal with such dense layers of complexity, as exhibited in this case? One answer could be that it does not and that its pronouncements are purely of an erratic political or ideological nature and its doctrines, such as the margin of appreciation, are only fancy window-dressing used to justify outcomes that have been decided in obscure and/or non-transparent ways (Amaya-Castro 2002). An extension of this view might also be that international justice is empty talk. This is not the line of argument I pursue in this paper. I will instead explore the doctrine of margin of appreciation as an attempt to create a framework of analysis to address what the limits of transnational adjudication of human rights are in delivering international justice. I will ask why the Court cannot operate without a distinction between international and national justice in order to organise and assign meaning to contested facts, as in the example of the Şahin case. I further aim to link the failure of the attempts to delineate boundaries between international and national justice to the frail and conflicting character of the international institutionalisation of justice in the world of sovereign states.

THE CONFLICTING FOUNDATIONS OF TRANSNATIONAL ADJUDICATION

The foundations of transnational human rights courts lie in international treaties. These courts have been given the task of adjudicating on the appropriate extent of the use of political power and coercion by states by making pronouncements on individual (or group) complaints. The point of human rights law is to constrain the exercise of power and the authority of states based on universal principles. International human rights courts seek to diffuse the monopolisation of power by the 'supreme authority within a territory' (Philpott 1999: 570), the sovereign state.[21] But this task ultimately depends on its recognition by states. Individual member states retain considerable competency and authority in facilitating the recognition of ECtHR judgments as authoritative pronouncements as well as the enforcement of these judgments. The delivery of international justice by transnational courts depends on how the courts perceive and organise their relationship with domestic legal and political orders and how much competency and legitimate

---

[21] For a view that this is a general problem for international law see: Shany 2006: 940.

authority they see fit to exercise in relation to the protection of the rights of individuals (Helfer and Slaughter 1997: 285). Even though one can argue that European human rights law operates at the level of a European legal community,[22] the very definition of that legal community remains contested.

Legal cosmopolitanism and the society of states approach offer two conceptions for organising the difficult relationship between international courts and states.[23] Legal cosmopolitanism puts greater emphasis on the task of these courts: the adjudication of human rights. The society of states approach taps into the normative dependency of the transnational human rights courts on sovereign states. These two approaches presuppose rival conceptions of the international legal community. Legal cosmopolitanism manifests a supranational account of the international legal community and sees international courts as guardians of that community. The society of states approach draws on a statist conception of the international legal community and sees international courts as having a limited and primarily consensual role.

Legal cosmopolitanism advocates that all domestic laws should be subordinate to the international legal order (Kelsen 1942; Koskenniemi and Leino 2002; Simma 2002), that international institutions should oversee the functioning of domestic orders (Held 1995) and that individuals, not nations, groups or states should be the main unit of moral concern (Pogge 1992; Caney 2005). Legal cosmopolitanism does not solve the problem of how different units should relate to each other, but it envisages a general framework of functional competency within a hierarchical order. The abolition of states is not necessary as long as supra-national legal (and political) authorities are empowered and the kinds of functions they perform can be differentiated from those of the states in an objective fashion. The ECtHR, in this conception, oversees the functioning of a European public order as the vertically located supra-national Court of that order.

The society of states approach points to the primacy of the sovereign authority of states over matters of law and order, the subsidiary nature

---

[22] *United Communist Party of Turkey v. Turkey* (Application No. 19392/92) 1998-I (1998) 26 EHRR 121, para. 45.

[23] I treat legal cosmopolitanism and 'society of states' approaches as broad umbrellas of thought offering normative rival conceptions for the organisation of international society and the appropriate role of states within that society. I therefore will not focus on the varieties of these approaches in the literature, but on their standard assumptions. On the variations of cosmopolitan and society of states approaches, Mapel and Nardin 1998; on divergences between political theory and international law in conceiving legal cosmopolitanism, Çalı 2006.

of international institutions in relation to states and the central role states play for the well-being of their individual members (Nardin 1983; Frost 1996; Jackson 2000).[24] Statism is a de facto form of legal pluralism in international affairs and it is not only advocated as an empirical explanation of current world affairs, but as a normative position about what kinds of political institutions are appropriate. Proponents of this approach do not see any conflict between the protection of human rights and statism (Frost 1996: 147–50). States provide individuals with a political status and recognition, which cannot be offered by family, civil society or a cosmopolitan community. The relationship between the ECtHR and the states in this conception is horizontal. The ECtHR is not the final arbiter of disputes in human rights protection, but a co-ordinator of the horizontal consensuses that exist between states with regard to human rights protection. The ECtHR does not have the moral or legal right to make a substantive intervention into the decision-making processes of a state.

These two conceptions illustrate conflicting commitments about the task of the ECtHR as a transnational human rights adjudicator. The key issue here is not whether the Court fails an ideal of international justice by making the definition of international justice sensitive to national justice. There is a deeper problem about properly understanding how international human rights courts position themselves as agents of international justice. This positioning has both functional and political aspects.

From a legal cosmopolitan perspective, when the Court is trying to define its sphere of competency with respect to domestic courts, including constitutional courts, and domestic political decision-making procedures, there are questions of functional competency at stake. Legal cosmopolitanism does not deny that international human rights courts should be assigned different levels of competency performing different functions to that of the state apparatus. It only insists that the division of labour is informed by its main unit of concern, individuals (and not states) and the protection of their rights. From a society of states perspective, international courts are secondary to states, both normatively and instrumentally. The human rights court needs to gain and maintain credibility and authority in the eyes of sovereign states to ensure compliance and enforcement. This requires the Court to find

[24] The society of states approach is different from theories of realism in international relations since it rests on the moral defence of state sovereignty as a fundamental organising unit rather than a defence of its material capacity as a powerful agent in international relations.

out for every case what the states have consented to.[25] The key concern for international human rights courts becomes their political legitimacy and the legitimate degree of coercive authority they can exercise vis-à-vis states.

The moment that the promise of international justice for human rights claims is institutionalised through the creation of international human rights courts, the modes of its delivery are compromised by questions of competency, authority and legitimacy. International human rights courts are pulled in opposite directions by the functional and political positioning of these institutions in relation to states. This institutionalised hosting of rival conceptions is the cost of pursuing international justice through international law (Meckled-García and Çalı 2006). If we are right in assuming that it is better to have international human rights courts than not, this is a cost that may be regarded as bearable. Functional differentiation and considerations of political legitimacy, however, are often interwoven. What may seem to be the failure of international justice in a particular case can also be read as the justifiable cost of institutionalisation of international justice to the extent that transnational human rights courts cannot divorce themselves from their statist foundations and legal cosmopolitan commitments.

These conceptions simultaneously co-exist in the work of the Court and they generate conflict about the identity and the legitimate sphere of operation of the Court. Margin of appreciation, in this respect, is not an interpretive principle offering solutions to this problem, but a very symptom of the problem itself. The emergence of the doctrine in the *(First) Cyprus Case* illustrates this point. This case concerned an inter-state application filed by Greece in 1956 against the United Kingdom. It involved allegations of atrocities committed by Britain in Cyprus, which then was a British colony (Simpson 2004: 924–88). The European Commission on Human Rights[26] in 1958 adopted the doctrine, although neither the United Kingdom nor Greece introduced it. In the words of the Commission, a state derogating from the protection of rights in a case of state of emergency enjoyed 'a certain measure of discretion in assessing the extent strictly required by the exigencies of

---

[25] See, illustratively, *Murphy v. Ireland* (Application No. 41179/98) 10 July 2003, 2 EHHR (2004) 181 para. 81.

[26] Protocol 11 to Convention for the Protection of Human Rights and Fundamental Freedoms, which came into force on 1 November 1998, abolished the European Commission on Human Rights and established the European Court of Human Rights as the sole body for the interpretation and application of the Convention.

the situation'.[27] In its original articulation of the doctrine, three points are striking. First, the Commission did not regard the margin of appreciation as a matter of right for the states, but as a tool to demarcate where its own boundaries lay in relation to its competency and authority. Second, it recognised that the Court had the authority to decide whether states should enjoy a margin or not. Third, it decided that the Court should give preferential treatment to the initial assessment of the state if it decided that the issues at stake fell under the legitimate powers of the state. What is clear from these points is that the margin of appreciation can be constructed both as a functional exercise about the limits and competencies of units in relation to one another and also as a blanket cover for difficult and sensitive questions about how much the Court should interfere in sovereign space. The introduction of the margin of appreciation, then, does not solve the problem about the divided identity of the Court as an agent of international justice, but perpetuates it in its case law.

OSCILLATING BETWEEN THE FUNCTIONAL AND THE POLITICAL

From its initial formulation in 1958, the meaning of the doctrine of margin of appreciation has expanded with regard to the situations it covers (Yourow: 1996). This incorporated a functional need to situate the Court in relation to domestic systems in terms of competency and also a political need to ensure respect and compliance from states. In efforts to demarcate its role functionally or politically, the Court aimed to make a distinction between matters that state authorities are better *placed* to decide and those that an international judge is better *placed* to decide. However, this does not prevent being better placed to be interpreted both as a matter of functional competency and as a matter of political legitimacy in the absence of an overarching principle setting out the object and purpose of transnational adjudication of human rights claims.

In the case of the functional delineation, the relationship between the Court and its domestic counterparts can be regarded as a matter of competency about establishing the facts by domestic trial courts and the relevant domestic law by higher domestic courts.[28] It is within the

---

[27] *Greece v. United Kingdom* (Application No. 176/1956) 26 September 1958 (1958–9) Report of the European Commission on Human Rights No. A42.048.

[28] *Taşkın and others v. Turkey* (Application No. 46117/99) 10 November 2004 (2004) (unreported).

bounds of legal cosmopolitanism to assert that an international court does not interpret what the domestic laws of a country are, since its role is the international supervision of the compatibility of these laws with standards of human rights. In the case of competency between government authorities and the Court, the Court aims to make a functional distinction between the responsibilities of governments in a democracy and judicial supervision of executive authorities. The Court recognises that 'the national authorities have direct democratic legitimation'.[29] Questions with central distributive consequences, such as economic and social policies,[30] and ones with consequences for the survival of the state (hence the rights of people under the jurisdiction of the state), such as national security, are placed in the zone where the states may enjoy a wide margin of appreciation from the standpoint of the Court. This view also reflects a common principle of judicial review based on the principle of separation of powers (Mahoney 1990).[31] The Court, furthermore, states that its international supervision does not altogether disappear and that in every single case the question of whether there has been a fair balance between the decision of the competent organ and the individual's fundamental rights will be examined, without the Court substituting it own views with that of the domestic organ.[32] What this means is that if the domestic organ is clearly competent in the issue that is discussed, the Court will reduce its scrutiny of the initial assessment made by that organ. Such an analysis requires focusing on the manifestly severe consequences of the rights restrictions for individuals rather than motivations put forward by states for restricting these rights.

The Court, however, does not limit its understanding of margin to delimiting the functional competencies of legal orders and to the adjudication of democratic processes of decision-making. It justifies the use of the margin where there is no existence of a common ground between horizontally organised states with regard to the protection of

---

[29] *Hatton v. United Kingdom* (Application No. 36022/97) 8 July 2003 (Grand Chamber) (2003) 37 EHRR 28 at 634.

[30] *Gasus Dosier-und Fordertechnik GmBH v. Netherlands* (Application No. 15375/89) 23 February 1995, Series A, Vol. 36-B (1995) 20 EHRR 403; *Markt Intern Verlag GMBH and Klaus Beerman v. Germany* (Application No. 10572/83) Series A-164 (1990) 12 EHRR 161.

[31] There is a long debate about how the boundary between democracy and rights protection is to be drawn. But the principle that it needs to be drawn is not refuted in the debate. See generally, Waldron (2001).

[32] *Hatton v. United Kingdom* (Application No. 36022/97) 8 July 2003 (2003) 37 EHRR 28 para. 129.

particular rights,[33] where it deems that 'local forces are in direct contact with vital forces' in countries,[34] where it thinks that the state is acting in the name of public interest, for example, protecting morals or rights of others, even if there are no distributive consequences attached to the action of the states[35] and where it thinks that a state's particular history justifies the actions taken.[36] In this respect, the margin of appreciation also operates as a mechanism to accommodate state sovereignty as a political principle at the expense of a common European legal order. This is a qualitative shift in the use of margin of appreciation. A judge of the ECtHR, Judge de Meyer, in the case of *Z v. Finland*, protested this shift as 'wrong in principle and pointless in practice'[37] precisely because it does not strive for a functional differentiation of division of labour:

> It is possible to envisage a margin of appreciation in certain domains. It is, for example, entirely natural for a criminal court to determine sentence – within the range of penalties laid down by the legislature – according to its assessment of the seriousness of the case. But where human rights are concerned, there is no room for a margin of appreciation which would enable the States to decide what is acceptable and what is not. On that subject the boundary not to be overstepped must be as clear and precise as possible. It is for the Court, not each State individually, to decide that issue, and the Court's views must apply to everyone within the jurisdiction of each State.[38]

The political conception of the margin of appreciation rests on the primacy of the state on two levels: first, the Court alludes to the consensual basis of authority in international law by invoking a 'common ground between the laws of contracting states'.[39] This view is compatible with a society of states approach. Since the Court is the creation of states, it regards itself bound to respect the sovereignty of states. The Court may act to verify the degree of consensus among states, but as a matter of principle it is committed to the idea of order and diversity

---

[33] X, Y and Z v. United Kingdom (Application No. 21830/93) 22 April 1997, 1997–II (1997) 24 EHRR 143; Frette v. France (Application No. 36515/97) 26 February 2002 (2004) 38 EHRR 21.
[34] Hatton v. United Kingdom.
[35] Z v. Finland (Application No. 22009/93) 25 February 1997 1997–I, (1998) 25 EHRR 371.
[36] Rekvenyi v. Hungary (Application No. 25390/94) 20 May 1999, 1999–III (2000) 30 EHRR 519, para. 48; Refah Partisi v. Turkey (Application Nos 41340/98, 41342/98, 41343/98 and 41344/98) 13 February 2003 (2003) 37 EHRR. But the Court may also take the opposite view, Buscarini v. San Marino (Application No. 24645/95) 18 February 1999 (2000) 30 EHRR 208.
[37] Dissenting opinion, para. III.   [38] Dissenting opinion, para. III.
[39] See for example, Frette v. France, para. 40.

between a society of states. Second, by referring to the exclusive right of states to act in the name of the public interest to protect morals and to regulate religion, it reifies the continuing influence of the nation-state in commonsense moral and legal thinking. Therefore, the state is regarded not only as having external sovereignty, but also internal sovereignty on matters where there are deep disagreements. The political conception is substantive and not merely functional.

As the Court does not operate with a clear set of principles, but copes with questions of its competency and authority on a case by case basis, what may at first seem like a functional argument about competency may also turn into an argument about the primary and political role of domestic justice. In the case of *Buckley v. United Kingdom*, which concerns a traveller who was denied planning permission to build a caravan on her own land, the ECtHR used a combination of a defence of proximity to the event and discretion to democratic governments in general policy matters as grounds for the legitimacy of national decisions:

> By reason of their direct and continuous contact with the vital forces of their countries, the national authorities are in principle better placed than an international court to evaluate local needs and conditions. In so far as the exercise of discretion involving a multitude of local factors is inherent in the choice and implementation of planning policies, the national authorities in principle enjoy a wide margin of appreciation.[40]

Are there any criteria that can establish how and when the Court chooses to defend its own political legitimacy against state sovereignty instead of engaging in exercises of functional competency? The answer is unclear. The Court states that it will look into (a) the nature of the right protected, (b) the nature and the degree of the interference with the right and (c) the circumstances and the context of the measures in question as key variables in its decision to invoke the margin of appreciation. However, there seems to be no coherent hierarchical order in the consideration of these variables and in the decision over which variable weighs heavier than the others.[41]

---

[40] *Buckley v. UK* (Application No. 28323/95) 28 September 1996, 1996-IV (1997) 23 EHRR 129 para. 75.

[41] Cases of torture and arbitrary killings seem to be one area that the Court asserts a hierarchy of human rights. See, *Chahal v. UK* (Application No. 22414/93) 15 November 1996 (1997) 23 EHRR 413; *Aksoy v. Turkey* (Application No. 21987/93) 18 December 1996 (1997) 23 EHRR (553).

In the case of *Dudgeon v. Ireland*, where criminalisation of homosexuality was justified by the government as part of its actions in the
public interest, the Court was confident in identifying homosexuality
as a 'most intimate aspect of private life',[42] but also highlighted that 'in
the great majority of the member States of the Council of Europe it is
no longer considered to be necessary or appropriate to treat homosexual practices of the kind now in question as in themselves a matter
to which the sanctions of the criminal law should be applied; the Court
cannot overlook the marked changes which have occurred in this
regard in the domestic law of the member States'.[43] It was, however,
unclear whether the Court had found a violation of right to privacy
due to the criminalisation of homosexuality because this was a key
concern for the well-being of the individual or because there seemed
to be a consensus about the status of adult homosexuality in Europe.
This ambiguity reflects the conflict between loyalty to legal cosmopolitanism and the need to affirm the primacy of the convergence of
states on the issue.

It may, however, be argued that this analysis does not have significant
practical consequences. At the end of the day in specific cases the Court
can be seen to have come up with 'successful' and 'progressive' final
decisions. The way the decisions are couched benefits the individual
claimant as a matter of outcome while contributing to a process of
incremental confidence building between states and the Court. The
problem with this attempt to find a balance between fundamental interests and consensus, however, is that it can go both ways as long as it is
not clear how consensus is constructed and why and to what extent it
should matter. Consensus and individual interests are not commensu-
rable values which we can weigh on the same scale. Their collusion as
a basis of decisions, therefore, is a part of the problem of the shortcom-
ings of delivering international justice. The ECtHR runs the risk of
failing to fulfil promises about transcending national sovereignties. It
also strengthens the hand of the monopoly of state control over the
political, social and cultural spheres of human action. The more the
standard of human-rights-law-compatible conduct is defined in relation
to how states are currently behaving, the more the Court looks like an
international relations pragmatist. When assessments of margin of

---

[42] *Dudgeon v. Ireland* (Application No. 7525/76) 23 September 1981 Series A, No. 45 (1981) 4
EHRR 149, para. 50.
[43] *Dudgeon v. Ireland* (Application No. 7525/76) 23 September 1981 Series A, No. 45 (1981) 4
EHRR 149, para. 50.

appreciation collapse into the legitimate use of authority by states domestically and internationally, the ECtHR is inevitably in a political zone (Brems 2003: 105), giving away any exclusive authority there may be for the international judiciary.

LEYLA ŞAHIN V. TURKEY: THE RETREAT OF THE ECtHR TO POLITICAL COMMENTARY

In the case of *Şahin* the ECtHR was faced with the question of finding its place in relation to Turkish Courts, but ultimately in relation to the Turkish Constitutional Court. The ECtHR has on many occasions declared that it is not a court of 'Fourth Instance', that is, an instance above the Constitutional Courts in a hierarchical order.[44] The ECtHR is not a court of appeal, which examines alleged errors of law or of fact which might have been committed by national courts acting within their areas of competence. Its supervision is of a horizontal nature. The ECtHR has to delineate what it is that it can do that a Constitutional Court cannot or what the added value of European supervision is to the supervision of rights protections by a Constitutional Court.

The Turkish Constitutional Court delivered two judgments discussing the compatibility of statutory law to allow headscarves to be worn with principles of the Constitution. Both judgments were made *in abstracto* and were not in relation to the application of the laws. The first one quashed the Higher Education Act of 10 December 1988, which made the wearing of headscarves covering head and neck permissible in higher education institutions. The second one interpreted the Higher Education Act of 1990 as not allowing for the wearing of headscarves.[45] The Constitutional Court in its judgments of 1989 and 1991 identified the problem not in terms of the rights of students to religious expression and rights to education, but in terms of the creation of a public space free of religious pressure. The Constitutional Court thought that the fact that the majority of the population in Turkey is Muslim was a special and decisive factor in the headscarves, particularly the *türban*, becoming a powerful religious symbol. Therefore, banning a powerful symbol from public spaces was regarded as protecting the constitutional principles of

---

[44] See for example, *Kemmache (3) v. France* (Application No. 17621/91) Series A No. 296 C (1995) 19 EHRR 349; *Öneryıldız v. Turkey* (Application No. 480939/99) Grand Chamber (2005) 41 EHRR 20.

[45] The Constitutional Court thought that clear interpretation was necessary since the Act provided 'Choice of dress shall be free in higher education institutions, provided that it does not contravene with the laws in force.' Law No 2547 of 25 October 1990.

secularism and freedom of religion.[46] The Court highlighted that freedom of religion in the private sphere was untouched. It was only restricted on public order grounds to defend secularism, which is the guarantor of rights of others as well as the constitutional order of the country.

The Constitutional Court did not engage in a factual analysis of how much of a threat wearing a headscarf posed to the rights of others in any specific context, but played the categorical trump card of secularism as a fundamental constitutional principle of the Republic with respect to restrictions of religious symbols in the public sphere. In the eyes of the Constitutional Court, the protection of rights depended on the principle of secularism and not vice versa. In other words, the Constitutional Court defended the political regime of the state as the necessary condition for the protection of human rights.

Given the structure of the defence for the restriction of the right, the ECtHR was not able to invoke any arguments regarding functional competency. The dispute did not depend on the establishment of facts by a competent tribunal or a series of complicated and fact-sensitive general policy assessments which can only be carried out by the executive authorities. Any use of the margin of appreciation only concerned political, therefore, substantive deference to the interpretation of state authorities in deciding the appropriate scope of rights. The Constitutional Court of Turkey resolved the dispute by making the legitimate existence of rights conditional upon a substantive theory of the state (i.e. secularism). If the European Court decided to invoke a margin of appreciation, it had to retreat fully from the province of a legal cosmopolitan conception of international adjudication. The cost of deferring to the state meant that the ECtHR had to give primacy to a comprehensive political theory of rights developed by the Turkish Constitutional Court, which makes rights dependent on the substantive policy of the advancement of a religion-free public space. The Court, of course, did not have to invoke the margin of appreciation. Two further routes were available to the Court. First, it might on its own independent assessment of the facts and circumstances, have found that there was no violation of the Convention. This would have required the Court to ask questions such as whether there were dangerous religious movements on Istanbul University Campus, whether the wearing of the *türban* by some of the students constituted a threat for non-*türban*

---

[46] Constitutional Court Judgment of 7 March 1989 and 9 April 1991.

wearing students, or whether there was coercion and intimidation on campus grounds. Second, it may have engaged with the coherency of the rights theory espoused by the Turkish Constitutional Court and may have reached a conclusion on whether this was the correct theory of rights for the ECtHR to operate with. This would have required the Court to defend a principled theory of human rights as a basis of its adjudication in Europe. Both of these routes require a legal cosmopolitan stance towards the authority of the Court. The Chamber judgment, however, showed that the Court was to rely on a margin of appreciation as a basis for its whole thread of reasoning:

> Where questions concerning the relationship between State and religions are at stake, on which opinion in a democratic society may reasonably differ widely, the role of the national decision-making body must be given special importance . . . A margin of appreciation is particularly appropriate when it comes to the regulation by the Contracting States of the wearing of religious symbols in teaching institutions, since rules on the subject vary from one country to another depending on natural traditions and there is no uniform European conception of the requirements of the 'protection of the rights of others' and of 'public order'.[47]

In placing the relationship between state and religion into a zone of sovereign discretion, the Court retreated to a role akin to that of a political commentator, taking more interest in explaining how events unfolded rather than displaying a supranational court's concern with whether a state's arguments are 'relevant and sufficient',[48] or pointing to a 'pressing social need' to justify the restriction, or showing the 'proportionality' of the measure to the legitimate aim concerned. The willingness of disaffiliation and the refusal of supranational authority were so stark in their reasoning that the Court could not but overlook some of its own principles of adjudication. The first was the omission that it was hard to suggest that there was no convergence in Europe about wearing religious symbols in universities.[49] By expanding the grounds of disagreement to all types of educational institutions, the Court collapsed the distinction between children and consenting adults with respect to decisions about wearing religious attire. The second was the

---

[47] Chamber Judgment, paras. 101 and 102.   [48] *Buckley v. United Kingdom*, para. 77.

[49] As pointed out by Judge Tulkens in the single dissenting opinion to the Grand Chamber judgment. In the case of *Odièvre v. France*, No. 42326/98 (2003) the same flaw of argument in the reasoning of the Court is picked by seven judges. See, Joint dissenting opinion of Mr Wildhaber, Sir Nicolas Bratza, Mr Bonello, Mr Loucaides, Mr Cabral Barreto, Mrs Tulkens and Mr Pellonpää, especially para. 16.

principle that the margin should be 'narrower where the right at stake is crucial to the individual's effective enjoyment of intimate or key rights'.[50] The general emphasis on the domestic context operated as a discursive strategy to refuse normative engagement with the specific matter at hand. In the final analysis, by active construction of a 'deep disagreement' and constantly changing views, the Court represented its agency in the matter as marginal. The intimacy of the right from the perspective of the applicant was severed both by references to the fact that she was continuing her education and had benefited from an amnesty and by the fact that the foreseeable consequences of the circular were known to the applicant.[51]

The Grand Chamber replicated the same line of reasoning, but strengthened even further the abstract and inductive reasoning of the Court and identically replicated the arguments made by the Turkish Constitutional Court about secularism and external religious symbols.[52] The particular interpretation of secularism put forward by the Constitutional Court was also supported with an unclear reference to 'gender equality' in the Grand Chamber judgment.[53] This interpretation was to the effect that the ban on *türban* promoted sexual equality by enabling a space for women to decide not to wear it.[54] This view, however, has no relevance to the facts of the case. The Istanbul Vice Chancellor did not ban the *türban* on campus because he was pursuing an agenda of 'gender equality' based on liberation from religious symbols. The substantive views of the Turkish Constitutional Court, which regarded its task as protecting rights according to the Constitution,[55] were, therefore, fully substituted by the views of the Court at the expense of the relevance of these views to the facts of the case. The Grand Chamber considered:

> this notion [of the Constitutional Court] of secularism to be consistent
> with the values underpinning the Convention. It finds that the uphold-
> ing of that principle, which is undoubtedly one of the fundamental

---

[50] *Dudgeon v. UK*, para. 51.   [51] Chamber Judgment, para.113.

[52] Grand Chamber Judgment, paras. 109–16.

[53] Grand Chamber Judgment, paras. 115 and 116. Cf. Dissenting Opinion of Judge Tulkens para. 12.

[54] This line of argument rests on a paternalistic assumption that the *türban* is intrinsically oppressive of women rather than the assumption that it can be an instrument of oppression. For criticisms of this position and its contradictions, see Shaheed 1998; Sunder 2003.

[55] Opening Address by Tülay Tuğcu, The President of the Constitutional Court of Turkey on the Occasion of the new Judicial Year of the European Court of Human Rights, 20 January 2006, Strasbourg, at www.anayasa. gov.tr, accessed on 15 February 2006.

organising principles of the Turkish state which are in harmony with the rule of law and respect for human rights, may be considered necessary to protect the democratic system in Turkey.[56]

The more the questions were addressed in terms of grand value conflicts, the easier it was to move away from the particular claims of this university student and why the Court should not conduct a fact-intensive questioning of whether the Istanbul University Vice Chancellor's circular was necessary in a democratic society to protect the rights of others.[57] The Court collapsed the particular query of the applicant into the 'question of the Islamic headscarf in the Turkish context' and made hypothetical references to the potential 'impact of the symbol on those who choose not to wear it'.[58] The Grand Chamber concluded by insisting that there was no uniform consensus on this matter in Europe and that disagreement was inevitable and tolerable (Dembour 2006: 86).[59] In sum, the Court found disagreement where there was a high level of uniformity.[60] The debates about religious manifestation were indeed diverse among Council of Europe member states on issues of the attire of civil servants, high school students, and even employees in private firms, but not concerning the dress code of university students. The Court also did not engage with the nature of the applicant's activities on campus and the political context in concrete terms.[61] This effort seemed to be directed at avoiding a politically sensitive issue, with the result of creating a deep internal contradiction within its own activities. At the end of the Şahin case, the Court looked like an institution with a deep identity crisis (Koskenniemi: 2000). Since the Court agreed with all of the arguments of principle put forward by the Constitutional Court, it also brought no added value to the debate from the perspective of any of the parties concerned. The judgments neither make the difficult tensions clearer nor highlight the difficulties of the ECtHR in adjudicating on the matter. The status quo regarding the domestic disagreement on the issue was also maintained and made even more complex by the addition of the transnational (non) involvement layer (Altıparmak and Karahanoğulları: 2005). This is not to suggest that the Court should always change the status quo or that changing the status quo

---

[56] Grand Chamber Judgment, para.114.   [57] Dissenting Opinion of Judge Tulkens, para. 10.
[58] Grand Chamber Judgment, para. 108.   [59] Grand Chamber Judgment, para. 109.
[60] Dissenting Opinion of Judge Tulkens, para. 3.
[61] Dissenting Opinion of Judge Tulkens, para. 2.

should be a benchmark for its success. The Court, however, was unable to bring a new perspective to standard arguments at hand as an agent of international justice. Did it not have an answer at all to questions about what the ECtHR could add to the debate? Was it because the ECtHR, unlike the Constitutional Court, was not up for discussing its theory of rights? This case shows that there is a significant gap between the expectations of the Court and what the Court sees itself as capable of delivering.

The applicant was absent from the Court's decision.[62] The Court further omitted any discussion of whether militant political Islam operating on the campus of Istanbul University was endangering the rights of students on campus. Domestic legal debates about the legal validity of University circulars on dress code were also lacking. The external power of the *türban* (not particularly of the applicant) *in abstracto* and the fundamental importance of the Constitutional interpretation of the principle of secularism were at the forefront of the judgment. The move away from the particular circumstances, claims of loss and harm to the applicant towards the defence of general principles emerged as an argumentative strategy that led to the no violation decision. These general principles, however, were also justified in reference to a heavily under-referenced and caricaturised historical narrative of Turkey in which Turkey emerged as a fragile political regime under constant danger from extremist political movements.[63] This meant not only that the Court did not adequately justify how the margin of appreciation operated in this case, but it also oversimplified the theoretical, legal as well as socio-political dimensions of the dispute.

CONCLUSION

The delivery of international justice through the creation of international human rights courts inherently involves compromise. International institutionalisation of human rights under the current system of international order has many costs attached. It can be argued that this discussion is only pertinent to the European Court of Human Rights, since other human rights bodies, such as the United Nations Human Rights Committee, are not fully committed to invoking a

---

[62] Judge Tulkens also highlights the absence of the voice of women in the Judgment: 'what is lacking in this debate is the opinion of women, both those who wear the headscarf and those who choose not to', Dissenting Opinion of Judge Tulkens, para. 11.

[63] Chamber Judgment, para. 99 and Grand Chamber Judgment, para. 115.

margin of appreciation.[64] It is, however, the strong, credible status and perception of the ECtHR that has resulted in the practice of the margin of appreciation (Donoho 2001: 465). In the case of the ECtHR, the more the Court regards itself as legitimate and authoritative, the more cautious it seems to be about jeopardising its authority through expanding its sphere of scrutiny to address difficult domestic political and legal choices.

I have aimed to show in the case of Şahin that the doctrine of margin of appreciation is used merely as a way of stating a conclusion rather than a way of reaching one. Because the margin of appreciation operates in regard to both the functional and the political delimitation of the Court's authority, it emerges as part of the problem rather than the solution to rival conceptions of the operation of international justice. In the Şahin case, the ECtHR's reasoning exhibits features pointing to the conclusion that it is not better placed to adjudicate. The Court, however, does not offer a general interpretative framework for the limits of transnational human rights adjudication.

This makes us revisit the question of the bearable cost of international adjudication mechanisms in human rights and what range of legitimate expectations one may have for a strong international human rights court torn between conflicting commitments to states and to individuals. A commitment to deliver 'international justice' through legal cosmopolitanism falls short in the face of the current system of horizontally negotiated international human rights treaties and the lack of explicit powers given to these institutions. This causes special problems in the domain of human rights protection, where the role of law is perceived as one that transcends nation-state authority. The same law, however, is also dependent on the coercive powers of states. The negotiation of international justice through international human rights courts is a fragile process when the stakes for the legitimacy of the supranational court are higher. It is not that international human rights courts fail to live up to their ideals. Rather, it is that they are trapped between competing conceptions of these ideals.

[64] In both cases there are isolated examples, referring to both functional and political legitimacy, but not an overarching doctrine of margin of appreciation. See Proposed Amendments to the Naturalisation Provision of the Constitution of Costa Rica, Inter-American Court of Human Rights, Series A, No. 4 (1984) para. 58 on discretion to member states to regulate naturalisation procedures and Herzberg v. Finland, Un Doc. A/37/40 (1982) para. 10.3 on lack of consensus on 'public morals'. In a banning of headscarf case for a university student from Uzbekistan, the Human Rights Committee found that the government did not fulfil the criterion of 'necessity': Hudoyberganova v. Uzbekistan, Decision of 18 January 2005, UN Doc. CCPR/82/D/931/2000 para. 6.2.

REFERENCES

Altıparmak, Kerem and Onur Karahanoğulları. 2004. Phrrus Zaferi: *Leyla Şahin/Turkiye*, AIHM/Hukuk, Düzenleyici İşlem/Kanun (Victory of Phrryus: *Leyla Şahin v. Turkey, ECHR v. Law, Executive Order v. Law*). In *Hukuk ve Adalet Dergisi* 249–75.

2005. After Şahin: The Debate on Headscarves is not Over. In *European Constitutional Law Review* 2: 268–92.

Amaya-Castro, Juan. 2002. *Dudgeon v. United Kingdom* and the Public Layers of International Adjudication. Paper presented at *Governance and International Legal Theory Conference*, Utrecht, 4–6 July 2002.

Arai-Takahashi, Yutaka. 2002. *The Margin of Appreciation Doctrine and the Principle of Proportionality in the Jurisprudence of the ECHR*. Cambridge: Cambridge University Press.

Asad, Talal. 2003. *Formations of the Secular: Christianity, Islam, Modernity*. Stanford: Stanford University Press.

Benevisti, Eyal. 1999. Margin of Appreciation, Consensus and Universal Standards. In *New York University Journal of International Law and Politics* 31: 843–54.

Brems, Eva. 2003. The Margin of Appreciation Doctrine of the European Court of Human Rights: Accommodating Diversity within Europe. In *Human Rights and Diversity: Area Studies Revisited* (eds.) David Forsythe and Patrick McMahon. Nebraska: University of Nebraska Press, 81–110.

Burgorgue-Larsen, Lawrence and Edouard Dubuout. 2006. Le port du voile à l'université. Libres propos sur l'arrêt de la Grande Chambre *Leyla Şahin c. Turquie du 10 novembre 2005*. In *Revue trimestrielle des droits de l'homme* 66: 183–215.

Çalı, Başak. 2006. On Legal Cosmopolitanism: Divergences Between Political Theory and International Law. In *Leiden Journal of International Law* 19: 1–15.

Caney, Simon. 2005. *Justice Beyond Borders: a Global Political Theory*. Oxford: Oxford University Press.

Dembour, Marie-Bénédicte. 2006. Diversity or Commonality? The Power to Toss the Human Rights Coin. In *Mediterranean Journal of Human Rights* 9: 65–91.

Donoho, Douglas Lee. 2001. Autonomy, Self-Governance and the Margin of Appreciation: Developing a Jurisprudence of Diversity with Universal Human Rights. In *Emory International Law Review* 15: 391–466.

Frost, Mervyn. 1996. *Ethics in International Relations: A Constitutive Theory*. Cambridge: Cambridge University Press.

Held, David. 1995. *Democracy and the Global Legal Order: From Modern State to Cosmopolitan Governance*. Cambridge: Polity Press.

Helfer, Lawrence and Anne-Marie Slaughter. 1997. 'Towards a Theory of Effective Supranational Adjudication.' In *Yale Law Journal* 107(2): 273–391.

Jackson, Robert. 2000. *The Global Covenant*. Oxford: Oxford University Press.

Kelsen, Hans. 1942. *Law and Peace in International Relations*. Cambridge, MA: Harvard University Press.

Knights, Shelly. 2005. Religious Symbols in the School: Freedom of Religion, Minorities and Education. In *European Human Rights Law Review* 5: 499–516.

Koskenniemi, Marti. 2000. The Effects of Rights on Political Culture. In *Human Rights in the European Union* (ed.) P. Alston. Oxford: Oxford University Press, 99–116.

Koskenniemi, M. and E. Leino. 2002. Fragmentation of International Law? Postmodern Anxieties. In *Leiden Journal of International Law* 15(3): 553–79.

Mahoney, Paul. 1990. Judicial Self-Restraint and Judicial Activism in the European Court: Two Sides of the Coin. In *Human Rights Law Journal* (1990)11: 54–85.

Mapel, David, R. and Terry Nardin. 1998. *International Society: Diverse Ethical Perspectives*. Princeton: Princeton University Press.

Meckled-García, S. and Başak Çalı. 2006. Lost in Translation: Human Rights Ideals and International Human Rights Law. In *Legalisation of Human Rights: Multi-disciplinary Perspectives on Human Rights and Human Rights Law* (eds.) S. Meckled-García and B. Çalı. Oxford: Routledge, 11–31.

Nardin Terry. 1983. *Law, Morality and the Relations of States*. Princeton: Princeton University Press.

Philpott, Daniel. 1999. Westphalia, Authority and International Society. In *Political Studies* 47: 566–89.

Pogge, Thomas. 1992. Cosmopolitanism and Sovereignty. In *Ethics* 103: 48–75.

Pufendorf, Samuel. *On the Law of Nature and of Nations (1672)*. In (ed.) Knut Hakkonssen, *The Work of Samuel Pufendorf*. Indianapolis: Liberty Fund.

Shany, Yuval. 2006. Toward a General Margin of Appreciation in International Law? In *European Journal of International Law* 16: 907–40.

Shaheed, Farida. 1998. The Other Side of the Discourse: Women's Experience of Identity, Religion and Activism in Pakistan. In *Shaping Women's Lives: Laws, Practices and Strategies in Pakistan* (eds.) F. Shaheed, S. A. Warraich, C. Balchin and A. Gazdar. Lahore: Shirkat Gah Women's Resource Centre 415–41.

Simma, Bruno. 2002. *The Charter of the United Nations: A Commentary*. Oxford: Oxford University Press.

Simpson, Brian. 2004. *Human Rights and the End of Empire: Britain and the Genesis of the European Convention*. Oxford: Oxford University Press.

Sunder, Madhavi. 2003. Piercing the Veil. In *Yale Law Journal* 112: 1399–472.

Sweeney, James. 2005. Margin of Appreciation: Cultural Relativity and the European Court of Human Rights in the Post Cold War Era. In *International and Comparative Law Quarterly* 54: 459–74.

Waldron, Jeremy. 2001. *Law and Disagreement*. Oxford: Oxford University Press.

Yourow, Howard. 1996. *The Margin of Appreciation Doctrine in the Dynamics of European Human Rights Jurisprudence*. The Hague: Kluwer Law International.

CHAPTER 6

GLOBAL JUSTICE, LOCAL CONTROVERSIES: THE INTERNATIONAL CRIMINAL COURT AND THE SOVEREIGNTY OF VICTIMS

Kamari Maxine Clarke

Though widely celebrated, the creation of the International Criminal Court (ICC), established in 2002 following the ratification of the Rome Statute by sixty nation states, has also been extremely controversial.[1] During the first few years of its existence, the controversies revolved around two central issues: the primacy of international law over national law, and the preference for pursuing justice through criminal prosecutions as opposed to amnesties or truth commissions. The Rome Statute[2] has been noted for revolutionising the ways in which people understand states' responsibility to 'humanity'. As the world's first permanent court with a specific jurisdiction to prosecute individuals who are responsible for genocide, war crimes, crimes against humanity and crimes of aggression, the ICC claims personal jurisdiction over all persons living in states that fall under the jurisdiction of the Rome Statute.

The ICC aims at ensuring that high-ranking government officials who commit crimes against humanity are apprehended and prosecuted through the action of an international body that works in conjunction with states that have both signed and ratified the Rome Statute. It thus creates a new relationship between international and national forms of justice. No longer embedded in the restrictions of citizenship that mark

---

[1] Many people contributed to strengthening this chapter, and for that I am appreciative. Special thanks to the following for their input: Lucia Cantero, Marie-Bénédicte Dembour, Ilana Gershon, Ariana Hernandez-Reguant, Tobias Kelly, Mahmood Mamdani, Mike McGovern, Beth Povenelli, Richard Wilson, Eric Worby.
[2] Rome Statute for the International Criminal Court, UN Doc. A/CONF.183/9 (17 July 1998) (hereinafter Rome Statute).

civil rights alone, the new order it establishes assumes that there is a 'natural harmony' of judicial interests between the national and the international that already exists to protect victims. According to this logic, there is no need to introduce additional spheres of justice-making that are not in keeping with juris-political spheres already offered through international and national litigation. However, in this chapter, by exploring the consequences of treating political agents as 'victims', I argue that there is a need to rethink the nature of jurisdictional sovereignty. This is because the jurisdictional claims of the ICC result in the production of a universalising category of 'victims' to be saved by 'global' human rights institutions that recasts – and denies – the political agency of victims. However, as I will argue, the sphere of victims' agency is also embedded in the sphere of sovereignty. To locate all agents in these terms is to expand that which constitutes the political in international, the national, and more circumscribed contexts.

In a bid to articulate how the universal application is to work, paragraph 10 of the preamble of the Rome Statute explicitly declares that the ICC exists in a complementary relation to national criminal jurisdictions, indicating that a case cannot be tried by the ICC if it is being investigated or prosecuted by a state that has jurisdiction over it.[3] But the preamble also identifies the international, rather than the national, as the principle unit for acting out of humanitarian concern. These principles are further detailed in Article 17 of the Rome Statute, which allocates complementary jurisdiction to the ICC over cases 'of sufficient gravity to justify further action by the Court' while ensuring that national courts retain initial jurisdiction. Thus, complementarity is meant both to represent a nod to the primacy of the nation state and to ensure that the standards of international adjudication are used as the ultimate measure of justice. In practice, however, the relationship between the international and the national spheres of governance is far from unproblematic (Schabas 2001). The forms of governmentality produced in attempts to enforce the Rome Statute at the intersection of the national and the international force us to reconsider the multiple domains of sovereignty that operate in contemporary global processes and to interrogate the politics of justice as it is played out in more circumscribed contexts.

---

[3] This is in sharp contrast to earlier tribunals such as the International Criminal Tribunals for the former Yugoslavia (ICTY) and the International Criminal Tribunal for Rwanda (ICTR), in which the sphere of the international simply claims primacy over the national (see further Brown 1998; Holmes 1999).

Unlike the nineteenth and early to mid-twentieth century that saw the management of violence collectivised through state institutions, contemporary management of violence is increasingly taking place through international institutions that are driven by supra-state organisations. A central component of this supranational governmentality is the emergence of new forms of sovereignty that range from the victims of violence to Non-Governmental Organisational (NGO) and Community Based Organisational (CBO) elites, some of whom are actively engaged in ensuring the protection of victims, while – I shall argue – also dispossessing them of their political agency as a precondition of political protection. Today neither the modern bureaucratic state nor the postcolonial state has ultimate control over the management of violence. Both sovereignty and the definition of justice have moved from the purview of the state to the realm of individuals and institutions, including non-governmental organisations, whose management of life and mechanisms for surveillance are expanding with the collectivisation of transnational human rights networks. These processes reflect an expansion of spheres of political contestation due to the involvement of new actors advocating the rights of victims on the world stage. This in turn is creating conflicts over how best to respond to various crimes against humanity in international justice domains.

As of August 2006, ten situations that have produced widespread victims of violence have been analysed by the ICC's Office of the Prosecutor (OTP) for possible prosecution. Three proceeded to investigation: one was in the Democratic Republic of Congo (DRC), the second in Sudan, and the third in Uganda and Sudan. An additional two cases concerning violence in Iraq and Venezuela were dismissed. As of autumn 2006, another five remain under analysis, including an investigative analysis of the situations in both the Central African Republic and The Ivory Coast (IBA Monitoring Report 2006). In January 2004 the ICC began the investigation into possible crimes against humanity and genocide committed in Uganda, the first state for which the prosecutor of the ICC claimed jurisdiction and later issued arrest warrants. This chapter examines how this international intervention has undercut local victims' attempts to come to terms with Uganda's violent past. At the same time it explores the competition over the expansion and restriction of the political sphere within which these contests are taking shape. The particular focus is on conflicting interpretations of justice and the role of various actors – the ICC, NGOs, traditional chiefs, perpetrators and victims – in contests over the ability of the Ugandan state to offer amnesties to its citizens versus the power of the ICC to prosecute perpetrators for war crimes and crimes against humanity.

The Ugandan context raises several important questions: At what point should the independent prosecutor of the ICC intervene in national contestations? Is national reconciliation alone sufficient? Are judicial interventions appropriate, or are there other ways in which justice for victims might be achieved? In the emergent corpus of human rights driven international law, the current trend requires states to prevent and punish various crimes against humanity and to restrict the space within which national amnesties can emerge (Laplante, this volume). The articulation of justice that advocates international law over national law reduces citizens in Uganda (and elsewhere) to victims whose very exclusion from political life is the necessary condition for political intervention by international legal regimes such as the ICC. The failure to treat Ugandans and other Africans as political agents creates the conditions for seeing Africans as victims in need of being saved by a benevolent West. I therefore explore the ways in which the management of the African population through contemporary human rights institutions, most of which originate outside of the African continent, creates forms of what Agamben calls 'bare life' (1998). Such forms of 'bare life', marked by a condition of pre-political absolute victimhood, exist in tension with the attempts to produce political beings found in the struggles of individuals from postcolonial African regions to implement their own forms of justice. Although such processes are often complex and contradictory, they can take shape through local refusals to comply with international legal demands and the creation or implementation of alternate forms of governance. This is made manifest in the conflict between international criminal prosecution and national/local reconciliation, highlighting the many unresolved issues of the ICC that are being brought to international attention by NGOs on both sides of the dispute.

There are two basic and interrelated sides of the dispute over the relationship between international criminal prosecution and national/local reconciliation. On one side is a disagreement over the use of judicial mechanisms in which, following Article 53 of the Rome Statute, a range of NGOs and legal experts in Uganda, as well as elsewhere, argue that in the 'interest of justice' the Prosecutor of the ICC should discontinue investigations and arrests in northern Uganda and allow Ugandan peace negotiations to take place. According to this argument, it is only by doing so that moral, legal and political issues can be interwoven into regionally and historically complex situations and local justice mechanisms implemented. On the other side is the prosecutor for the ICC and its global institutions, working alongside the UN Secretary-General Kofi Annan and various international human rights NGOs whose global advocacy seeks to promote the refusal of the ICC to comply with national amnesty provisions. Producing campaigns that equate amnesties with 'turning a blind eye' that lead to the 'undermining of durable peace', advocates of this movement have been central in the fight to maintain prosecution-driven justice.[4] In the middle are more complex positions that are intent on using the language of international criminal and humanitarian law instrumentally, but do so in bad faith. Others master the basic discourse of internationalism and Rule of Law in order to make a living but are ultimately concerned with ethnic and family matters, regardless of the political implications.

In interrogating the meaning of a path to international justice, therefore, it is critical to explore how, in the context of international criminal law, various understandings of justice overlay and contradict others. Especially pertinent are those paths to peace or justice that fulfil the immediate needs of victims where the Rule of Law may cause more suffering long before anything resembling peace will be possible. As the legal anthropology literature has shown, diversity in justice conceptions is vast, ranging from different views on the basis for justice (Rosen 1989; Wilson 2001; Clarke 2006), to differences in how people conceptualise rights (Mutua 2002) to differences in how they understand the duties of the individual versus ethnic, cultural, religious, or family groups (Maurer 2003; Moore 2005; Merry 2006), as well as related differences in the perceived appropriateness of punishment (An-Na'im 1999, 2005). Given this diversity, we should be asking whether the expansion of different meanings of justice provides a new language by which people can defend the persecuted or unrepresented in ways not already available to societies. In this way we can ask whether both human rights movements and the emergent international criminal law movement can provide support for local discourses of justice, instead of merely colonising existing cultural expressions or replacing them with new norms.

Beyond the question of justice, in a context where victims have been living in camps for displaced people in northern Uganda for over eleven

---

[4] See Gaertner (2006).

years, and where they are tired of its extreme poverty, the larger theoretical question is what kind of victims does the ICC require northern Uganda's citizens to be? This line of questioning highlights the ways in which the ICC mechanisms of political control mean that citizens can so easily represent 'bare life'. Scholars such as Agamben have argued that politics contains two conceptions of life: either *zoe*, that is bare life, or *bios*, that is politically or morally qualified life. *Bios* reflects the form of life found in a thriving community. The process of determining the strategy for maintaining life involves the distinction between political and human life versus bare existent life, and is what enables the ICC to claim jurisdiction and intervene through the exclusion of *zoe*, bare life, from political life. Bare life exists outside of the realm of the political whilst political life is managed by the political subjects of power relations. It is this process that decides which lives matter.

Nevertheless, of late in Uganda, victims, who have been otherwise excluded from judicial and quasi-judicial proceedings, are now through NGOs and other governmental initiatives central players in the justice-making process. This inclusion of victims has taken shape as a bid toward reconciliation and new paths toward traditional justice. In this regard, chiefs and townspeople use the language of 'rights' and 'forgiveness' and, according to Norbert Mao, chairman of the northern Uganda's Gulu district at the heart of the conflict, insist that 'justice does not necessarily mean punishment', thereby 'aiming for a higher target of seeking a peaceful and reconciled society in which we can pursue our own ancient reconciliation rituals to end one of Africa's longest wars'. This leads me to end this chapter with a section highlighting that Uganda no longer requires that victims exist as 'bare life'. To the contrary, victims are constantly enmeshed in relational connections that leave them situationally, but never a-contextually, vulnerable. Unlike the people treated as 'bare life' victims by the ICC, the Ugandan Amnesty approach allows victims and perpetrators to engage in rituals of reconciliation that reproduce themselves as political beings.

As we will see, whether perpetrators can or should be reintegrated into communities is at issue precisely because victims and their rights take centre stage. Thus, the clash between NGOs, the Ugandan government and the ICC is not simply over the nature of perpetrators and how best to respond to their crimes. Rather, the clash is over the nature of victims and how best to treat them as social/political beings and as sovereign individuals with the power to decide the exception. That is, whether Uganda, as a postcolonial state, should be able to exercise the constituent power of constitutional self-government in which they choose to apply the constitutional terms of their Amnesty Act.

THE UGANDAN AMNESTY ACT AND THE DIFFICULTIES OF COMPLEMENTARITY IN ACTION

The Acholi-speaking people of Uganda are from the Luo ethnic group, who are said to have travelled to northern Uganda from southern Sudan. By the end of the seventeenth century they settled in northern Uganda and set up chiefdoms headed by rulers known as *Rwodi*. By the mid-nineteenth century, sixty small chiefdoms existed in eastern Acholiland. During Uganda's colonial period, the British encouraged political and economic development in the south of the country, but in the northern regions the Acholi and other northern ethnic groups supplied the south with manual labour and military might. This military power peaked with the coup d'état of Acholi General Tito Okello and ended with Okello's defeat in a military coup during a five-year guerrilla war led by the National Resistance Army's leader, Yoweri Museveni.

President Yoweri Museveni assumed power non-democratically, in a country fraught with ethnically motivated conflict and political struggle. However, with pledges to restore peace, end ethnic strife and rebuild Uganda's economy, three successive presidential elections in 1996, 2000 and 2006 confirmed his rule and commenced a period of relative economic stability.[5] But violence throughout the late 1980s, 1990s and into the twenty-first century has continued to affect the northern region. A prime example is the Lord's Resistance Army (LRA), formed in 1987 as a popular resistance movement against Museveni's National Resistance Movement (NRM) government and now transformed into a rebel paramilitary group. Until 2006 the LRA engaged in a violent campaign across northern Uganda, often spilling over into parts of southern Sudan.

---

[5] A particularly unique aspect of Museveni's democracy is the current prohibition of party campaigning, put in place to avoid political party building along ethnic lines. However, this provision seems to have resulted in disadvantaging contenders to the presidency – a result to which a range of groups have objected. Under the current democratic system, candidates for both presidential and parliamentary elections are expected to campaign as individuals and not as representatives of a party. In this context they are not expected to commence their electoral campaign by engaging as a permanent opposition party. Rather, once potential candidates succeed in achieving nominations, they can contest the elections. This and other aspects of governmental policies have inspired violent resistance struggles against the Museveni government.

The LRA emerged from several splinter groups of the former Ugandan People's Democratic Army, and consists predominantly of ethnic Acholi who have been displaced by Museveni's 1986 seizure of power and are angry at what they see as unfair governance. The leader of the LRA, Joseph Kony – a spirit medium who emerged after his initial success with the growing Holy Spirit Movement – has characterised its goal as replacing Museveni's parliamentary government with an administration that would enforce the Biblical Ten Commandments (rather than a national constitution).[6] United Nations officials have classified the contemporary violent struggles in Uganda as the world's worst forgotten humanitarian crisis, blaming the LRA for regular attacks against civilians in northern Uganda that have claimed the lives of over 23,000 persons and displaced over 1.2 million. The LRA has been accused by members of the national and international communities of attacking and abducting some 20,000 children; looting and destroying civilian property; killing civilians; and torturing, raping and mutilating girls forced to serve as concubines for senior commanders.[7]

Responding to international pressure to end the northern violence and establish political and economic stability, Uganda signed the Rome Statute on 17 March 1999 and ratified it on 14 June 2002, thus becoming the ICC's sixty-eighth state member. On 29 January 2004, President Museveni referred the jurisdiction for investigating criminal offences allegedly committed by the LRA to the lead prosecutor of the International Criminal Court, Mr Moreno-Ocampo. This occurred at a time when the Ugandan government was also drafting a legislative bill in order to implement the terms of the Rome Statute into national law. Moreno-Ocampo determined that, due to conflict of law provisions surrounding the national Amnesty Act, Uganda was unable to effectively investigate LRA crimes committed in Uganda after 1 July 2002.[8] Thus on 29 July 2004 he determined that there was sufficient basis to start planning the first investigation of the ICC. In the summer of 2005, indictments for crimes against humanity were prepared by the ICC against LRA leader Joseph Kony and his top five commanders, and unsealed and presented arrest warrants were issued in winter 2006. The

---

[6] The suggestion that if the LRA was in power, religion rather than law would represent the new order is part of a larger rhetorical strategy being used by various spokespeople. However, there is widespread agreement throughout the country that such articulations of Christianity point to the political and not spiritual motives of LRA leaders.

[7] Human Rights Watch (2003); Foundation for Human Rights Initiative (2004).

[8] This is the date on which the Rome Statute came into force and thus the temporal jurisdiction of the ICC started.

indictment has raised a range of challenges concerning Uganda's sovereign right to resolve the conflict in alternative ways.

This is particularly so given the parallel and largely irreconcilable history which was evolving on the national scene. The bill implementing the Rome Statute was submitted to the cabinet for approval on 25 June 2004. Contrary to what would have been required under the Rome Statute, it failed to remove governmental immunities and amnesties, including the Ugandan Amnesty Act passed by parliament in January 2000. In late 2005, a Ugandan high court judge issued a ruling pronouncing that amnesty under local law remained available to all LRA rebels, including those indicted by the ICC. Furthermore, on 3 July 2006, Museveni announced that Uganda would grant Kony total amnesty as long as LRA leader Joseph Kony responded 'positively' to the Southern Sudan mediated peace talks and abandoned terrorism. This affirmation of state primacy came after the president, originally an ICC ally, criticised both the UN and the Democratic Republic of Congo's government for failing to capture Kony in the Garamba National Park of Congo and to initiate peace talks with the LRA.[9]

In a country with a violence-ridden past, amnesty has come to be seen by many Ugandan citizens as the best way of rebuilding the nation. Especially in the Acholi region most heavily hit by the recent warfare, the various traditional reconciliation processes of *mato oput* have been seen as complementing the amnesty pardons offered by the state. This path to justice, however, is hardly complementary to the ICC path.

AMNESTY AND THE 'TRADITIONAL' ACHOLI PATH FOLLOWED BY UGANDA

An amnesty bill was introduced by the Ugandan government in 1998 in an attempt to use pardons for insurgents to end what looked like an intractable conflict.[10] Previously, de facto and de jure amnesties under the NRM had already offered pardons to various parties and rebel groups/movements that had engaged in rebellion.[11] The Amnesty Statute of 1987 is a landmark in this history. It was passed by the

---

[9] The southern Sudanese experience, where the twenty-two-year-long war recently ended, further complicates efforts to establish peace in northern Uganda by, as it were, setting the stage for Ugandan peace talks (Anderson 2006).

[10] Bill No. 13. See *Uganda Government Gazette* No. 58 Volume XCL, 22 September 1998.

[11] Notably the UPDM/A and the UPF/UPA.

National Resistance Council (NRC) and professed to encourage various fighting groups and sponsors of insurgency to cease their activities. In particular, the statute targeted those Ugandans in exile afraid to return home for fear of possible prosecution. Admittedly, four offences – genocide, murder, kidnapping and rape – were considered too heinous to be included in the statute. The subsequent 1998 statute similarly sought to exclude certain offenders from amnesty. Nonetheless to many people subjecting all the LRA members to formal prosecution did not seem a valid or effective alternative path towards peace.

Building on the tradition of the Amnesty Statute of 1987, the government adopted a second Amnesty Act in January 2000 for Ugandans involved in 'acts of a war-like nature in various parts of the country'. The 2000 Act provides that 'an Amnesty is declared in respect of any Ugandan who has at any time since the 26th day of January, 1986 engaged in or is engaging in war or armed rebellion against the government of the Republic of Uganda by actual participation in combat; collaborating with the perpetrators of the war or armed rebellion; committing any other crime in the furtherance of the war or armed rebellion; or assisting or aiding the conduct or prosecution of the war or armed rebellion'. The amnesty depends on individual application to the authorities for a 'certificate of amnesty', along with a statement that the person concerned 'renounces and abandons involvement in the war or armed rebellion'. The Act defines amnesty as 'pardon, forgiveness, exemption, or discharge from criminal prosecution or any other form of punishment from the State'. The granting of amnesty for insurgency-related offences confers an irrevocable immunity from prosecution or punishment within the borders of Uganda (but not outside). This immunity is underwritten in the Ugandan Constitution and has been established by the Ugandan Amnesty Commission (UAC).[12] The UAC is the statutory body set up by the Ugandan government to give a blanket amnesty to surrendering rebels. Crucially, it promotes 'appropriate mechanisms of reconciliation in the affected areas'.[13]

In the Ugandan Acholi language, 'amnesty' is usually translated as '*kica*'. The term resonates with historically embedded practices. Many people in that region see the mediation of the 'traditional' chiefs (*rwodi*) as a particularly appropriate means to resolve disputes in 'the traditional

---

[12] See Article 25 (10) of the 1995 Ugandan Constitution.
[13] Section 9c of the 2000 Amnesty Act.

ways'. The *mato oput*, as it is popularly known, is presented as a cere-mony of the clan group, especially its inner family, in which the perpe-trator acknowledges his or her wrongdoing, offers compensation to the victim and culminates with the sharing of a symbolic drink.

Mato oput are being supported and institutionalised by governmental as well as non-governmental organisations throughout the northern region as an alternate path to national and international justice.[14] For example, in a project supported by the Belgian government, the *rwodi* of all the Acholi clans were reinstated and the *lawi rwodi* (head chief) was elected by the other *rwodi* in Pajule. A group *mato oput* ceremony was held in November 2001, which involved about twenty recently returned LRA combatants. The ceremony was intended to demonstrate the support of the wider Ugandan community and was attended by rep-resentatives from NGOs and churches, as well as Acholi returnees and government officials, the amnesty commissioners and senior army com-manders. Since 2001, the district of Kitgum in northern Uganda has regularly earmarked funding for elders to carry out similar atonement rituals elsewhere and ceremonies have taken place in Pabbo, Gulu dis-trict, and others have been planned for different parts of the Acholi region.

A recent *New York Times* feature article welcomed the recourse to tra-ditional justice in seeking reconciliation through *mato oput*:

> The other day, an assembly of Acholi chiefs put the notion of forgiveness into action. As they looked on, twenty-eight young men and women who had recently defected from the rebels lined up according to rank on a hilltop overlooking this war-scarred regional capital, with a one-legged lieutenant colonel in the lead and some adolescent privates bringing up the rear. They had killed and maimed together. They had raped and pil-laged. One after the other, they stuck their bare right feet in a freshly cracked egg, with the lieutenant colonel, who lost his right leg to a bomb, inserting his right crutch in the egg instead. The egg symbolizes innocent life, according to local custom, and by dabbing themselves in it the killers are restoring themselves to the way they used to be. Next, the former fighters brushed against the branch of a pobo tree, which symbolically cleansed them. By stepping over a pole, they were welcomed back into the community by Mr. Acana (i.e. the paramount chief) and the other chiefs. 'I ask for your forgiveness,' said Charles Otim, 34, the rebel lieu-tenant colonel, who had been abducted by the rebels himself, at the age of 16, early in the war. 'We have wronged you.' (Lacey 2005)

[14] Even though the guilt and submission implied by the term *'kica'* are resented by the LRA.

Not only *mato oput*, but also individual cleansing rituals have taken place whenever former LRA members have returned to the community. As described, the rituals involve the political sphere alongside the spiritual sphere, in which both the traditional institution as a political force and the spiritual realm of godly justice are seen as reuniting ex-combatants with victims.

A range of organisations are actively participating in ensuring that these revived rituals are integrated into the reconciliation process. In an interview by Janet Anderson of the Institute for War and Peace Reporting, Betty Bigombe, a key peace negotiator from Northern Uganda, insisted: 'There is tremendous support in Northern Uganda for approaches that will lead to national peace . . . .We have been calling for the ICC to back off in order to give local peace initiatives, based on traditional reconciliation methods, a chance to end the war.' Archbishop John Baptist Odama adds, 'The ICC's decision to get involved in northern Uganda's tragedy has undermined their own efforts to build the rebels' confidence in peace talks' (quoted in Anderson 2006).

Acholi reconciliation traditions are becoming popularised as a result of the efforts of international development organisations, NGOs, media reporters, as well as western researchers sympathetic to local struggles. My findings have also shown that talk of forgiveness is part of a larger discursive process that notably intersects with cultural familiarity and ethnic celebration in the midst of ethnically related violence. When given a choice between Acholi traditions and international displays of 'justice', most choose that which is familiar. However, contradictions abound and many are engaged in complex negotiations over the basic meaning of justice in this contemporary period. This is not because they agree with non-judicial sanction for the perpetrators of Ugandan violence, but because they regard it as being embedded in the desired domains of local ethnic control and culturally familiar spirituality. Thus, I am neither raising these alternative methods in order to romanticise traditional forms of justice as reconciliatory in nature, nor am I suggesting that social healing rituals reflect the totality of people's understandings of justice. Rather, Acholi 'traditional justice' mechanisms represent ritualised public expressions of wrongdoing and corrective measures towards reconciliation that have adapted symbolic meanings to contemporary social circumstances. While these various justice-making mechanisms provide alternatives to the hegemony of international legal regimes, they are also likely to perpetuate inequalities (Nader 2002), as increasing numbers of victims – disenfranchised and impoverished – gain access to the political sphere. For example, I have met people in the region who have been disillusioned by social rituals that lack judicial power. Some of these were people from afflicted villages and communities who argued that some ex-combatants, especially those who do not believe in the power of spiritual redemption, cannot be reconciled using traditional justice mechanisms. Instead, favouring international and national juridical paths to justice, they argued that the old systems of traditional justice no longer work.

Others, such as Ugandan non-governmental organisations like the Victims Rights Working Group, remain sceptical of the efficacy of traditional justice mechanisms and have lobbied for victims' interests to be taken into account through the exercise of judicial mechanisms – both international and national (Victims Rights Working Group 2006). This has meant rebutting the interest of peace by those advocates like Betty Bigombe who call for peace at all costs. These NGOs have argued that only judicial paths will achieve sustainable peace. For them, the absence of law is the absence of justice and, as such, will undermine victims' rights and dismiss their suffering as unimportant. As their literature indicates

> impunity might serve as a quick, short-term solution, but it cannot root out the seeds that led to the conflict nor deter future crimes. Indeed, denying justice can lead to further human rights violations. For example, they announce that reports from northern Uganda indicate that amnestied rebels continue to mete out abuses on victims even when they have been released from captivity in the bush . . . . International obligations to ensure justice for crimes under international law should be upheld. (Victim's Rights Working Group 2006)

Not surprisingly various international NGOs, such as Amnesty International and other NGOs that are part of the Coalition for the ICC support this position and are working alongside the ICC in order to block local attempts at amnesty. The net result is that Uganda sees itself as facing the political challenge of having to convince international institutions to respect its chosen path towards peace, while at the same time having to put in place processes of justice-based accountability.[15] Thus, on 21 July 2006, under the guardianship of the Government of Southern

---

[15] Uganda is not the only country in this situation. Rwanda has become famous for its recourse to 'traditional' *gacaca* courts alongside international and national justice options in its path to reconstruction. *Gacaca* is geared toward facilitating the trials of the over 100,000 people imprisoned since the Rwandan genocide. It is used as a form of 'reconciliation and healing'. Rather than serving prison sentences, those convicted are being called upon to confess before elected judges. The judges are then asked to give testimony to what they saw, heard and experienced

Sudan, the Lord's Resistance Army and the Ugandan Government began peace talks in Juba, Southern Sudan. This effort to end the war in northern Uganda reflects a path towards reconciliation that has been seen by all parties as being long overdue, and has stipulated that the LRA meet all four of the following conditions: (i) renounce and abandon all forms of terrorism, (ii) cease all forms of hostilities, (iii) dissolve the organisation and hand over all arms and ammunition in its possession together with their inventory, and (iv) assemble in agreed locations and demobilise and disarm. Upon successful conclusion of the talks, the Ugandan Government has offered to: (i) reintegrate ex-combatants into civilian life, (ii) fund educational training and locate economic sustenance, (iii) provide assistance with resettlement into civilian life, and (iv) provide cultural, religious leaders with the resources to allow ex-combatants to engage in social rituals and traditional justice mechanisms such as *mato oput* in order to reconcile with their community.

For the ICC and its supporters, however, there are different challenges ahead. These include creating the conditions through which its legal primacy can be established as well as taking into account a consideration of victims' needs that are in the interest of justice. At the heart of these issues are questions concerning whether the chief prosecutor of the ICC should pursue investigations and arrests prior to the end of the war in northern Uganda, or whether 'in the interest of justice' he should deem his findings inadmissible and instead support the Ugandan President Museveni's bid for peace. This would enable the Ugandan government to apply its national legislation, the Amnesty Act, and grant amnesty to the perpetrators of crimes against humanity – some of whom were victims of war – while also applying traditional justice mechanisms to Ugandan paths to justice.

'IN THE INTERESTS OF JUSTICE': RECASTING VICTIMS FROM THE POLITICAL SPHERE

One of the greatest innovations of the Rome Statute is the central role accorded to victims. As noted in one of the reports from the Office of the Prosecutor:

> For the first time in the history of international criminal justice, victims have the possibility under the Statute to present their views and

during the genocide. To give a second example, the African Union has recommended incorporating traditional forms of reconciliation to resolve the Darfur crisis in the Sudan.

observations before the Court . . . The experience of the Court to date proves that understanding the interests of victims in relation to the decision to initiate an investigation is a very complex matter. While the wording of Article 53(1)(c) implies that the interests of victims will generally weigh in favour of prosecution, in practice it is conceivable that . . . the interests of the victims may weigh against ICC action, especially when the victims themselves voice these concerns . . . There is rarely a homogeneous reaction among victims to atrocities: reactions and priorities vary for many different reasons. (OTP Report 2006b)

Since the release of the first set of ICC-related arrest warrants, there have been several discussions about the meaning and possible interpretation of Article 53 of the Rome Statute in which considerations of the clause 'in the interests of justice' have become a central factor in the admissibility of a criminal case. Article 53 describes the substantive rules for an investigation and prosecution of crimes under the subject matter jurisdiction of the ICC. In detailing the initiation of a prosecution, it indicates that 'the Prosecutor shall, having evaluated the information made available to him or her, initiate an investigation unless he or she determines that there is no reasonable basis to proceed under this Statute'. It then outlines the considerations for deciding whether to initiate an investigation.[16] If the Prosecutor determines that there is no basis upon which to proceed, then he or she is expected to inform the pre-trial chamber of this. The Prosecutor is then expected to inform the inflicted state, in this case Uganda, of the finding and reasons for such a conclusion. In determining whether there is sufficient basis for a prosecution, subsection (c) refers to inadmissibility where it is determined that proceeding with the prosecution is not in 'the interests of justice'. However, deciding on what is and what is not in the interests of justice is controversial and remains one of the most underdeveloped and contested concepts in the Rome Statute. This is primarily because the concept of acting in the interests of justice extends well beyond the exercise of criminal justice, extending into the political and moral arenas.

In June 2006, in response to questions about the political motivations of the court, the Office of the Prosecutor circulated to various

---

[16] Article 53 (1) The prosecutor shall consider whether:

(a) the information available to the prosecutor provides a reasonable basis to believe that a crime within the jurisdiction of the court has been or is being committed;
(b) the case is or would be admissible under article 17; and
(c) taking into account the gravity of the crime and the interests of victims, there are nonetheless substantial reasons to believe that an investigation would not serve the interests of justice.

international NGOs and consultants two draft documents that further expanded on the OTP's selection criteria for judicial investigations and clarified the criteria being used by the OTP in pursuing cases (OTP 2006a, 2006b). The determinations for cases were described as being shaped by four guiding principles: independence, impartiality, objectivity and non-discrimination; however, the most critical were the justifications of decisions to proceed or not proceed with judicial action in the 'interests of justice'. These determinations require legal analytic tests guided by the purposes of the court as well as larger political determinations that are connected to victims' justice. The legal tests include ending impunity while also guaranteeing respect for international justice, and in so doing justifying further action that balances the interests of justice in relation to both the gravity of the crime and the interests of the victims to end violence.

In the Uganda cases, the OTP reported that they conducted twenty missions to listen to the concerns of representatives of local communities. These meetings provided increased awareness of the differences among victims and their notions of justice, and have drawn attention to the dangers of alternative justice mechanisms. Accordingly, the OTP has continued to express their sensitivity to the deep scars that victims of the conflict have endured. Nevertheless, it has insisted that 'only in exceptional circumstances will they conclude that an investigation or a prosecution may not serve the interests of justice'.

Many developments in the last fifteen years point to a consistent trend in establishing the duty of states to prosecute crimes of international concern committed within their jurisdiction.[17] This trend is also present in the language of the Preamble to the Rome Statute, paragraph 6, in which states recognise that 'it is the duty of every State to exercise its criminal jurisdiction over those responsible for international crimes'. This view of the states that have ratified the Rome Statute appears to be supported by the United Nations Commission on Human Rights (now Human Rights Council), which has adopted an updated set of principles for the protection and promotion of human rights.[18] As argued by

---

[17] See UN Security Council Press Release, 22 June 2006, on 5474th meeting.

[18] Updated set of principles for the protection and promotion of human rights. Report by Diane Orentlicher updating the Joint Principles. UN COMMISSION ON HUMAN RIGHTS E/CN.4/2005/102/Add.1 Sixty-first session, 8 February 2005. See in particular Principle 19: *duties of states with regard to the administration of justice*: States shall undertake prompt, thorough, independent and impartial investigations of violations of human rights and international humanitarian law and take appropriate measures in respect of the perpetrators, particularly in the area of criminal justice, by ensuring that those responsible for serious crimes under international law are prosecuted, tried, and duly punished.

Moreno-Ocampo, the interpretation of the concept of 'interests of justice' should be guided by the objects and purpose of the Statute. Accordingly, the pursuit of those responsible for crimes under the jurisdiction of the Court subject to Article 17 of the Rome Statute, such as LRA perpetrators, is warranted. The above OTP draft document makes it clear that respect for victims in relation to the 'degree of legitimacy and the extent to which serious efforts had been made to respect the rule of law would be among the important factors the Prosecutor may take into account in considering national approaches'. Ultimately, the Office will seek to work with various persons in order to ensure the maximum impact.

Human Rights Watch, among a range of other international NGOs, has agreed with the OTP position. As noted by one of its Executive Directors, Richard Dicker:

> International law rejects impunity for serious crimes, such as genocide, war crimes, crimes against humanity and torture. International treaties, including the UN Convention against Torture, the Geneva Conventions, and the Rome Statute of the International Criminal Court, require parties to ensure alleged perpetrators of serious crimes are prosecuted. Uganda has ratified each of these in addition to numerous other human rights treaties . . . . The creation of the International Criminal Court and other international criminal tribunals to prosecute genocide, war crimes, crimes against humanity or other serious violations of humanitarian law illustrates the strong international commitment to justice for serious crimes.

In questioning amnesty and various traditional justice mechanisms, various representatives from Amnesty International's New York office have argued that amnesties as solutions for peace and reconciliation only lead to undercutting durable peace. Says Richard Dicker, Executive Director of Human Rights Watch:

> How long can a peace based on this kind of deal last? [To supplement investigation and prosecutions by the International Criminal Court] Uganda also should conduct meaningful prosecutions in its own courts. The Ugandan government should establish a truth commission or another truth-telling process that would allow people in northern Uganda a forum to speak about the human rights abuses that occurred during the war. This process could work alongside traditional reconciliation measures in which those affected wish to participate.

A range of local Ugandan NGOs, however, have insisted that the ICC's 2005 indictment of five LRA leaders should not preclude these talks from taking place nor should it obstruct amnesty as one of many 'paths to justice.' The intervention by various international NGOs such as Amnesty International and Human Rights Watch is often interpreted by various Ugandan NGOs as undermining the local NGO authority. Some, but not all, Ugandan NGOs feel the differences in strategies and approaches between local and international groups is typical of the micro-politics of collaboration with international NGOs. Various people with whom I developed a close relationship insisted that 'this was not unusual', and argued that one of the ways that Africa has been pathologised in world history has been through the implicit assumption that African societies are unable to address their own problems, and are therefore in need of western interventions. This intervention is symptomatic of this bias, highlighting the way that various African organisations are often made to comply with the strategies promoted by the leadership of NGOs from the US and western Europe. Arguing that international law recognises Uganda's sovereign right and obligation to resolve conflict peacefully and to address alleged offences, the Executive Director of The Refugee Law Project, Zachary Lomo, and James Otto of Uganda's Human Rights Focus have argued that the UN Charter upholds the principle of self-determination of peoples, and under the Rome Statute's principles of complementarity and admissibility, Uganda also has a right to assume responsibility for dealing with criminal charges (Lomo and Otto 2006).

On both sides of the debate are questions about what is actually in the interest of victims. The answer to that question is central to the reconfiguration of sovereignty today. In the absence of monarchs and absolutist states, and given that we have moved beyond the period of non-interventionist state sovereignty of the early twentieth century, it is clear that the new (transnational) must consider victims as central.

VICTIMS AND THE NEW *NEW* SOVEREIGNTY

In *The New Sovereignty: Compliance with International Regulatory Agreements* (1995), Abram Chayes and Antonia Handler Chayes argue that the exercise of sovereignty by states in the late twentieth century was characterised by membership in good standing to various international networks. By dismissing approaches to sovereignty that focus on a model of coercive enforcement, they proposed a new 'managerial' model of treaty compliance in which the new sovereignty could be described as an elaboration and application of treaty norms.

Accordingly, membership in the international system is the major pressure for compliance with treaty obligations. Cast this way, the continuing dialogue between international officials and non-governmental organisations generates pressure to resolve problems of non-compliance. Chayes and Chayes argue that the new sovereignty no longer 'consists of the freedom of states to act independently in their perceived self-interest'; rather, 'membership in reasonably good standing makes up the substance of international life' (1995: 27). Contending that in order to be competitive and relevant in the world economy, nation-states must submit to impositions of the international system and in so doing be accepted in a complex web of regulatory agreements, they suggest recasting the language of sovereignty in more complex terms that articulate the growing webs of obligation with that of international membership.

Although membership in the international order is certainly a critical consideration for how and why national states act, it is also important to recognise that definitions of compliance are no longer being managed solely by the state. Complex and undecided relationships between the international and the national (including constitutional provisions and legal norms) characterise the new regime. The struggles it generates over state and international authority are controversial, as multiple international and supranational organisations compete to set the parameters of international membership. The inherent inequalities involved in the process are what Giorgio Agamben (1998, 2005) has referred to as the 'state of exception', in which constituent power (the actual power to create government) is outside of the judicial order. Such an approach to sovereignty locates power both in the realm of victims of violence and in the realm of organisations and governments who participate in the decision-making process.

SOVEREIGNTY, EXCLUSION AND BARE LIFE

In ancient Roman law, the *homo sacer* was someone who could be killed with impunity but whose death had no sacrificial value. For Agamben, this figure offers the key to understanding political power and explains the 'paradox of sovereignty' as actually the essence of sovereignty. The sovereign was the person 'who decides on the state of exception'. As such, that person grants the exception the highest status for the formulation of positive rights, expressing at once the limits of sovereign power and its legitimisation. Only insofar as the value of positive rights can be suspended in a state of exception are claims to sovereignty able to define the standards for normality. Therefore, following Agamben's argument, it is not the exception that trumps the rule itself, but the rule, through its ability to suspend itself, that gives rise to the exception. It does so by always maintaining a relation to the exception, and in so doing constitutes itself as a rule (Agamben 2005).

The state of exception describes the authority to suspend the law in the name of an emergency. In the context of ethnic violence, that emergency might be one in which citizens use paramilitary coups to condemn fellow citizens to the status of 'bare life', using police, army militia or death squad resources to reduce life to death. The state of exception is also reflected in the power of individuals working through global institutions to manage international justice mechanisms and suspend national-level processes. This is directly relevant to the competition between the ICC and national-level strategies for justice in Uganda, as it relates to the power to decide when and with respect to whom the law does or does not apply. The International Criminal Court relies on states to implement its laws by eliminating national laws that conflict with them. This expectation of international supremacy points to the relative power of states in relation to international courts. Although the 120 states that initially signed the Rome Statute for the ICC participated in the writing of its statute, being central to its development and the passage of amendments, cloaked in the language of the universalism of the ICC are relations of dominance that have brought into being particular norms of juridical justice over others. This is because the conditions for inclusion in the International Criminal Court already make particular presumptions about the supremacy of international law over quasi-judicial mechanisms. During the United Nations Assembly of State Party (ASP) meetings and the UN-based General Assembly in which the provisions of the Rome Statute were established, politically 'weak' states are not always in positions to overpower 'stronger' states. As such, the relations between different nation-states and international institutions resemble contests over the power of authority – the decision to claim universal jurisdiction and form alliances with international institutions, or to implement amnesty laws and defer to state sovereignty.

This path to international justice cloaks an unequal distribution of power for the sake of a new form of governmentality through which violence can be managed internationally or in various spheres of invented tradition. The result is what Suarez-Orozco and Suarez-Orozco (2001) has referred to as the hyper-presence and hyper-absence of the state, a concept that I articulate here with reference to the ultra-expansion of statecraft, but not necessarily the state, as a result of the globalisation of governance based in networks of international, national and local spheres of individual and institutional power. Crucially, these networks do not themselves constitute sovereignty. Rather, they work alongside states and operate through such institutions as international courts and human rights agencies in strategic relation to states, by which the coordination and determination of new disciplinary principles are mobilised in strategic relation to each other.

Various extra-national tribunals have become forums for the development of new paths to extra-national justice in African postcolonial state contexts. The management of contemporary forms of violence can no longer be understood as operating through single forms of sovereign power that reflect one path or one hegemonic notion of justice within the state alone. Rather, the modernity of international criminal law, alongside the work of NGOs who propel human rights imperatives, represents a range of forces that interact with each other and produce hybrid articulations of justice. This supranational sphere of governmentality is being propelled through the legal advocacy of elite cosmopolitans operating within discrepant orders complicated by persisting postcolonial histories of deeply entrenched social divisions. The paradox of sovereignty, therefore, is its ability to make real the notion of the universal in a way that reconstitutes inequalities through the language of jurisdiction and membership. How is this possible?

Jurisdictional arrangements contribute to the creation of categories and relations between persons (Ford 1999), and therefore, through legal and political processes, law contributes to inequalities within and outside of the legal realm.[19] The international criminal law regime reproduces a relation of exclusion[20] in which these various institutions for the production of justice serve as conduits for the normative category of victim and perpetrator. According to this position, 'victims' are represented through the jurisdictional claims of the ICC as a category of individual to be saved by global human rights institutions. This process, in which international organisations take on concerns on behalf of victims for the purposes of humanitarianism, reflects the limits of international cooperation, highlighting the relegation of victims'

---

[19] See Collier, Maurer and Suarez-Navaz (1995).
[20] Also see Hansen and Stepputat (2005), and Simon Turner's contribution in the same volume.

agency to outside of the political sphere. For in the local realm, victims are included and central to reconciliation. However, in the international realm it is through their very exclusion as political agents that they are included in victims' protection and compensation programs. They are included in the international political arena by virtue of their experience as dispossessed agents.

Though many scholars of sovereignty studies have heralded this age of globalisation as an age of international cooperation and respect among different actors – the state, NGOs and victims – the space for the inclusion of victims and postcolonial sovereignty has not produced the possibility for a new immanent form of justice-making. Rather, the paths to international justice have not gone beyond producing what Partha Chatterjee (2005) calls a 'public rhetoric of moral virtue' in which a specific set of techniques for the production of democratic consent are deployed to insure the expansion of the international force of law. As such, victims are not expected to act, interpret and exercise legal power in their own right, other than by testifying in legal proceedings when called upon. To some extent, the same can be said of 'perpetrators'. They are not expected to exercise the sovereign right to negotiate terms of the peace accords or the type of justice regime they prefer. The new site of international power represents the power to declare the exception through the moral imperative of justice, as well as to take on the task of educating, disciplining and training (Chatterjee 2005), as well as to determine the terms of punishment.

However, a range of new national punishment approaches have combined both retributive justice models (in which the punishment imposed is seen as repayment or revenge for the offence committed) and rehabilitation models (in which society assists the accused in changing his/her behaviour) with forms of restorative justice which emphasise the harm done to persons and relationships rather than the violation of the law. The latter, by focusing on both the victims of crime as well as the offenders, as with 'traditional' justice mechanisms in Uganda, highlight the possibility of enabling the offender to recognise the injustice he or she has committed and participate in negotiating restoration by emphasising the need for community involvement in addressing criminal behaviour. Such notions of restorative justice as practised in the west have been shaped by Christian principles of personal salvation and peacemaking, forgiveness and healing. They became secularised in the 1980s and 1990s and have been incorporated in judiciaries in the

United States, Canada and parts of Europe, as well as in a range of non-secular legal contexts, such as that of Uganda in which traditional justice is being used in the midst of a failed judicial system. My point here is not that only such restorative justice mechanisms are viable in contexts in which civil war and ethnic hatred have led to the decimation of communities, but that the choice of rebuilding and supporting Uganda's judiciary alongside its various traditional restorative justice mechanisms as viable strategies for peace should be considered in the interest of justice. The reality however is that today, to speak of the new sovereignty is to speak of the movement of the force of law, its techniques of coercion and the disciplinary mechanisms that make the new world order possible.

Such an approach to understanding the myth of sovereignty opens up new sites of power in which the rule of international law, by suspending the possibility of national jurisdiction (in Uganda this being the application of amnesties), can render irrelevant or relevant the exercise of traditional justice mechanisms. In doing so, it denies local responses to injustice and treats victims as docile agents who need to be saved. These moralities of universalism disregard difference and enable the perpetuation of exclusion through the rule of law.

As a far from neutral project, international criminal law does not operate in an explicitly heavy-handed way through mechanisms blatantly forcing people to submit to its teachings. Rather, the contemporary effectiveness of international criminal law is in its promises of the transcendence of injustice while effectively excluding that which it seeks to protect. This ranges from the exclusion of Ugandan victims from participating in the terms of justice for LRA combatants, to the exclusion of displaced persons from determining the future of international justice deliberations. These justice hegemonies work alongside a growing regime for the universal establishment of rule of law and represent new pressures towards the supranational management of not only crime, but also of new reporting mechanisms that require international organisations to document, account for and manage the human body in particular ways, in accordance with particular treaty laws and regulations. The new sovereignty provides rationalities through which to understand the utility of contemporary democracy as a viable form of government in the late twentieth and early twenty-first centuries, and point to what international law needs in order to reshape the bio-political subject outside of the parameters of state institutions.

156

Through the moral and political force of humanitarianism, these invocations of justice as universal contribute to establishing a new moral economy according to particular human rights principles, always clarifying what is legal and illegal, acceptable and unacceptable – and, as such, participating in maintaining the norms of the good life – within 'normal' spheres of life relations – the building of a home environment free of violence, the possibility of food and economic resources to sustain education and family life. Such conditions also mark membership and belonging to the prestige of the global, which is already in alliance with the geography of rights – the spatialisation of universal jurisdiction as a widespread good. However, the nexus of conflict between social actors and institutions represents a domain in which law is mediated by power relations, and, as such, is productive of underlying exclusions that underpin the contests over, for example, amnesties versus international adjudication.

Today, institutions such as the ICC and its complex web of interlocutors are constituted by the interaction between states, institutions, international and national NGOs, victims and even rebel groups that are vying to participate in shaping the law under which they will submit. These various segments constitute international justice networks, representing the new governmentalities central in new paths to international justice and the rule of law.

Thus, I end here with a proposition for rethinking core conceptions of sovereignty that clarify various paths to international justice by locating them not just as the production of justice itself, but the production of the indirect and direct control of the prerogative within which appropriate paths to justice are made, naturalised and controlled. The complexities of Uganda's relationship to the International Criminal Court, therefore, bring into focus the power of international law to separate political beings from 'victims', while simultaneously gaining power over them by making them the subject of their political control.

CONCLUSION

While national and international contests over law-making seem to hold the potential to suspend each other and thereby suspend their norm-generating capacities, the reality is that postcolonial African states and African perpetrators of violence are engaged in uneven competitions with international legal bodies whose dominance is upheld by those UN member states most powerful on the world scene. In the midst

157

of such uneven social relationships, the ICC does not represent justice in and of itself; rather it represents the shifting locus of 'the real' through the engagement of new processes within which new norms of justice-making are reinforcing a dual presence and absence of governance within new global spheres of power. This move from the absolute jurisdictional sovereignty of nation-states to the jurisdictional reconfiguration of international bodies to adjudicate international grievances is reflective of new sovereignties of the twenty-first century, but does not constitute their totality. This is because the central issues for me here are not embedded in contests over the rituals of reconciliation versus rituals of international adjudication in relation to how to treat perpetrators of the worst crimes against humanity. Rather, the central struggles are struggles over the place of victims and how best to treat them as social/political beings. By working on behalf of victims – 'bare life' survivors whose existence is maintained by virtue of their exclusion as political agents – it is important to recognise that the power of the decision over what constitutes the life that is thereby taken outside of the political sphere (the polis) is actually the site of sovereignty. Thus, sovereignty is not a historically constituted form of political authority that arises out of the modern nation-state. It is the force of law – its techniques of coercion and the disciplinary mechanism – that makes possible the new world order of justice and politics. However, it is the essence of the political – that which is made possible by an exclusion of bare life from political life – that simultaneously makes bare life a condition of politics.

The way forward, however, is not to eradicate ICC judicial paths to justice altogether. Human rights work continues to be an important ideal in the achievement of global rights and protection against those who take the life of others in their own hands. But, we need to think more precisely about the meaning and enactment of justice and politics in local contexts – how it should work, whom it should include and whom it excludes. We must rethink the conditions within which we envisage justice in the first place, and expand the basis within which we locate political beings.

REFERENCES

Agamben, G. 1998. *Homo Sacer: Sovereign Power and Bare Life*, trans. Daniel Heler-Roazen. Stanford: Stanford University Press.
2005. *States of Exception*. Chicago: University of Chicago Press.

Allen, Tim. 2006. *Trial Justice: the International Criminal Court and the Lord's Resistance Army*. London: Zed Books.

Anderson, Janet. 2006. World Court Faces Biggest Challenge. In *Africa Reports*. The Hague. AR No. 67, 16 June.

An-na'im, Abdullah. 1999. Universality of Human Rights: An Islamic Perspective. In *Japan and International Law: Past, Present and Future* (eds.) Nisuke Ando. The Hague: Kluwer Law International, 311–25.

2005. Globalization and Jurisprudence: an Islamic Law Perspective. In *Emory Law Journal* 54: 25–51.

Brown, B. S. 1998. Primacy or Complementarity: Reconciling the Jurisdiction of National Courts and International Criminal Tribunals. In *Yale Journal of International Law*. 23: 383.

Chatterjee, Partha. 2005. Empire and Nation Revisited: Fifty Years after Bandung. In *Inter-Asia Cultural Studies* 6(4): 487–96.

Chayes, Abram and Antonia Handler Chayes. 1995. *The New Sovereignty: Compliance with International Regulatory Agreements*. Cambridge: Harvard University Press.

Clarke, Kamari M. 2006. Internationalizing the Statecraft: Genocide, Religious Revivalism, and the Cultural Politics of International Law. In *The Loyola of Los Angeles International and Comparative Law Review* 28(2).

Collier, Jane, Bill Maurer and Liliana Suarez-Navaz. 1995. Sanctioned Identities: Legal Constructions of Modern Personhood. In *Identities* 2(1 and 2): 1–27.

Ford, Richard. 1999. Law Territory (A History of Jurisdiction). In *Michigan Law Review* (February) 97: 843.

Foundation for Human Rights Initiative. 2004. The Bi-Annual Human Rights Reporter. Kampala, Uganda.

Gaertner, Hannah. 2006 (28 July). Uganda: No Amnesty for Atrocities. Human Rights Watch. Unpublished Paper.

Hansen, Thomas Blom and Finn Stepputat. 2005. *Sovereign Bodies: Citizens, Migrants, and States in the Postcolonial World*. Princeton: Princeton University Press.

Holmes, J. 1999. The Principle of Complementarity. In *The International Criminal Court: The Making of the Rome Statute – Issues, Negotiations, Results* (ed.) R. S. Lee. The Hague: Kluwer, 41–78.

Human Rights Watch. 2003 (July). Abducted and Abused: Renewed War in Northern Uganda. New York.

IBA Monitoring Report. 2006 (April). Monitoring Report: International Criminal Court. Available at www.ibanet.org/images/downloads/hri/04_2006_IBA_Monitoring_Report.pdf.

Lacey, Marc. 2005. Atrocity victims in Uganda choose to forgive. *New York Times*, April 18. Also see www.globalpolicy.org/intljustice/icc/2005/0418forgive.htm.

Lomo, Zachary and James Otto. 2006. Not a Crime to Talk: Give Peace a Chance in Northern Uganda. Human Rights Focus and Refugee Law Project. July 24. Available at: www.refugeelawproject.org/papers/reports/JubaPeaceTalksPressRelease.pdf.

Mutua, Makau. 2002. *Human Rights: A Political and Cultural Critique.* Philadelphia: University of Pennsylvania Press.

Maurer, Bill. 2003. On Divine Markets and the Problem of Justice: Empire as Theodicy. In *Empire's New Clothes* (eds.) Paul Passavant and Jodi Dean. New York: Routledge.

Merry, Sally Engle. 2006. *Human Rights and Gender Violence: Translating International Law Into Local Justice.* Chicago: University of Chicago Press.

Moore, Sally Falk. 2005. *Law and Anthropology: A Reader.* Boston and Oxford: Blackwell Publishing.

Nader, Laura. 2002. *The Life of the Law: Anthropological Projects.* Berkeley and Los Angeles: University of California Press.

New Vision (Kampala). 2006 (18 July). Uganda: Govt Position on Kony Peace Talks in Juba. Available at allafrica.com/stories/200607190114.html.

OTP. 2006a (June). *Criteria For Selection of Situations and Cases.* ICC-OTP draft document. Available at www.icc-otp.int/library/about/newsletter/archief.html.

2006b (13 June). The Interests of Justice: Internal OTP Discussion Paper. ICC-OTP draft document. Available at www.icc-otp.int/library/about/newsletter/archief.html.

Rosen, Lawrence. 1989. *The Anthropology of Justice: Laws as Culture in Islamic Society.* New York: Cambridge University Press.

Schabas, William. 2001. *An Introduction to the International Court.* New York and Cambridge: Cambridge University Press.

Suarez-Orozco, Marcelo and Carola Suarez-Orozco. 2001. *Children of Immigration.* New York and Cambridge: Harvard University Press.

Turner, Simon. 2005. Suspended in Space: Contesting Sovereignties in a Refugee Camp, in (eds.) Hansen and Stepputat.

Victims Rights Working Group. 2006. *Ugandan Peace Talks: Victims Rights Must Be Respected.* August. Available at www.vrwg.org/Publications/1.html.

Wilson, Richard. 2001. *The Politics of Truth and Reconciliation in South Africa: Legitimising the Post-Apartheid State.* New York and Cambridge: Cambridge University Press.

CHAPTER 7

HUMAN RIGHTS LAW AS A PATH TO INTERNATIONAL JUSTICE: THE CASE OF THE WOMEN'S CONVENTION

Sally Engle Merry

The importance of laws in exploring paths to international justice cannot be overlooked. International laws such as human rights conventions are critical components of international justice.[1] Over the last fifty years, an extensive body of laws and principles guaranteeing human rights has been developed and accepted by the large majority of the countries of the world. The six major human rights conventions constitute the legal basis for international human rights. These conventions govern civil and political rights, economic, social and cultural rights, racial and gender discrimination, torture and the rights of the child. These conventions are binding only on those nations that ratify them, but these nations are expected to incorporate the conventions' principles into their domestic law. All conventions have been ratified by at least 140 countries and some by over 180.[2] Some human rights conventions are so widely accepted that they are considered international customary law, or *jus cogens*. International customary law governs even in the absence of national consent.

[1] Research for this paper was generously supported by a grant from the National Science Foundation, Cultural Anthropology Program and Law and Social Sciences Program # BCS-9904441 and by a Visiting Fellowship at the American Bar Foundation. I am grateful for comments from Jane Collier, Marie-Bénédicte Dembour, Mindie Lazarus-Black, Frances Raday, Judith Resnik, Austin Sarat and Hanna Beate Schoepp-Schilling. Portions of this paper appeared in *Law and Social Inquiry* 28(4): 941–79, 2003.
[2] According to a UN website updated 3 May 2006, ratifications of the major conventions numbered as follows: Convention on the Rights of the Child 192, Convention on Racial Discrimination 170, Convention on Economic, Social and Cultural Rights 153, Convention on Civil and Political Rights 156, Convention on the Elimination of all forms of Discrimination Against Women 182, and Convention on Torture 141. See untreaty.un.org/ENGLISH/bible/englishinternetbible/bible.asp.

However, the mechanisms that enforce these conventions lack the force of nation-state laws. Because their origin rests in a body of sovereign states that have collectively developed these principles but cannot impose them on any individual state, the means of implementing them are quite different from nation-state mechanisms. This system grows out of a structure of state sovereignty and an international regime with little coercive power over its member states. Because treaty bodies, the committees charged with monitoring compliance with human rights treaties, work within this global structure of sovereignty, they are not empowered to impose sanctions on non-compliant states. They generally lack any direct form of sanction or coercion but work through forms of shaming, internal and external pressure, and negotiation and reciprocity. Indeed, the implementation of international laws bears some similarity to that of customary village law.

What kind of path does this provide for international justice? This article considers two critical questions. First, are these conventions successful, in the sense of articulating a set of rules and enforcing some degree of compliance with them? Clearly, their enforcement powers are severely circumscribed, but I argue that there are important dimensions of cultural transformation that come out of the monitoring process. Second, in what sense is the process of articulating and monitoring these conventions 'international'? What does international mean in this context? Using the Convention on the Elimination of all forms of Discrimination Against Women (called the Women's Convention or CEDAW) as a case study, this chapter examines these two questions. It notes some areas of success in developing new cultural concepts for gender equality as a result of the conventions and the monitoring process. It also points to limitations in the concept of 'international' behind these efforts. Although the treaty bodies are internationally representative, this is defined largely in terms of region rather than ethnicity, social class or national affluence.

I argue that CEDAW operates as quasi-law, as the creator of new international cultural categories rather than as a set of rules that are enforced. Influence rather than coercion is the prevailing mode of enforcement. Success means disseminating new standards and intervening in the negotiations that take place within national delegations. This negotiation is influenced to varying degrees by nations' desires to appear 'civilised' before the international community, defined as compliance with human rights treaties. At the same time, it is also influenced by the capacity of domestic (in-country) groups' ability to pressure and expose government misconduct. Despite the formal structure of international representation of the CEDAW Monitoring Committee, however, in practice large and wealthy countries and their cosmopolitan elites participate far more extensively than do small, poor countries and non-elite individuals.

THE CEDAW MONITORING PROCESS

The thirty articles in the Women's Convention cover a broad array of social issues such as political participation, education, employment, health and the special difficulties faced by rural women. States parties are required to eliminate discrimination in the exercise of civil, political, economic, social and cultural rights both in the public domain and in the family (DAW 2000: 5). CEDAW not only proscribes discrimination but also advocates positive steps such as the elimination of sex-role stereotypes in the media and educational materials and the creation of 'temporary special measures' to benefit women, measures which are not forms of discrimination but efforts to overcome past disabilities. The Convention focuses on legal regulations that selectively disempower women such as regulations requiring women to have their husband's permission to acquire a passport. It presumes that producing equal rights for women requires transformations of marriage laws, access to education and employment and gender images within the media.

CEDAW is law without sanctions. But a closer examination of the way the CEDAW process operates suggests that although it does not have the power to punish, it does do important cultural work by articulating principles in a formal and public setting and demonstrating how they apply to the countries under scrutiny. The central regulatory feature of the Women's Convention and its hearings is the definition and naming of problems and the articulation of solutions within a prestigious global forum. National and international NGOs as well as other international actors endeavour to shame non-compliant governments. This is a cultural system whose coin is admission into the international community of human-rights-compliant states. At the heart of the legal process of monitoring this international human rights convention is the cultural work of altering the meanings of gender and of state responsibility for gender equality. Much socio-legal scholarship suggests that similar processes are basic to the way state law regulates behaviour as well. Only a small fraction of conflicts actually become cases in court and compliance depends largely on individual consciousness of law (see Merry 1990; Ewick and Silbey 1998).

Despite its lack of sanctions, CEDAW can be considered part of an emerging global system of law. As global law has expanded, it has acquired greater influence over national and local systems of law. In the late twentieth century, global social reform movements such as feminism and human rights advocacy have increasingly turned a transnational gaze on local and national laws and practices and found them wanting.[3] International human rights law offers new opportunities to pressure offending governments. Keck and Sikkink's study of transnational NGOs shows the critical role they play in defining social problems, giving them names, and doing the research necessary to document their scope and severity (1998). Indeed, it shows how the category of violence against women itself was cobbled together by NGOs out of several distinct issues. Since the end of the Cold War the idea that legitimate sovereignty rests on democratic governance and humane treatment of citizens has been growing, so that the new international 'standard of civilisation' includes acceptance of human rights (Foot 2000: 11). During the 1990s, sovereignty was increasingly defined as contingent on a country's human rights performance (Foot 2000: 251–2). The primary mechanism for inducing compliance with these treaties, including CEDAW, is the preparation of periodic reports that are presented by national governments to an oversight committee, called a treaty body, at the UN headquarters in New York. Treaty bodies monitor compliance with ratified treaties by requiring countries to write periodic reports detailing their efforts to put the treaty into force. The committee reads and comments on the report. The process of preparing, presenting and discussing reports for the CEDAW committee encourages governments to think about situations within their countries relevant to the treaties and to consider ways of improving them. Pressure is exerted through exposure, shaming and appeal to the international standards articulated in the Convention. Committee members see the process as a 'constructive dialogue' in which they pose questions to governments.

The monitoring and surveillance procedures of the six treaty bodies are the centrepiece of the legal implementation of human rights. In a recent major study of the six treaty bodies, Bayefsky concludes: 'It is the legal character of these rights which places them at the core of the international system of human rights protection. For these rights generate

---

[3] This process is analogous to the constant renegotiation of the boundaries of federal, state, and local control in the US (see Resnik 2001: 670–79).

corresponding legal duties upon state actors, to protect against, prevent, and remedy human rights violations' (2001: 5). Some countries have produced twenty or more reports and the most frequently reporting country, the UK, has produced thirty-eight (Bayefsky 2001: 244–51).

However, committees have little recourse against states that prepare thin reports or cover up discriminatory practices. They cannot prevent a government from providing evasive or scanty answers although they can write critical 'concluding comments' that are sent to governments and posted on the internet. Overall, compliance depends on the will and commitment of national political actors and pressures from other countries and non-governmental organisations (NGOs). This does not translate into widespread conformity with the terms of the conventions. Bayefsky's study of the treaty bodies concludes '. . . the gap between universal right and remedy has become inescapable and inexcusable, threatening the integrity of the international human rights legal regime. There are overwhelming numbers of overdue reports, untenable backlogs, minimal individual complaints from vast numbers of potential victims, and widespread refusal of states to provide remedies when violations of individual rights are found' (Bayefsky 2001: xiii).

I observed part or all of four CEDAW sessions – two in 2001 and two in 2002 – each of which lasted three weeks and considered reports from about eight countries. I interviewed seven experts serving on the Committee and talked to NGO representatives from reporting countries and from international NGO groups. I also talked to local activists from Fiji, India and Hong Kong after they returned home from attending CEDAW hearings (see Merry 2006).

At these hearings, held at the UN headquarters in New York, the CEDAW Committee encourages governments to change national and local laws, institutions and cultural understandings that discriminate against women. The Convention articulates the principle of gender equality in the enjoyment of human rights and in the elimination of gender-based discrimination in marriage, work, education, politics, the legal system and the family. Like other human rights discourses and instruments, it is committed to universalism: to the idea that there are minimal standards of human dignity that must be protected in all societies (An-Na'im 1992; Ignatieff 2001; Schuler 1992; see Wilson 1997). Universal gender equality requires eliminating those laws and institutional practices that treat women in discriminatory ways. It advocates eliminating discriminatory practices and introducing compensatory measures for past inequalities.

CEDAW has an Optional Protocol that allows individuals to file complaints directly to the Committee.[4] It entered into force by late 2000 and has been ratified by seventy-eight states as of 2006.[5] It allows individual women or groups to submit claims of violations of rights protected under the Convention to the CEDAW Committee, but only after all domestic remedies have been exhausted and only in countries that have ratified it. Thus, it allows the Committee to inquire into situations of grave or systemic violation of women's rights (DAW 2000: 7).

The reasons why a nation would choose to ratify CEDAW and subject itself to periodic reporting and examination are not obvious. They are linked, I think, to claims to civilised status in the present international order, much as ideas of civilisation provided the standard for colonised countries during the imperial era. Fanon's famous after-word to *Wretched of the Earth* (1963) testifies to the power of this idea as he urged decolonising nations to look to sources of moral virtue other than the ideas of the rights of man established by Europe. Bayevsky notes that states may consider ratification an end in itself and, given the relatively brief and infrequent monitoring process, are not seriously concerned about the national consequences (2001: 7). On the other hand, the work of Foot and many others emphasises the importance of compliance with human rights instruments for participation in the international community and for benefits such as aid, trade relations and foreign investment.

By 2006, CEDAW had been ratified by 182 nation states. The United States is one of very few countries that have not ratified it. There has been considerable discussion of the US failure to ratify this Convention as well as several other core human rights conventions, with explanations ranging from the lack of domestic political support by a constituency that feels its rights are already adequately protected to the nation's system of popular sovereignty which means that ratification requires a legislative vote rather than an executive order (Ignatieff 2001). Despite its declared support for human rights abroad, there has been considerable resistance to the domestic application of human rights in the US.

States that ratify CEDAW are obliged to incorporate it into their domestic legislation (see Cook 1994). According to Schoepp-Schilling,

---

[4] Complaints and inquiry procedures are particularly important for the Commission on Human Rights/Human Rights Council, which has, since 1978, appointed special rapporteurs, representatives, and working groups to carry out investigative procedures (see Foot 2000: 34–6). This happens outside of a treaty mechanism.

[5] Information from www.untreaty.un.org/ENGLISH/bible/englishinternetbible/bible.asp, accessed 3 May 2006.

a member of the CEDAW Committee for twelve years, 'States Parties are obliged to undertake all legislative and other appropriate measures to eliminate discrimination against women without delay' (2000). She notes that this contrasts with other conventions, such as the International Covenant on Economic, Social, and Cultural Rights which obliges states to take steps to 'progressively' achieve the full realisation of rights. Nevertheless, she notes that states often hide behind financial shortfalls and other difficulties as excuses for not initiating reforms. Indeed, in the hearing on the Burundi country report in 2001, there was widespread recognition by CEDAW committee members that in a largely rural country undergoing a protracted civil war, relatively little could be anticipated in the way of reforms to benefit women. It is common for states of the global South to complain that they need more financial help from the global North in order to make the desired changes.

States may ratify CEDAW with reservations to particular items of the Convention by declaring that certain parts of the treaty are not binding on it. The Committee discourages this and endeavours to persuade ratifying states to remove their reservations. In the past, this Convention had more reservations to it than any other (DAW 2000: 6; see also Cook 1990). A recent study shows that CEDAW is not now the most reserved Convention, yet it still has 123 reservations, declarations and interpretive statements, which are in effect reservations. Three quarters of these (76 per cent) refer to the substance of the text itself rather than to its procedures (Bayevsky 2001: 66). Forty-nine states parties, or 30 per cent of those which have ratified CEDAW, have entered reservations.[6] Some of the reservations are to core portions of the Convention, such that they undermine the purpose of the convention itself. Egypt, for example, entered a general reservation on Article 2, explaining that it is 'willing to comply with the content of this article provided that such compliance does not run counter to the Islamic Shari'a' (Egyptian NGOs Coalition 2000: 5). Yet Article 2 embodies the core of the Convention, stating: 'States Parties condemn discrimination against women in all its forms, agree to pursue by all appropriate means and without delay, a policy of eliminating discrimination against women, and to this end undertake . . .' and lists a variety of constitutional, legal

---

[6] In comparison, the Convention on Civil and Political Rights has 181, 88 per cent of which are normative, representing 35 per cent of states parties. The Convention on the Rights of the Child has 204, 99.5 per cent of which are normative, from 32 per cent of states parties. Thus, like CEDAW, these conventions are heavily circumscribed by reservations.

and legislative measures to eliminate this discrimination. Bayevsky notes that Article 2 has five general reservations, another eight normative general declarations and interpretive statements, and twelve more specific reservations, while there are twenty-five reservations to Article 16, the article that requires equality in marriage and family law (2001: 66, 717–18).[7] The CEDAW Committee is concerned that reserving on Article 2 constitutes failure to adopt the spirit of the Convention. On the other hand, as Schoepp-Schilling notes (2000), even states with significant reservations present reports and engage in dialogue with the committee's experts, so this may be constructive.

THE COMMITTEE HEARINGS

The dialogue between a country and the Committee occurs during the regular meetings of the CEDAW Committee. At these hearings, the Committee of twenty reads the report and meets with a delegation from the country, often a high-ranking minister for women's affairs. The committee members, called experts because of their knowledge and experience in the field, ask questions about discrepancies between the actions of the country and the obligations it assumed when it ratified the Convention. The experts are expected to act independently and not to speak for their national governments. They bring impressive credentials in terms of scholarship and publication, NGO activism, extensive government service and strong backgrounds in international participation in the process. Most have a strong background in women's issues.

The tenor of the hearings is always serious and although it is unfailingly polite, it sometimes takes on an edge of criticism. Rarely are criticisms explicit, however. More often, experts speak of 'concerns' or of the need for more information. Privately, some experts commented to me on how frustrated they felt about one or another country's report, such as its abysmal gender-based statistics or failure to implement policies, but they did not level such accusations against governments in the hearings. If a country acknowledges that it has had difficulty in

[7] The CEDAW committee has said that Articles 2 and 16 are core provisions of the Convention and that reservations which challenge central principles are contrary to the provisions of the Convention and to general international law. 'Reservations to articles 2 and 16 perpetuate the myth of women's inferiority and reinforce the inequalities in the lives of millions of women throughout the world. The Committee holds the view that article 2 is central to the objects and purpose of the Convention . . . . [R]eservations to article 16, whether lodged for national, traditional, religious, or cultural reasons, are incompatible with the Convention and therefore impermissible . . . .' (from CEDAW, A/53/38/Rev.1, paras. 6, 8, 15, 16, 17); quoted in Bayevsky 2001: 69).

implementing CEDAW, the experts tend to be more supportive than if a country tries to cover up its failures.

The experts present a united front in these hearings, although they do differ on some issues, such as abortion and the value of separate legal systems for different religious communities within a country. Those more closely connected to NGO or academic communities tend to challenge governments more than those employed by their national governments. The latter tend to be less confrontational and more inclined to praise a country's efforts than to condemn its shortfalls. Despite these differences, the hearings give a sense of unanimity among the experts as they pose questions to government representatives.

The CEDAW Committee, which has been meeting since 1982, was originally restricted to meeting once a year for two weeks. Members who participated in those early days say that governments did not take them seriously and there was little interest in who served on the Committee. That interest has now increased, along with the meeting time. In 1995 it expanded to three weeks a year and in 1997 three weeks twice a year. In 2002, it held an exceptional third meeting to catch up with the backlog of reports and with another meeting in 2006. Country reports were initially only two to three pages according to a long-standing member of the Committee, but now routinely run to sixty pages and occasionally up to 150 pages. By March 2000, CEDAW had considered 104 initial reports, 72 second reports, 45 third reports, and 13 fourth periodic reports (DAW 2000: 8). By 2001, it was common practice to hear two or even three periodic reports from the same country at once. However, a substantial number of ratifying states have failed to file a report at all or have fallen behind. By mid-2001, 49 states had not filed an initial report, 65 were late in filing their second periodic report, 42 the third periodic report, 52 the fourth, and 41 were late in their fifth periodic report. Several states that ratified in the early 1980s have never filed a report and thus appear in all of these lists, such as Brazil, Bhutan, Congo, Costa Rica and Togo (Secretary-General Report 2001: CEDAW/C/2001/II/2).

The focus of the CEDAW Committee's work is reading the periodic reports of signatory countries, asking questions and writing concluding comments. Every ratifying country is obligated to provide an initial report within one year of ratification on the legislative, judicial and administrative measures it has adopted to comply with the Convention and obstacles it has encountered and to prepare subsequent reports periodically every four years. For initial reports, the

Committee uses a two-stage process. First, the national delegation presents its report and the committee members, sitting in a large conference room at the UN building in New York, go through it carefully and ask questions, request clarification, and note contrasts with other countries' experiences with these particular reforms. Second, the national delegation returns to the Committee two or three days later and provides answers to these questions. Some answers are brief and inconclusive and some issues are not addressed, but the Committee can do little under these circumstances.

For subsequent reports, a subcommittee consisting of a representative from each of four geographical regions meets at the end of the previous session to read the report and pose questions to which the national representatives should provide written responses within forty days. At the next meeting of CEDAW six months later, government representatives present an updated overview statement of perhaps one hour and are asked further questions by the experts to which they reply immediately. This process is thorough: one country complained that it had received sixty-four additional questions before the meeting. The questions and the replies, as well as the country reports, are available to all the members of the Committee.

The goal of the reporting process is to promote change in the government by forcing it to review domestic law, policy and practice and to assess to what extent it is complying with the standards of the Convention. According to the Division that supports the process, 'Strengths and weaknesses are submitted to public scrutiny, while consideration of the report by CEDAW provides a forum for discussion with a wholly independent body whose brief is to provide constructive assistance so that States meet their treaty obligations' (DAW 2000: 8). Questions by experts frequently point out the need for more information, particularly disaggregated by sex, in order to assess the relative participation of women in school, government and the workplace, for example. Their questions show how the Convention applies to the country giving the report, pinpoint areas where there is not compliance, and provide comparative information about how other countries have handled these issues. The tenor is unfailingly polite and courteous, although questions are sometimes pointed. The experts I have talked to emphasise that their goal is to be constructive as well as critical. One expert said that this was a political process, and, if a country chooses to ignore it, there is nothing the Committee can do. Sometimes governments find the experience of reporting helpful. One of the government ministers said that the attention and concern of the international community about women's rights energised her and supported her work.

After hearing these reports, the Committee meets in closed session to develop its 'Concluding Comments' for each country which praise or express concern about its efforts to comply with the Convention as well as recommendations to be considered at the next review four years hence. These comments are publicly available and posted on the internet. Governments differ in the extent to which they make these comments public, but NGOs may publicise them in an effort to shame the government into more action. There is, as long-term expert member Beate Hanna Schoepp-Schilling notes, little sanctioning power beyond the capacity to 'shame' non-compliant states parties (2000).

In recent years, NGOs have begun to offer important support for this process (see Afsharipour 1999: 157). Although their input was described as minimal in the 1980s, the situation is changing (Jacobson 1992: 467). NGOs are encouraged to write 'shadow reports' which provide their version of the status of women in their countries, and are often offered training in producing these reports by UN agencies such as UNIFEM (United Nations Development Fund for Women) or UNDP (United Nations Development Programme) (see, e.g., Afsharipour 1999: 165; Economic and Social Commission for Asia and the Pacific 2000). Some representatives of NGOs appear at the committee meetings in New York where they are not allowed to speak but can sit in the conference room and informally lobby the experts, suggesting questions to ask. Their shadow reports are available to the Committee. A second source of information for committee members are reports by other UN agencies such as FAO, UNICEF, UNIFEM, and the ILO on the status of women in a particular country. Finally, a US-based NGO, the International Women's Rights Action Watch (IWRAW) and its Asia-Pacific office based in Malaysia (IWRAW-AP) have aided in training NGO representatives and regularly produced shadow reports on the countries under examination (see, e.g., Afsharipour 1999: 165). IWRAW began as a channel for NGOs to get information to committee members, initially summarising information and presenting it to committee members in the 1980s (Jacobson 1992: 467). In the last few years, IWRAW-AP has focused on bringing national NGOs to the CEDAW hearings in New York and encouraging them to write their own shadow reports. Both IWRAW and UNIFEM fund NGO representatives if possible. The CEDAW Committee sets aside an afternoon to hear NGO presentations at the beginning of each session. The government delegations are not present. At the January 2002 meeting, which I attended, most of the members were present to hear the NGO representatives make their oral statements. Country hearings are attended by representatives of international NGOs such as Equality Now, IWRAW, and national NGOs from that country as well as a scattering of students. The results of these hearings are made available to other UN agencies such as the Commission on the Status of Women (CSW), the Economic and Social Council (ECOSOC), and the General Assembly. However, it does not appear that they are considered extensively by these bodies, based both on my own observations of CSW meetings and comments by Jacobson (1992: 463–5).

There are a variety of ways for countries to escape scrutiny. One is to fail to write a report or to do so only after a long delay. The list of countries that are neglectful in their production of reports is very long. By 1 January 2000 there were 242 overdue reports to CEDAW from 165 states parties. Fifty-three states had initial overdue reports. Overall, 78 per cent of all states parties had overdue reports, although the average for all treaty bodies is an equally high 71 per cent (Bayevsky 2001: 471). The second is to write a superficial or partial report. Sometimes reports just recite the provisions of the constitution or other legislation or are very brief and do not offer candid self-evaluations of a state's compliance with its treaty obligations (Jacobson 1992; Bayevsky 2001: 21). The third is to send low-level government representatives instead of high-level delegations of ministers or assistant ministers. In 2002, Uruguay, complaining that it was financially strapped, asked its UN mission in New York to report and sent no one from the country, much to the displeasure of the CEDAW Committee. The UN mission rarely is as informed about national issues as leaders of women's ministries. A fourth means is to evade direct answers to questions. A fifth is to promise changes that do not in fact take place. A sixth is to reserve on important articles on the grounds that they conflict with basic cultural, legal or religious tenets of the country. A seventh is to refuse to present a report even after it has been submitted (Bayevsky 2001: 23).

Although the NGO community is present at CEDAW hearings to help publicise the discussions and conclusions, treaty body meetings such as the CEDAW hearings are quite different from the major meetings of governments and NGOs common at the end of the twentieth century such as the Beijing Conference of 1995 or the Beijing Plus Five meeting in New York in 2000. Participation is far smaller than at these conferences or at meetings such as the Commission on the Status of

Women or the Commission on Human Rights, now Human Rights Council. Moreover, participation varies significantly depending on the country and the number of NGOs it has as well as funding for attending and for staying in New York. During the discussion of Egypt's report in January 2001, a large audience of NGO representatives attended, making up an audience of perhaps thirty people. Egypt has a large NGO community. Burundi and Kazakhstan had smaller audiences, and relatively few NGOs attended the report on the Maldives. Similarly, in the July 2001 CEDAW meetings, discussions of very small countries with few NGOs – such as Andorra – generated very few NGO observers, while more – about fifteen to twenty – came to hear the reports of Vietnam, Nicaragua and Guyana. Nevertheless, NGOs make a critical contribution to the process. Based on her detailed survey of all six treaty bodies, Bayevsky concludes 'the treaty bodies have been heavily dependent on information from NGOs in preparing for the dialogue with states parties. State reports are self-serving documents that rarely knowingly disclose violations of treaty rights' (2001: 42).

Clearly, governments can escape this system, but they face internal pressure from national NGOs, who may be supported by international donors and therefore active even if the country does not have enough wealth to support them. In theory, they face pressure from other countries as well as via their own NGOs, as Keck and Skikkink argue in their boomerang metaphor (1998), but I saw little evidence of pressure by other nations. Instead, it was primarily domestic NGOs who used the hearings to exert pressure on governments to comply. Countries are concerned about their reputation in the international community, but they clearly differ in their vulnerability to international pressure depending on their size, wealth, form of government and dependence on the international community for trade, aid and other symbolic and material forms of exchange. Countries that are economically and politically dominant, such as the United States, may resist the system by failing to ratify at all.

To what extent is this process successful in inducing compliance? Its success seems to depend on at least two factors. First, the extent to which a national government cares about the opinions of the international community affects its willingness to report, to participate and to seek to comply with the requests of the committee. For example, Guinea's report, heard in the July 2001 CEDAW meetings, sought to show that Guinea was a modern nation. This was Guinea's initial report, but also its second and third periodic report since it had not filed any reports since ratifying the Convention in 1982. In the opening speech and in the country report, the delegation from Guinea emphasised the extent of gender equality in its constitution and its laws. There are equal rights to work, to unionise, to strike, to own land, to freedom from discrimination at work and to be elected to political office. The penal code is equal for all. All work for the same task is to be paid equally. Moreover, the government representatives argued that Guinea has carried out huge efforts to implement the Convention, despite wars and a heavy burden of foreign debt. It is now drawing up a plan for the country for the next ten years, endeavouring to strengthen civil society to benefit women, to encourage the private sector, to develop a national program for youth and for population management and to support programs for village communities. The government is working on a document to reduce poverty and holding workshops that will develop a poverty-alleviation initiative. This initiative will include gender studies and attention to women in the informal sector.

Thus, both the delegation and the report present Guinea as a modern country engaging in planning and fully committed to the principle of gender equality. It described itself as eager to pursue democratisation based on a liberal development model and as a country with vast mineral resources dependant on foreign partnerships (2001: 6–7). Appearing to promote the human rights of women is critical to economic development since it marks the nation as modern and suitable for foreign investment (CEDAW/C/GIN/1 2001: 32).

Second, countries that face more scrutiny from their NGOs and from other countries contend with more pressure at home after the hearings. Some countries face severe and effective external pressure, as Fiji did in 2000 when the ethnic Fijian population overturned a duly elected premier of Indian ancestry. Others are able to ignore this pressure, particularly if they are large and economically successful, like China. In some historical circumstances, these hearings have particular weight, as they did in Hong Kong in the early 1990s during the fear of the 1997 handover to China and the loss of rights.

Thus, the impact of CEDAW and its monitoring process is indirect, filtered through pre-existing global inequalities. As the process defines problems and frames social issues in the language of human rights and freedom from discrimination and gender equality, however, it provides a language of argument that resonates with the values of a secular global modernity. Ratifying covenants, submitting periodic reports, and attending UN meetings and conventions offer the elites of many nations opportunities to circulate in the global space of modernity. Many of these elites had already been students in global modern spaces. Circulating in this domain opens doors for trade, investment and foreign aid, while those who refuse to participate can face economic and political penalties.

Adherence to international standards has both symbolic and material benefits. For example, at a March 2002 meeting of the National Assembly of Nigeria to put in motion a framework to repeal all laws that inhibit the protection of fundamental human rights, the chairman of the occasion, Chief Phillip Ume, said that the subject of human rights has become so important all over the world that 'it is now the benchmark for the assessment of good governance and good governments. As well as being the pre-qualification and pre-condition for the grant of aids by international donor agencies' (from article in *Punch*, 4 March 2002 by Clara Nwachukwu Owerri, circulated by womensrightswatch-nigeria@kabissa.org March 14, 2002). Foreign aid and tourism are often connected to maintaining a good reputation as well (see Foot 2000). Clearly, the appeal of global modernity is economic as well as cultural, similar to the appeal of the concept of civilisation during the era of empire. In the postcolonial era, the glamour of the modern is still juxtaposed to backward others, but now it includes those who are 'developing' but still burdened by 'traditional harmful practices'. Human rights are of course a fundamental part of the global modern. The fight against 'culture' is a deeply cultural one.

THE ROLE OF NGOs

NGOs play a critical role in making the documents known, and the documents themselves represent an important resource for them. They pressure governments and join with allies in other countries to pressure their governments. As Keck and Skikkink (1998) note, they may use a boomerang tactic in which the NGO from one country links with the NGO of another, more powerful one, which then puts pressure on its government to push the less powerful government to change. Government representatives at UN meetings often refer to the importance of 'civil society' and its essential role in their activities. They are obviously pointing to practices of exposure, pressure and monitoring. It is notable that the NGOs pay a great deal of attention to the documents and are deeply engaged in trying to influence what they say.

But, the relationship is not as mutually supportive and positive as this analysis suggests. The CEDAW Committee is far more supportive of NGO input than the government-based UN bodies such as the Commission on the Status of Women (CSW) or the Commission on Human Rights, now Human Rights Council. Despite talk about the importance of civil society, NGO access to governmental decision-makers in UN meetings such as CSW, the Commission on Human Rights, and even Beijing Plus Five, is extremely limited. Important decisions are often made in closed-door negotiating sessions as governments strive to hammer out a consensus on a document. NGO representatives may wait outside the door, hoping to talk to their national representatives, but they are not allowed to participate. At the resolution drafting sessions of the Commission on Human Rights (now Council) in Geneva, some chairs would allow NGOs to be present, but not to speak. Even those who allowed them to submit language in writing paid little attention to their suggestions. For example, in a session in 2001 drafting a resolution about trafficking that I observed, an NGO suggested developing some mechanism for dealing with the demand rather than only the supply of trafficked women, something such as retraining male customers in wealthy countries. She was permitted to submit this suggestion only in writing, not orally. Governmental representatives from Japan and Europe quickly quashed the suggestion as too vague.

NGOs are also allowed to speak from the floor at the Commission on the Status of Women and the Commission on Human Rights (now Council) meetings, but are given very short time periods and are required to present their statements in written form in advance. The attention of the government delegates is typically less during NGO interventions, with more talking and walking around, than during other deliberations. Government representatives are often uncomfortable about NGO statements, worried that they will try to embarrass them and expose problems. Some NGOs say that governments fear they will be too radical. Many governments wish to restrict NGO speaking time and to know in advance what they are going to say. Thus, opportunities for NGO input into the discussion and document production process are highly circumscribed. NGO representatives typically describe their task as lobbying their government representatives and often see this as their central mission. Some governments, such as the US, hold regular formal briefings for NGOs at major meetings such as CSW or Beijing Plus Five to inform them about the US delegation's activities. These are typically settings where NGOs are to listen rather than give feedback.

In contrast, many of the members of the CEDAW Committee are quite positive toward NGOs and make an effort to listen to them informally and to come to the NGO briefing, which was attended by at least eighteen of the twenty-three members at the 2002 meeting. Those experts who have NGO backgrounds are particularly receptive to NGO representatives. I have often heard these experts pose the questions to the government representatives that NGOs suggested. In this sense, the NGO presence at CEDAW meetings is very important and successful.

But, in order to gain access to the space where any of these UN meetings are held and government representatives are available for lobbying, an NGO must receive consultative status from the UN. While this was a relatively easy process in the past, there has recently been a great increase in applications and a tendency to scrutinise applicants far more closely.[8] In order to gain consultative status, an NGO must apply through a complex procedure and describe in detail the nature of the organisation, its mission, its membership and its financial status. The decision can take over a year.[9] As the number of NGOs has expanded, the pressure on the UN to accommodate them has also increased, as has the difficulty of determining which groups should earn this status. Without consultative status, an NGO cannot participate in these meetings. The UN recognises that the process for achieving consultative status is difficult and may deter small organisations in developing countries. It has made efforts to make the process more accessible, but it is still difficult, particularly for NGOs in developing countries for whom the faxing and communication difficulties loom large.

Many of these NGOs are based on large established religions or are funded by transnational philanthropy or government grants. Although

---

[8] The website for the Conference of NGOs in Consultative Status with the United Nations Economic and Social Council (CONGO) (www.congo.org/ngopart/constat.htm) describes the process of gaining consultative status as follows: 'The basis for the consultative relationship between the United Nations and non-governmental organisations was set forth most recently following an extensive intergovernmental review that culminated in ECOSOC Resolution 1996/31. This relationship is the principal means through which ECOSOC receives input from NGOs into its deliberations at public meetings and in its subsidiary bodies as well as in UN international conferences and their preparatory bodies. Each year the approximately 2,000 NGOs now holding consultative status receive the provisional agenda of ECOSOC. They have certain privileges to place items on the agenda of ECOSOC and its subsidiary bodies; they may attend meetings, where they may submit written statements and make oral presentations to governments.'

[9] The criteria for consultative status are: (1) The applying organisation's activities must be relevant to the work of ECOSOC; (2) The NGO must have a democratic decision-making mechanism; (3) The NGO must have been in existence (officially registered) for at least two years in order to apply; (4) The major portion of the organisation's funds should be derived from contributions from national affiliates, individual members or other non-governmental components (www.un.org/esa/coordination/ngo, March 2002).

there are some radical NGOs, such as the Women's International League for Peace and Freedom, most are mainstream organisations such as professional businesswomen's associations or the Girl Scouts. The left, progressive, social activist NGO is the minority. These groups vary significantly in their political views of social change and how agents of change should be empowered. The more conservative groups seem content to give vulnerable groups such as battered women a voice, while the more radical ones want to focus attention on economic and structural inequalities.

It is obviously expensive and difficult for South NGO members to attend UN meetings in Europe or the US. Many who do come are working in projects with international donors, but this does not guarantee that they will be able participate on a regular basis. Yet only those NGO representatives who go year after year develop the expertise in personnel, lobbying strategy and the texts of documents essential to making an impact on the document drafting process. NGO representatives who know the language used in past documents and how to find it are much more influential in lobbying than those who lack this expertise since there is usually a preference for using 'agreed-upon' language from some other document rather than forging new wording. Consequently, the leading NGO representatives tend to be experienced heads of major US, Canadian and European organisations. I heard little complaint about this situation by developing countries' NGO representatives, however. Instead, there is generally a sense of camaraderie and support as well as openness to learning from one another. Nevertheless, the hurdles for NGO participation from poorer parts of the world are quite substantial and it seems that many who come are sent by an NGO receiving substantial funding, usually from Europe or North America.

Despite the celebrated interdependence of civil society and the international system of law, the relationship between states and NGOs is fraught with tension and ambivalence. While some governments welcome NGO participation, others resist. Some do not want NGOs to be involved in the process at all and insist that the UN is a body of governments. Some governments of the South are uncomfortable about criticism and embarrassment from NGOs. They fear public exposure and will be angry at the NGOs when they get back home. One NGO representative from Africa said that some governments even threaten treason trials against outspoken NGO representatives, and many are unhappy about NGO criticisms. The US also resists criticisms by

NGOs. My observations of briefings by the US delegation to the NGOs at the CSW in 2001 and 2002 as well as at the Beijing Plus Five Conference, for example, show that they focus on providing information about US government activities rather than looking for NGO input or criticism. At a March 2002 US briefing to NGOs, a representative from the Women's International League for Peace and Freedom pointed out that discussions of gender and poverty need to take into account the way US economic policies are producing global poverty. The US team was annoyed by this comment and one member accused the NGO representative of being unpatriotic.

While there is general recognition that NGOs perform a valuable service in identifying issues, doing research to support them and advocating for particular causes, an important task of many NGOs is exposing government failures. This makes many governments uneasy, particularly since the task of representatives to these global forums is to portray their countries in the most favourable light. The CSW begins with hours of speeches in which each country emphasises its accomplishments in the field of women's issues. It is not surprising that the CEDAW process is far more open to NGO participation than the commissions and world conferences that are made up of government delegations. The system of shadow reports and NGO briefings has institutionalised NGO input into the process, yet even here, aside from the separate briefing meeting that lasts about an hour and a half, NGOs have no formal space to speak and some experts are more interested in NGO input than others.

As in so many other areas of UN activity, this relationship is a developing and changing one. NGOs are gradually gaining more acceptance and a stronger voice, but still face considerable resistance to their participation among some governments. And like many other areas of international activity, the sharp resource disparities between North and South radically limit the ability of some NGOs to participate in the process. It is common for North foundations and governments to fund NGOs from the South. Issues of importance to the North tend to take precedence, and these issues change. Trafficking in women is a new issue, for example, which responds to North concerns about immigration as well as moral reform. Human rights documents create the legal categories and legal norms for controlling violence against women, but the dissemination of these norms and categories depends on NGOs seizing this language and using it to generate public support or governmental discomfort. This is a fragile and haphazard process, very vulnerable to existing inequalities among nations and the availability of donors.

AN INTERNATIONAL PROCESS?

In what sense is this process international? Experts are chosen to represent the international community broadly and are drawn from all the ratifying states. There is a system of formal equality in international representation with pre-established regional groupings each assigned a specific number of representatives, a system used throughout the UN to guarantee equal regional representation. But experts are also selected on the basis of political manoeuvring. Although experts act in their personal capacity rather than as representatives of their governments, they must be named by their governments and supported by them. They are nominated by their national governments and elected for four-year terms by the state signatories to the Convention. Indifferent in the past, governments now put forward candidates and lobby energetically for their election. According to one expert, she was selected because the NGOs in her country encouraged her government to nominate her and her government then negotiated with other governments to get its candidate elected.

Experts are lawyers, diplomats, government bureaucrats, scholars, judges, medical doctors and educators (Schoepp-Schilling 2000). Based on the biographies they provided to the UN as candidates for election to CEDAW, of the 2002 Committee over half (fourteen) have primarily NGO/academic backgrounds of whom two are also in elected political positions and one recently joined her government after an NGO career. Four of these are full professors, coming from Israel, Sri Lanka, Sweden and Turkey. They bring considerable academic expertise and independence to the process. About one third (eight) are primarily employees of their national governments in the foreign service or women's ministries. This adds up to twenty-two: one committee member was recently brought on, for whom I did not have information, and a second just replaced another member, so I used the information for the previous member. The experts generally have considerable previous exposure to UN activities and are often educated in other countries. Of the twenty-two for which I have information, at least fifteen studied at some point in Europe or North America and at least sixteen attended other UN meetings and conferences. This is a highly educated and transnationally active group of people (CEDAW/SP/

1996/3, CEDAW/SP/1998/3, CEDAW/SP/2000/6). Only two men have served as experts since CEDAW hearings began in 1983, both in the early 2000s.

There is circulation between national elites and CEDAW experts. Many experts are employed by their governments, often as ambassadors. Experts may return to politically prominent positions in their home countries, as did the expert from New Zealand. Country delegations can include former experts. For example, the chair of the Egyptian delegation was a former member of CEDAW. She said that things had really changed since the early days when the Committee was thought of as a group of women pestering governments. In general, experts serve in addition to holding regular jobs and devote considerable time to their responsibilities, for which they receive expenses but little remuneration.[10]

Thus, although the experts are chosen to represent the world, in practice they do not. Geographically they are international, but in terms of social class, cosmopolitanism, education, they are surprisingly similar. Poor villagers are not here from any part of the world. Moreover, insofar as this process of norm implementation depends on NGOs, there are enormous global inequalities in the number and distribution of NGOs, determined to a large extent by the money available for this activity. NGO funding comes largely from government and private sources in the global North, even if activists come from all countries. Activists from poorer countries find it far more difficult to travel to CEDAW meetings than those from wealthier places. Finally, although the expectation is for all ratifying countries to report every four years, there are clearly enormous differences in reporting patterns, with some countries reporting very irregularly and others not at all. By and large, it is the poorer countries of the global South that report less often; for some it is a significant expense to produce the report and attend the meetings.

The human rights regime articulates a particular cultural system, one rooted in an idea of the international as secular transnational modernity. The experts and the Convention work with a conception of the international grounded in modernist ideas that often disregards the value of local customs, practices and religions. Alternative cultural systems such as religious nationalism or customary practices are not viewed supportively. CEDAW, like the rest of the human rights regime,

---

[10] They are paid only $3,000 a year for eight weeks of meeting time and considerable preparation between meetings (Bayevsky 2001: 99).

assumes that culture, custom or religion should not condone violations of human rights. The committee members often present a united front against recalcitrant or evasive government representatives. They uniformly condemn injurious cultural practices that discriminate against women, a position which is clearly articulated in the text of the Convention. This universalising approach is structured by the Convention itself. The Committee's mandate is to apply it to all countries equally. Countries that ratify it assume the burden of conforming to its requirements, regardless of their specific cultural attributes. This is the mission that the Committee adopts.

Thus, the Committee is not simply promoting transnational modernity but is pressing governments to conform to the terms of a convention that embodies many of the ideals of that modernity. The Convention is the product of global negotiation and consensus building by government representatives within several UN deliberative bodies such as the Commission on the Status of Women and the General Assembly (Jacobson 1992: 445–6). It offers a universal vision of a just society in which local differences do not justify continuing discrimination against women. In other words, claims to culture do not justify deviation from the culture of transnational modernity. Cultural differences are respected, but only within limits. Cultural difference does not justify assaults on the bodily integrity of vulnerable people. The human rights community generally resists seeing claims to cultural difference as a valid justification for practices that they define as harmful to women, children or other vulnerable populations. This is an understanding of the international not as a mosaic of different cultural practices but as a universal set of standards and ideals. It is not surprising that the highly educated, cosmopolitan group of national leaders who wrote the Convention in the first place developed these ideas, or that the urbane, sophisticated, transnational people who now serve on the monitoring Committee, support it. Thus, the formal internationalism of equal regional representation obscures the extent to which the international, in practice, is more culturally homogeneous.

CONCLUSIONS

CEDAW is clearly a powerful site of cultural production. It is one facet of the generation of documents by a large body of sovereign states through a consensual process that confers international legitimacy on the documents. These processes follow a fairly consistent set of procedures and are organised around a key set of concepts such as political will, human rights and capacity building. The documents themselves name problems, specify solutions, articulate areas of global consensus and offer moral visions of the good society, replicating language developed in one setting in the next. That this vision is articulated in law-like documents produced through quasi-legislative processes increases its creative cultural possibilities. This is a form of global legality that depends deeply on its texts, not for enforcement but for the production of cultural meanings associated with modernity and the international. Compliance requires generating political pressure on states from the CEDAW Committee, from sympathetic leaders within a country, and from international and national non-governmental organisations. But there are ways to slip through this grid of surveillance. The success of CEDAW depends on cultural conversion rather than coercion. This is a nuanced process depending on negotiation domestically and internationally in the face of indirect social, political and economic pressures.

Like law within nation states, CEDAW's role is culturally constitutive in that its effects depend on the extent to which individuals develop a consciousness of themselves in terms of these legal categories (see Merry 1990; Sarat and Kearns 1993; Ewick and Silbey 1998). Both international and nation-state law engage in the cultural production of norms. In both forms of legality, law operates more in the routines of everyday life than in moments of trouble. Compliance depends on the extent to which legal concepts and norms are embedded in consciousness and cultural practice. Legal documents in both situations name problems, specify solutions and articulate goals. Both state law and international human rights treaty law influence cultural meanings and practices beyond the reach of their sanctions. The critical feature of the CEDAW process is its cultural and educational role: its capacity to coalesce and express a particular cultural understanding of gender. Like more conventional legal processes, its significance lies in its capacity to shape cultural understandings and to articulate and expand a vision of rights (see Ewick and Silbey 1998; Merry 2000).

However, despite its claims to be international, the Convention and its monitoring process promote a particular understanding of justice for women, one that is framed in terms of gender equality rather than complementarity. In contrast to many religious traditions that see different and complementary roles for men and women, CEDAW expresses an ideal of social justice for women rooted in gender equality derived from a secular modernity. The committee members are generally supportive of norms of transnational modernity such as equal human rights for women and sceptical of some of the social and religious practices that deny women these rights. As educated, transnational activists, they speak international languages such as English and share similar views of social justice. Although CEDAW and its Committee looks international as a formal body, the social positions of these representatives suggest a narrower representation. By defining international as balanced regional representation by country and the principle of one country, one voice, the Committee produces a formal structure of equality that papers over the vast inequalities in power endemic to the international system.

REFERENCES

Afsharipour, Afra. 1999. Empowering Ourselves: The Role of Women's NGOs in the Enforcement of the Women's Convention. *Columbia Law Review* 99: 129–73.

An-Na'im, Abdullahi Ahmed. 1992. *Human Rights in Cross-Cultural Perspectives: A Quest for Consensus*. Philadelphia: University of Pennsylvania Press.

Bayefsky, Anne F. 2001. *The UN Human Rights Treaty System: Universality at the Crossroads*. Ardsley, NY: Transnational Publishers.

Cook, Rebecca J. 1990. Reservations to the Convention on the Elimination of All Forms of Discrimination Against Women. *Virginia Journal of International Law* 30: 643.

———. 1994. State Accountability Under the Convention on the Elimination of All Forms of Discrimination Against Women. In *Human Rights of Women: National and International Perspectives* (ed.) Rebecca J. Cook. Philadelphia: University of Pennsylvania Press, 228–57.

DAW (Division for the Advancement of Women), Department of Economic and Social Affairs, United Nations. 2000. Assessing the Status of Women: A Guide to Reporting under the Convention on the Elimination of All Forms of Discrimination Against Women. New York: United Nations.

Economic and Social Commission for Asia and the Pacific. 2000. Using CEDAW at the Grass Roots: Convention on the Elimination of all Forms of Discrimination Against Women in the Pacific. New York: UN Publication E.01.11.F9. UN DAW Resource Room.

Egyptian Non-Governmental Organizations Coalition. 2000. *CEDAW: The Shadow Report*. Cairo: Egyptian NGOs Coalition. (Photocopied document, on file with the author.)

Ewick, Patricia and Susan Silbey. 1998. *The Common Place of Law*. Chicago: University of Chicago Press.

Fanon, Frantz. 1963. *Wretched of the Earth*. New York: Grove.

Foot, Rosemary. 2000. *Rights Beyond Borders: the Global Community and the Struggle over Human Rights in China*. Oxford: Oxford University Press.

Ignatieff, Michael. 2001. *Human Rights as Politics and Idolatry*. Princeton: Princeton University Press.

Initial Reports of States Parties: Guinea. 2001. Consideration of reports submitted by States parties under Article 18 of the Convention on the Elimination of all Forms of Discrimination Against Women. United Nations CEDAW/C/GIN/1.

Jacobson, Roberta. 1992. The Committee on the Elimination of Discrimination Against Women. In *The United Nations and Human Rights: A Critical Appraisal* (ed.) Philip Alston. Oxford: Oxford University Press, 444–72.

Keck, Margaret E. and Kathryn Sikkink. 1998. *Activists Beyond Borders: Advocacy Networks in International Politics*. Ithaca: Cornell University Press.

Merry, Sally Engle. 1990. *Getting Justice and Getting Even: Legal Consciousness among Working Class Americans*. Chicago: University of Chicago Press.

2000. *Colonizing Hawai'i: The Cultural Power of Law*. Princeton: Princeton University Press.

2006. *Human Rights and Gender Violence: Translating International Law into Local Justice*. Chicago: University of Chicago Press.

Resnik, Judith. 2001. Categorical Federalism: Jurisdiction, Gender, and the Globe. In *Yale Law Journal* 111: 619–80.

Sarat, Austin and Thomas Kearns (eds.). 1993. *Law and Everyday Life*. Ann Arbor: University of Michigan Press.

Schoepp-Schilling, Hanna Beate. 2000. CEDAW: A Key Instrument for Promoting Human Rights of Women. Talk delivered in St Petersburg, 13 November 2000.

Schuler, Margaret (ed.). 1992. *Freedom from Violence: Women's Strategies from Around the World*. New York: UNIFEM.

Secretary-General, Report. 2001. Status of submission of reports by States parties under article 18 of the Convention. CEDAW, United Nations. CEDAW/C/2001/II/2.

Wilson, Richard A. 1997. Introduction: Human Rights, Culture and Context. In *Human Rights, Culture and Context: Anthropological Perspectives* (ed.) Richard A. Wilson. London: Pluto Press.

PART 3

. . . JUSTICE

Plate 1: The house at the centre of *Brumărescu v. Romania* at the European Court of Human Rights.

CHAPTER 8

THE HOUSE OF GHOSTS: POST-SOCIALIST PROPERTY RESTITUTION AND THE EUROPEAN COURT'S RENDITION OF HUMAN RIGHTS IN *BRUMĂRESCU V. ROMANIA*

Filippo M. Zerilli and Marie-Bénédicte Dembour

Most non-criminal court cases are instigated by an individual 'applicant' whose name appears in legal commentaries only because it gives the case its title.[1] Individual lives, motivations and expectations are typically ignored; so is the impact the judicial process has on individual lives and society. The socially stripped 'applicant' hardly matches the 'real person' who lives behind the legally constructed figure. This discrepancy, which produces an objectifying and distancing effect,[2] is rarely noted in legal scholarship.[3] This chapter illustrates how the absence in the law of the person of the applicant and of other social actors produces a truncated view of the context in which law operates and of its actual achievements.[4] Reading a verdict of violation in international human rights law, it is easy to assume that the judgment will

---

[1] This chapter is the result of a genuine cooperative effort between the imagination of two scholars. Nonetheless, in order to satisfy Italian academic expectations and practice, the authors are happy to attribute the writing of its odd- and even-numbered pages to Dembour and Zerilli, respectively. They thank the participants to the workshop, especially Jane Cowan, Emily Haslam and Richard Wilson, as well as Cristina Pantiru (Sussex PhD student) and Françoise Tulkens (Judge at the European Court of Human Rights) for their constructive comments on earlier drafts. Zerilli expresses his gratitude to Dan and Sanda Brumărescu for their generous participation in an ongoing and enriching conversation. He also thanks Mircea Mirescu warmly for discussing with him various aspects of the case. Dembour acknowledges her helpful conversations with Crina Sandru (Registry of the European Court of Human Rights). The usual disclaimers apply.
[2] Wilson (1997) has documented the same effect in the production of human rights documents by NGOs such as Amnesty International.
[3] For an exception, see Halley (2004: 69). The former Registrar of the European Court of Human Rights, Petzold (2000: 1578), notes the discrepancy, but only in respect of decisions of (in)admissibility.
[4] Following a well-established anthropological tradition from Geertz (1983) to Latour (2002).

directly and effectively have impacted on the legal and social reality with which it deals. The case study presented here suggests that such a straightforward transformation is unlikely.

Brumărescu v. Romania was decided on its merits in 1999.[5] It was the first case in which the European Court of Human Rights (hereafter, Court) found an ex-socialist state in violation of the European Convention on Human Rights (hereafter, Convention) in relation to claims arising in respect of a property which had been expropriated during socialism. *Brumărescu* instantly became a 'leading case' and has already been followed by the Court in dozens of other cases against Romania, with more cases pending and awaiting decisions. It has inspired judgments by the Court in respect of other eastern and central European countries. It is often referred to in domestic processes, both in Romania and elsewhere. The case is well known in European human rights law and it has been the object of numerous commentaries (see e.g. Popescu 2000).

Not surprisingly given the way law works, these commentaries hardly say anything about the house which was the object of the litigation. In particular they do not mention that it became known as 'the house of ghosts' in the Bucharest neighbourhood where it is located, following an incident which we shall recount below. This label gives its title to our contribution because we feel it usefully directs attention to the multiple spectres, both from the past and related to present concerns, which feed into the relationship various social actors entertain towards the house – or rather, towards each other and society at large. The house of ghosts at the centre of the *Brumărescu* case can be approached, we suggest, as a microcosm of Romanian society, which is continually haunted by its past. The house constitutes a site where complex social relations are embedded which rest on particular memories of family histories, contested images of present Romanian society and disputed visions of the way the individual has related and continues to relate to the state. It also testifies to the existence of various ways of relying on a diversity of national and international institutions to articulate and legitimise claims to justice.

One of us (Zerilli) has met 'the applicant', Dan Brumărescu, on numerous occasions between 1999 and 2005, as well as, more episodically, 'the intervener' in the case, Mircea Mirescu. Mirescu's family had

---

[5] Judgment of 28 October 1999, application no. 18342/95 (2001) 33 EHRR 35. The judgment can also be found on the website of the Court at: www.echr.coe.int.

acquired the ground floor flat of the house under socialist rule. Even though Mirescu is a major protagonist in the dispute, not least in Brumărescu's perspective, he is hardly mentioned in the Strasbourg judgment. A European Convention case is always built around an applicant, a defendant state and the Court, irresistibly evoking a triangular representation of human rights.[6] An ethnographic perspective makes this triangular model explode. In *Brumărescu*, the players are not just Brumărescu, the Romanian state, the Strasbourg Court and even Mirescu, but also include other tenants, associations representing interests of former owners and tenants, a multitude of national courts, not to mention the Romanian legislative and other institutions such as the municipality of Bucharest.

This chapter is the fruit of a collaboration between a legal expert on European human rights law and an anthropologist of Romania. It will hopefully encourage others to pursue such an interdisciplinary collaboration which, despite its prestigious pedigree going back to *The Cheyenne Way* (Llewellyn and Hoebel 1941), remains all too rare and certainly unprecedented in the field of European human rights law. Our chapter starts by offering a summary of the *Brumărescu* case devoid of any social context – which lawyers would characterise as black-letter; its aridity shows the way human rights law is taken to operate. It then renders the dispute at the centre of the case understandable by providing its political context: the turmoil of legislative activity in Romania during the last fifteen years around the restitution of real estate property confiscated during socialism. Its third section examines the way the main protagonists in the dispute creatively participate in producing the context of the dispute, using various means – including gossip. Here we seek to render the sense of morality, justice and citizenship the participants develop when they reconstitute their family histories and reflect upon what was, what is and what should be Romania and being Romanian. The last section returns to international human rights law. It stresses that the rulings of the European Court of Human Rights have not provided any sense of closure in Romania. It also asks what kind of human rights – in a four-fold conception of rights as given, agreed upon, fought for and talked about – the Court can be expected to work with and, in fact, delivers. The conclusion locates the contribution by reference to the overall themes of this volume.

---

[6] See Mutua (2002: 10–38) for the denunciation of the implicit representation of human rights as involving a 'victim', a 'savage' and a 'saviour'; Kennedy (2001: 254).

BRUMĂRESCU V. ROMANIA: A BLACK-LETTER LAW SUMMARY

On 28 October 1999, the European Court of Human Rights decided that Romania had violated Article 6 para. 1 of the Convention (fair trial) and Article 1 of Protocol no. 1 (peaceful enjoyment of possessions)[7] in the *Brumărescu* case. To understand why and in what sense the Court found a violation of these provisions, it is useful to present the circumstances of the case, as recorded by the Court in its judgment.

The house at the centre of the case was built in 1930 by the parents of the applicant, Dan Brumărescu. In 1950 the applicant's parents lost possession of the house in an alleged application of Decree no. 92/1950 on nationalisation. They remained in one of the flats of the house as tenants of the state. In 1973, the state sold the ground floor flat of the house to the Mirescu family, who had been occupying it as tenants of the Brumărescus since 1939 (paras. 11–13 of the judgment).

In 1993, the applicant started an action for recovery of possession as the beneficiary of his parents' estate. The Bucharest Court of First Instance held on 9 December 1993 that the nationalisation of the house had been a mistake because its owners belonged to a category of persons exempted from nationalisation under Decree no. 92/1950, so that the state had never had any title to the house.[8] The Bucharest court ordered the return of the house to the applicant. No appeal was lodged against this decision. The applicant ceased to pay rent on the flat he was occupying and started, from April 1994, to pay land tax on the whole house (paras. 14–19 of the judgment).

The heir of the brothers who had acquired the ground floor flat in 1973, Mircea Dan Mirescu, requested the Procurator-General of

---

[7] By the time the Convention was signed in 1950, no formulation as to what the human right of property would cover had been agreed. Despite its central place in liberal ideology and the perceived need to prohibit totalitarian expropriation, the fear that the Court might end up protecting 'the right of the well-to-do' was too great for those who did not want to see set in stone an unfair pattern of property ownership (Nicol 2005: 162). The right was included in the first Protocol to the Convention.

[8] Decree 92/1950 was purportedly aimed at ensuring 'the proper management of dwellings which wealthy capitalists and exploiters . . . have allowed to fall into dilapidation as a means of sabotage [and at depriving] exploiters of an important means of exploitation' (Article 1). It specifically targeted 'immovable property belonging to former industrialists, owners of large estates, bankers, owners of large trading enterprises and other representatives of the wealthy capitalist class' (s. 1 of Article 1) and 'immovable property belonging to real-estate exploiters . . .' (s. 2 of Article 1). Such nationalisation was to occur without compensation (Article 3). Specifically excluded from the Decree's ambit was the 'immovable property of workers, civil servants, small artisans, persons working in intellectual professions and retired persons' (Article 2). These provisions are reproduced in para. 34 of the Strasbourg judgment.

Romania to lodge an application with the Supreme Court of Justice to have the judgment of 9 December 1993 quashed on the ground that the Court of First Instance had exceeded its jurisdiction.[9] Such proceedings were instigated, as was possible under Article 330.1 of the Romanian Code of Civil Procedure. The Supreme Court quashed the 1993 judgment on 1 March 1995, on the ground that the state had demonstrated title to the house under the nationalisation decree (paras. 20–4 of the judgment).

Brumărescu lodged an application at Strasbourg on 1 May 1995. He also lodged an application for restitution with the Romanian Administrative Board established in Romania in 1995 for dealing with restitution of property.[10] On 24 March 1998 the Board vested him with ownership of the first floor flat he was occupying as tenant of the state; it awarded him financial compensation for the rest of the house. Brumărescu challenged this decision of the Board in the Bucharest Court of First Instance in an attempt to get the whole house returned to him.[11] This application was dismissed on 21 April 1999. For the purpose of taxation, the house (except for the flat he was occupying) was reclassified state property as from 2 April 1996.

On 28 October 1999, the Strasbourg Court found Romania in violation of Article 6 of the Convention. This was because 'the Supreme Court of Justice [had] set at naught an entire judicial process which had ended in . . . a judicial decision that was [as recognised by the Romanian Supreme Court] "irreversible" and thus [what lawyers call] res judicata – and which had, moreover, been executed' (para. 62 of the judgment). This infringed the principle of legal certainty, a fundamental aspect of the rule of law which requires, amongst other things, that 'where the courts have finally determined an issue, their ruling should not be called into question' (para. 61 of the judgment).[12] The finding of violation of Article 1 of Protocol 1 followed from this finding on Article 6. In the words of the Strasbourg Court, it was '[i]n

---

[9] In other words, Mirescu's aim was to have the Supreme Court declare the 1993 judgment should never have been adopted and was to produce no effect because the Court of First Instance had never had the judicial competence to adopt it.

[10] Under Law no. 112/1995 (on which, see below).

[11] He notably argued that Law no. 112/1995 only applied to lawful expropriations, which had not been the case of his parents' house. While we understand their property had been listed in the annex to the Decree, the Brumărescu family did not fit the categories mentioned in Article 1 of Decree 92/1950.

[12] Moreover, the finding by the Supreme Court that the courts had no jurisdiction whatsoever to decide civil disputes such as the action for recovery of possession in the instant case amounted to a denial of the right of access to a tribunal guaranteed by Article 6 (para. 65 of the judgment).

consequence of the judgment of the Supreme Court of Justice [that] the applicant was . . . deprived of the rights of ownership of the house which had been vested in him by virtue of the final judgment [of the Court of First Instance of 1993] in his favour' (para. 77 of the judgment).

THE SOCIO-LEGAL CONTEXT OF HOUSE RESTITUTION IN POST-SOCIALIST ROMANIA

The *Brumărescu* case has been widely reported in Romania and remains mentioned to this day when property restitution is debated. It is perceived to be about property, not fair trial. This legally slightly misguided perception is understandable, given the political context which forms the background to the case, namely, the problem – common to most post-socialist eastern European countries (CeFRes 1997; Offe 1997; Pena 1998) – of having to decide what to do with privately owned properties which had been nationalised, confiscated or expropriated by the state during socialism.

In Romania, the problem became represented as a conflict involving at one end a group of capitalists thirsty for revenge and set on regaining rights they had acquired through labour or heritage and at the other end a mass of poor workers threatened with eviction despite arguable entitlements to property having emerged through time and use. The impression which has been created is that the controversy arose from a clash between two social groups claiming distinct concepts of property. In actual fact, the two groups share a paradigm of exclusive property rights typical of a neo-liberal ideology (Zerilli 2006). Neither group contests the concept of private property. On the contrary they both hold it as a 'sacred value' and consider it a 'natural right' of which they had been deprived. The bipolar representation, carried out in the media and in political and popular discourse, fails to highlight how individuals from both groups have sought to appropriate for themselves prestigious residential buildings, especially in the capital city of Bucharest. It also wrongly suggests that the state might have been able to act as an independent arbitrator on the issue. This would not have been possible given that the emerging political, economic and cultural elites were centrally implicated, with huge interests – both personal and collective – at stake (Bârsan 1997: 304–19).

The first democratically elected Romanian government promptly – though not unequivocally – provided for the restitution of agricultural land through Law 18/1991, which was subsequently amended many times (Verdery 2003: 94–104). However, it largely ignored the problem of the restitution of residential units. Decree Law 61/1990 and Law 85/1992 were admittedly passed, arguably for electoral gains. They made it possible for tenants to buy, at very advantageous prices, state flats built from 1950 onwards in what were locally known as 'blocks'. Individuals from families representing almost 4 million Romanians availed themselves of this opportunity, often referred to as 'the Revolution's gifts'. This contributed to ensuring that the incumbent party coalition was returned to power in the second general election of November 1992.

In the same period, former owners of private properties were trying to recuperate properties that either they or their forebears had lost under socialism. For most of them, restitution in kind was the only way they envisaged for securing their rights. They began addressing state institutions by way of letters, memoranda and petitions requesting the restitution of their properties. Between 1992 and 1995, approximately 1,500 former owners addressed national courts in individual actions aimed at recovering properties, especially in urban areas where expropriation had occurred on a massive scale. Many a former owner, including of course Brumărescu in 1993, won in the courts (Vasiliu 2001).

The political parties in power, with a self-proclaimed commitment to the defence of the rights of tenants living in nationalised houses, did not welcome these judicial developments. In May 1994, President of Romania Ion Iliescu, a founder and prominent leader of the Social Democrat Romanian Party (PDSR, now simply PSD), publicly contested the legitimacy of the judicial decisions in his famous 'Satu Mare speech' (named after the Transylvanian town he was visiting).[13] Iliescu reproached the courts for trying to solve a problem which was being debated in Parliament and was expected shortly to give rise to a national restitution law.

This is the context in which successive General Prosecutors, pressured to act by tenants threatened with eviction and with claims legitimised by the coalition in power, resorted to the extraordinary procedure of *recurs in anulare* (a judicial action towards annulment) provided in the Code of Civil Procedure, in order to have numerous definitive and irrevocable court verdicts that were favourable to the former owners quashed

---

[13] Iliescu's discourse is reproduced in Aviz consultativ nr. 1 din 5 iulie 1994 privind propunerea de suspendare din funcție a Președintelui României, 'Monitorul Oficial', n. 166, (16 July 1994).

by the Supreme Court, on the grounds that no tribunal was allowed to pronounce a judgment before the adoption of a national legislation. This stance was backed by the full Supreme Court of Justice which adopted, by 25 votes against 20, decision no. 1 of 2 February 1995 holding that the courts were not allowed to judge any claim concerning immovable property nationalised under Decree no. 92/1950. This decision was immediatly stigmatised by civic associations and legal scholars (e.g. Cosma 1995) for seriously infringing the constitutional right granting access to justice.

Former owners were strongly discouraged from undertaking any new judicial action at national level. At the same time, it became clear that the tenants did not aim so much at preserving their status of tenant (which an extension of their lease with state institutions could have guaranteed) as at emulating the right gained in the early 1990s by tenants living in 'blocks' of buying their dwellings (built by the state). Tenant associations largely won this fight: with minor restrictions, Law 112/1995 allowed the tenants of nationalised assets to buy the flats they were occupying. As a result, an important number of nationalised houses and flats were sold to tenants during the first right-wing legislature of 1996–2000 led by the Democratic Convention,[14] at the same time as Law 112/1995 was heavily criticised both by Romanian human rights NGOs (especially APADOR-CH) and the international community.[15]

A 1996 electoral promise to modify the law came to nothing. However, legal regulations were adopted in order to secure former owners access to justice, including through a limitation of the powers of the General Prosecutor. Law 17/1997 amended the Code of Civil Procedure, limiting the temporal application of the extraordinary *recurs in anulare*. On 28 September 1998 the full Supreme Court departed, this time unanimously, from its ruling of February 1995 and held that 'courts have jurisdiction to entertain any action concerning an alleged infringement of the right of property'.[16] Pressure from the European

---

[14] A coalition formed by the 'historical parties' of the Christian-Democrat National Peasant Party and the National Liberal Party, the Democrat Party and the Democrat Union of Hungarians of Romania.

[15] See notably the Council of Europe's Parliamentary Assembly Resolution no. 1123 of 24 April 1997 and Resolution no. A4-0428 of 3 December 1998 adopted by the European Parliament, both inviting Romania to modify legislation regarding property restitution. The US House of Representatives also adopted a Resolution (no. 562 of 1 October 1998) on the property expropriated by former totalitarian regimes calling for restitution in kind whenever possible.

[16] See Hotărârea nr. 1/1998 a Curți Supreme de Justiție – Secțiile Unite.

institutions negotiating Romanian accession to the European Union led the government of Adrian Nastase (the most prominent figure of the Social Democrat Romanian Party alongside Iliescu) to adopt Law 10/2001 and purportedly ensure restitution 'in kind'. However, the law subjected restitution and compensation to many conditions and excluded from its ambit buildings used by the state for public interest (hospitals, schools, museums, headquarters of legally-registered political parties, diplomatic residences, etc.). Legal pratictioners immediately denounced Law 10/2001 for amounting to 'a new expropriation' (Vasiliu 2001). Here ends our presentation of the (historically not completed)[17] socio-legal context which framed Brumărescu's judicial adventures and life experiences.

'AS TO THE FACTS'

The impression one gets reading the 1999 *Brumărescu* judgment of the Strasbourg Court is that the applicant's main dispute was with the Romanian state. When one talks to Brumărescu, however, it immediately appears that he regards Mirescu, the heir of the former tenants of his parents, as a protagonist far more important than the state (which is nonetheless not irrelevant). Mirescu's sidelining in the Strasbourg case law is due to the way the Convention works: a violation can only be established under the Convention if it is attributable to a state party to the Convention. An individual applicant must therefore put into brackets any dispute he has with another individual or at least rephrase it so that it can be read as a dispute with the state, under the jurisdiction of which he falls. This is what Brumărescu did. When Mirescu heard of his application to Strasbourg, he successfully asked the Court to be able to intervene (para. 8 of the judgment). His submissions are briefly summarised in the judgment, but not otherwise referred to by the Court which seems to have decided the case without paying much attention to Mirescu's stake in the house. The presentation by the Court of 'the facts' of the case – to use the language of lawyers – hardly alludes to what the case is really about according to the main protagonists to the dispute.

---

[17] The successive legislature (2004 to current time) saw a right-wing coalition, called Alliance Justice and Truth (and consisting of Liberals and Democrats, supported by the Hungarian Union), coming into power again. Law 247/2005 affirms the principle that property assets must be restituted 'in kind' to former owners 'whenever possible' (i.e. when the goods in question materially exist).

This section reports families' stories which Brumărescu and Mirescu have recounted in the informality of private conversations with the anthropologist. One might be tempted to dismiss much of this talk as inconsequential gossip of anecdotical character and often consisting of no more than unsubstantiated insinuations. These 'facts' would certainly not retain the attention of lawyers (as both protagonists perfectly understand). Social anthropologists, however, have demonstrated the significance for social life of the minutiae of an ordinary daily practice such as gossip (Gluckman 1963; Paine 1967; Haviland 1977, 1998; Van Vleet 2003). Here, each protagonist reflects upon his own personal attitudes and those of the other, assigning and imputing personal, social and cultural behaviour. What they say of each other brings to the fore issues of legitimacy and morality, thus highlighting how social identities are symbolically constituted and manipulated, in turn creating moral divides and new politics of difference in a context of rapid social change. The observations they offer produce and reproduce, but also challenge and transform, social meanings in a cultural order which is never 'given' but always 'made' through performed actions and speech which make sense at a local level.

FAMILY STORIES

Brumărescu has welcomed Zerilli into his house many times, presumably in an effort to acquaint the anthropologist with his perspective on and knowledge of the case, truncated not only by the Court but also, and more importantly from his point of view, by the media.[18] He explains that the house had been built by his parents in 1930 as a *casă de clan* (clan house) where his family, conceived as an extended unit, would live. While he traces the gradual disappearance of this model of the family and its replacement by a nuclear family model to socialist rules and housing policies, in his life story he also associates this transformation to changes in the spatial use of the house. These were inaugurated when the Mirescu family came to occupy the ground floor flat at the eve of World War II. International political turmoil had led Romanian citizens inhabiting the north-eastern part of the Moldova

---

[18] Brumărescu seems to want to convey a deep understanding of his life experiences of deprivation and humiliation both in socialist and post-socialist times. This would explain why he refused to participate in Florin Călinescu's acclaimed television show on private chain PRO-TV, but accepted to paint his family portrait on a special forty-minutes documentary (part of the series 'The Bucharest Memorial' directed by Lucia Hossu Longin) concerning the old inhabitants of the quarter Cotroceni on the public television chain TVR 1.

region, also known as Bessarabia, to flee in fear of a Soviet annexion (which did occur in 1941). This is the region from which Mirescu's family came to Bucharest in 1939. Brumărescu remembers generosity, altruism and most of all national solidarity towards 'refugees' from threatened Bessarabia to have presided over the informal rental arrangements (no contract had existed). By contrast, Mirescu thinks that pecuniary interest and possibly need were the principal factors which had motivated the Brumărescus to let the flat to his family – then composed of his grandmother and her five sons. Despite these discrepancies over which family was more helpful to the other, Brumărescu and Mirescu's accounts concord on a number of points. They both recall that the two families were on good terms and used to be pretty close – so much so that Mirescu owes his middle name 'Dan' to Brumărescu. They also agree that both families could claim a 'genuine' Romanian origin (which in Romania conventionally means Orthodox, not Hungarian, not Jewish and, most of all, not Gypsy).

The two families were evidently part of the small portion of Romanians who could be identified as belonging to an expanding urban bourgeoisie. They belonged neither to the rural nor worker population (70 per cent according to Popescu 1998), nor to the industrial or capitalist class (0.1 per cent, according to the same author), although Mirescu once proudly and ironically remarked that his family was 'perhaps *boierească*' (i.e. of aristocratic origin). We have noted above how the ordinary representation of the conflict over property restitution as an expression of a sociological divide between socialist workers (the tenants) and capitalist exploiters (the former owners) is an oversimplification. It may be worth in this respect to illustrate further the social position of the two protagonists. Dan Brumărescu is a retired (hydraulic) engineer. His father was also an engineer, and had been director general of an important private enterprise which specialised in the construction of works of public interest (such as roads) until he was appointed as executive of the company after the nationalisation of industries in 1948. Mircea Dan Mirescu currently works as a researcher for a private IT company in Bucharest. His father and four uncles were all university educated; they respectively became an accountant, a lawyer, a literary critic, an agronomist and an engineer.

The close class origin of the two families and the similar professional status of the two contenders invite us to explore how they assert different social positions in relation to the dispute. Our account attempts to identify how the strategies they adopt and the political and symbolic ends they pursue differ or, on the contrary, follow similar lines.

THE GROUND FLOOR APARTMENT'S SALE

In 1974,[19] the Mirescu family bought the flat they had been occupying as tenants for over three decades (from 1939 to 1950 as tenants of the Brumărescus and from 1950 to 1973 as tenants of the state). The sale occurred in the context of a growing financial crisis to which the state responded by putting on sale a portion of the real estate property sector. Among different decrees and provisions Article 42 of Law 4/1973 regulated, only for a few months, the sale of nationalised assets to tenants living in them. It is under this provision that the Mirescu family became owners of the ground floor flat of the house. Brumărescu and Mirescu recall the 1974 transaction very differently.

According to Mirescu, the transaction was not only fully legal but it also occurred with the express agreement of Brumărescu's father. Brumărescu contests the legal basis of the transaction arguing that the buyers could not ignore that the state was not the legal owner. He remembers Victor, one of Mirescu's uncles, telling his father they wanted to buy the flat, but he observes it would not have been possible to raise any objection without suffering severe consequences. Moreover, Brumărescu recalls that, at that time, his family had also wanted to buy the first floor flat in which they were constrained to live as tenants of the state but that the Central Committee of the Communist Party had refused them permission to buy. He asks, polemically, why they could not buy while others effectively did, in a subtle insinuation that the Mirescu family was close to the communist *nomenklatura*, a fact which he moreover connects to the short-livedness of Article 42 of Law 4/1973 which allowed only a few tenants (including the Mirescus) to buy the nationalised assets. Mirescu refutes Brumărescu's allegation on an altogether different and at the same time similar ground, i.e., by recalling that he (Mirescu) did not have a passport and could not travel abroad during socialism, while Brumărescu frequently visited western Europe, suggesting links to the *Securitate*, the socialist's regime secret police.

Both Brumărescu and Mirescu construct and order social positioning in terms of distance/proximity to the communist *aparatchik*, a

---

[19] The Strasbourg judgment seems erroneous in putting the year of the sale as 1973.

measurement they use retrospectively to bolster or undermine their respective family and personal social status. Prestige and reputation – precisely the ground on which gossip flourishes (Haviland 1977) – are at stake here. Another memory illustrates this further. An accountant, Mirescu's father kept the books of a state company. During socialist rule, he was convicted of a 'crime against state security' and sentenced to six years of detention. For his son, the imprisonment plainly demonstrates his father's anti-communism. Brumărescu suggests instead that the conviction was for *delapidare*, i.e., personal appropriation (a suggestion about which Mirescu said later to Zerilli that he would never forgive Brumărescu). The memory of the same episode is used by both protagonists to testify to (presumably) irreconcilable truths.

THE HOUSE OF GHOSTS: IMAGINING ROMANIA

Dishonesty is a recurrent theme in Brumărescu's portrait of Mircea Mirescu and his father. Striking in this respect is his account of the more recent history of the ground floor flat. This flat has remained empty ever since the double suicide on New Year's Eve 1987 of the last surviving two of the five Mirescu brothers, explaining why children scream – according to Brumărescu – 'the house of ghosts' when passing his house.

According to Brumărescu the two brothers drank a fatal cocktail they had prepared by mixing red wine with a sleeping potion. Their bodies were found six days later. A letter of apology to Brumărescu and his wife from the two brothers failed to provide the reasons for the double suicide. Brumărescu has an explanation. One of the brothers was seriously ill and depended for his care on the other. Fearing that the second brother would die first leaving the first without assistance, the two lonely brothers decided to die together. This hypothetical explanation is not necessarily implausible. It may nonetheless be more revealing of the way Brumărescu wants to portray Mircea Mirescu. In his conversations with Zerilli, Brumărescu insists over and over again that no tie of friendship united the uncles and their nephew Mircea: 'The brothers did not allow him to enter their home! Never!'. Brumărescu also claims that Mirescu fell under police inspection upon the discovery of the bodies. He furthermore alleges that Mirescu possibly became sole inheritor of the ground floor flat by usurping the rights of his sister (now deceased). He offers other 'facts', which need not be mentioned here, which concur in revealing Mirescu as fraudulent, violent and dishonest.

Mirescu's purported lack of morality should not be taken as denoting simply a trait of personal or filial character. Instead it is framed and assessed by Brumărescu as an illustration of the moral degeneration which affects postsocialist Romanian society, as evidenced by the presence of 'sharp businessmen' (*afacerişti*), i.e., profiteers or speculators. Brumărescu insists that Mirescu has no emotional attachment to the ground floor flat to which he was allegedly never admitted in his uncles' lifetime. He presents Mirescu's interest as purely pecuniary, aiming to destroy the unity of the house, in sharp contrast to himself, Brumărescu, who wants to recreate what he calls an 'unconditioned property', i.e., a family house at a single owner's disposal. The repeated attacks on Mirescu's moral probity are obviously meant to undermine Mirescu's property title – which Brumărescu characterises as having been 'vitiated' right from the start.

Mirescu presents a very different story. He portrays himself as the favoured nephew who took care of his beloved uncles. He also has a different vision of what may happen to the house if it were to return wholly to Brumărescu. Brumărescu's octogenarian status leads Mirescu to speculate that the house would be 'lost' as soon as it was inherited by Brumărescu's wife and two sons. Brumărescu's comparatively young wife Sanda, from a second marriage, is pictured as having married for profit rather than out of genuine love, which Mirescu plays out through gossip, alleging sexual infidelity. Sanda's presumed Jewish origin leads him to suppose that she would most certainly sell the house and very quickly leave for Israel. Moreover, Brumărescu's two sons being well established abroad – one in Germany, the other in France – leads Mirescu to conclude that, if returned to Brumărescu, the house would soon fall to 'foreign hands'.

These attitudes correspond to different visions of Europe and what it is to be a good Romanian. For Mirescu, Europe primarily entails a loss of national sovereignty. For Brumărescu, who is also deeply attached to the notion of a Romanian national heritage but in a different way, Europe represents the promise of rescuing the past and embarking on a healthy future. The comments that one makes of the other should therefore not be treated in a sociological analysis as simply defamatory gossip. They must be understood in reference to a wide-ranging social logic which considers 'exterior pressures' as one of the greatest challenges facing contemporary Romanian society. Verdery accurately predicted that 'the national idea', which had played a major role in cultural production during socialism, would keep its prominent place in

Romanian culture in the post-Ceausescu era (Verdery 1991: 318). This indeed has proved to be the case, with the ongoing cultural work and struggle over national sentiment in Romania an activity in which most citizens (not just the Romanian political elite and the intellectuals) are involved. This is evident in ordinary discourses and practices, including everyday talk such as gossip. Elaborating on the future destination of the contested house, Mirescu once said that he feared Romania would be put up for sale for western disposal. 'I am not a nationalist', he immediately added, 'nevertheless it is important to defend the interests of one's country.' To be sure, this badly disguised national(ist) rhetoric also applies to Brumărescu, although it is articulated in different ways given that he is – as one newspaper put it in a title – 'the Romanian who has beaten the Romanian state' when he addressed a *supra*national institution.

Brumărescu and Mirescu's reciprocal accusations must also be understood in reference to the specific national legal and ideological context which in Romania, throughout the 1990s, privileged the principle of the 'protection of tenants'. This is most clear in the passing of Law 112/95 which emphasises property as a right acquired through time and use,[20] against the idea of restitution of property 'in kind' (*restitutio in integrum* or *in natura*) as claimed by Brumărescu and former owners' associations. In this legal and social logic (the legislation is fed and supported by public discussion), it is not surprising that Brumărescu does not advertise the fact that he is seeking the restitution of other real estate properties.[21] It is also understandable that he tends to conceal the size of his house (twenty windows on the facade, a ground floor of approximately 200 square metres), located in the Cotroceni district, a select green residential area of early twentieth-century Bucharest which is part of a zone where prices are among the highest in the capital. In what could be seen as a parallel move, Mirescu told Zerilli when he first met him in 1999 – at a public protest promoted by a tenants' association against a bill modifying Law 112/95 in favour of former owners – that he was living in his uncles' flat and had sold the flat which he previously owned. This is certainly not true. While both Brumărescu and Mirescu proclaim their full adhesion to proprietary models and neo-liberal market economy ideals, they also shy away from defending this logic in public. Presumably they are afraid of accusations, such as that of having

[20] See especially Articles 7–11 in Chapter III ('Protection of Tenants') of Law 112/1995,
[21] As two applications currently pending at Strasbourg demonstrate (applications 2922/2004 and 41185/2004).

more than one dwelling asset, which could be used by the other to construct a lack of morality on their part, and possibly influence those who judge them – where 'judging' is not restricted to the prerogative of the judiciary institution.

Before concluding this section on 'the facts' of the case, it is worth signalling that there are other tenants in the house who are not mentioned in the Strasbourg rulings or in the local press, yet again showing a very selective factual account. The second floor flat was occupied until very recently by a family of three who had moved in in 1972 (they were evicted in 2005 following a national court judgment); in 1992, the basement flat was allocated by the City Hall to a single man. When explaining their personal histories, attitudes and behaviour, Brumărescu describes all these people, who have never recognised him as the entitled owner, as being of Gypsy origin, thus evoking standardised images of Gypsyness (such as dirtiness, dishonesty, etc.) widespread in Romania. Furthermore, he presents the occupant of the basement flat as having homosexual tendencies.[22] We could say that while the ground floor flat is crowded with Mirescu's 'ghosts' in the sense that we have seen, the rest of the house is also full of 'ghosts', here to be conceived of as a Romanian's social stereotyped nightmares. These hardly coincide with the European values promoted by the Council of Europe and the European Union and thus highlight how 'Europe' is a symbolic construction which is strategically used to different ends in different contexts. To Brumărescu, they illustrate the most negative aspects of a transitional society; they are symbols that should enable social change by calling attention to what people, and society, should and should not be and do. Thus, here gossip and rumours become a means of imagining and enacting social justice, reinforcing legal reasoning and action and sustaining individual moral expectations in conditions of extreme legal uncertainty – one that the second Strasbourg judgment has hardly dissolved as we shall argue in the next section.

SPHERES OF JUSTICE

From a European human rights law perspective, the significance of the *Brumărescu* case rests first and foremost in its affirmation of the need in a democracy to promote legal certainty, which had been negated by the

---

[22] On negative Romanian attitudes on homosexuality and the impasse this raises for European law, see Stychin (2004: 960–3).

Supreme Court's annulment of a judicial decision which national law had considered final (Leach 2005: 253; but for a different interpretation see Carss-Frisk 2001). This procedural aspect, however, is generally ignored by non-specialists who take the case, which is a constant topic of media commentory in Romania, to be exclusively about property – even though the Strasbourg Court found first a violation of Article 6 of the Convention (on fair trial) and only then a violation of Article 1 of Protocol 1 (on peaceful enjoyment of possessions). Interestingly, neither the 1999 verdict of violation (dealing with the 'merits' of the case) nor the judgment which followed in 2001 on 'just satisfaction' (stating how the situation should be put right) have put an end to the litigation: the question of who owns the house at the centre of the dispute remains unsolved. More generally, the Strasbourg rulings have brought no closure to political and popular debates concerning property restitution in Romania. What has happened is that Strasbourg has become a symbolic resource amongst others in local and national politics, deployed and manipulated by social actors to specific ends. This situation calls for exploring the limits of international justice and alerts us to possible functions of human rights law beyond straightforward recognition of a natural right's entitlement, notably in terms of participation in the reinforcement of the rule of law and assertion of protest in the face of humiliation and spoliation.

The second Strasbourg judgment: the failure of success?[23]

In its judgment of October 1999, the Strasbourg Court had considered that the question of the application of Article 41 of the Convention, on 'just satisfaction', was not ready for decision (para. 84 of the judgment). The Court ruled on this aspect on 23 January 2001 in a second set of proceedings. During these, Mirescu, using a phrase which was at that time recurrent in the discourse of tenants, submitted that the Court should not 'commit a new injustice' by returning the flat he owned to Brumărescu. He suggested that the Court award Brumărescu pecuniary compensation. In keeping with the principle that a dispute at Strasbourg occurs between the applicant and the defendant state (and no one else), the Court did not follow this route. It ruled that 'the state should . . . restore the applicant's title to . . . the house . . . without prejudice to any claim which Mr Mirescu might have to ownership of the flat on the ground floor, which claim would fall to be determined in

---

[23] In a reversal of Cowan's evocative title (this volume).

the domestic courts'.[24] It further decided that the house should be returned to the applicant within six months or, failing such restitution, that Romania must pay the applicant within the same period of six months a given sum of money (para. 31 of the judgment).

Within the legal parameters of the case, restitution makes sense: human rights law's aim is to erase the violation whenever possible. In a case such as *Brumărescu*, restitution (if possible) would be the best way to put the applicant in the situation he would have been in if the violation had not existed. But the ownership of the ground floor flat by a third party, while irrelevant to the Strasbourg case, obviously makes restitution highly problematic in practice. This is presumably why the Court offered Romania a second course, namely, financially compensating Brumărescu for the part of the house he did not himself occupy. Things, however, took an altogether different course.

Relying on the Strasbourg judgment of January 2001, Brumărescu asked the Procurator-General to instigate proceedings so as to have the Supreme Court of Justice quash the decision it had adopted on 1 March 1995 (whereby the Supreme Court had quashed the 1993 final first instance decision which had declared Brumărescu owner of the house). Such proceedings were instigated, and on 24 July 2001 the Supreme Court quashed its 1995 judgment.[25] The judgment of 1993 was therefore reinstated and, in its wake, Brumărescu's title to the ownership of the whole house.

The last proceedings before the Supreme Court were highly ironic: they resulted in the application of more or less the very mechanism for which Romania had been found in violation of the Convention at Strasbourg in the first place![26] The Supreme Court cited amongst the facts of the case both the Strasbourg judgments of 1999 and 2001; the former – and most important in European human rights law as it explains why there is a violation – rather briefly, the latter more

---

[24] In a context where rising applications threaten the efficacy of the Court (Woolf 2005), legal commentators have noted this passage for indicating that the Court was finally opening up to the idea that it should not just *declare a violation* but should also facilitate the execution of the judgment by *indicating how the violation should be repaired* (Leach 2005: 98). However, our account dissipates any hope that the ruling may have helped to resolve the national situation and to make applications to Strasbourg by people in a situation similar to Brumărescu unlikely.

[25] Supreme Court judgment no. 61/2001.

[26] The European Court had found Romania in violation of the Convention in 1999 because the Supreme Court had quashed, under Article 330 para. 1 of the Romanian Code of Civil Procedure, the 1993 final judgment of an inferior court. In 2001, the Supreme Court relied on Article 330 para. 4 of the same Code to quash a previously successful action in annulment before the Supreme Court. The logic of Article 330's paras. 1 and 4 seems similarly unsatisfactory from the perspective of legal certainty.

extensively. A conspiracy theorist might be inclined to argue that Romania was pretending to respect the European Convention while maintaining the legal uncertainty for which it had been condemned. Putting it less strongly, it is clear that the limited transformation of the Code of Civil Procedure (the introduction of a six-month limit in respect of Article 330.1) may have appeared to satisfy the requirements of the European Convention but was in practice insufficient to ensure that ways of doing acquired in the past would not continue to operate. This demonstrates, if need be, the complexity of the relationship between the international and the national.[27]

The net result of the Supreme Court decision of 2001 is highly problematic, for there are now two individuals recognised to be the rightful owners of the same property: Mirescu, whose title to the ground floor flat has never been invalidated nor even challenged, and Brumărescu whose title to the full house has now been reinstated (for a second time). Not surprisingly, the Bucharest City Hall declared itself unable to return a flat which was not state property. The Romanian government decided the best course was to compensate Brumărescu for the ground floor flat, valued at US dollars 42,000 by the Strasbourg Court in its 2001 judgment.[28] Brumărescu, interested in restitution not compensation, failed to disclose to the Government the number of a bank account to which money could be transferred.[29] This would not have prevented the case from being closed at Strasbourg,[30] but things remain in flux at the national level. It is very difficult to predict what will happen next. Mirescu's title does not appear threatened right now, though a new piece of legislation (admittedly not currently tabled)

---

[27] The Strasbourg Court was not in a position to assess whether the reform of Article 330.1 was sufficient to satisfy the requirements of Article 6 of the Convention (on fair trial); nor was it asked to rule on Article 330 para. 4, which was unaffected by the reform of the Code of Civil Procedure. [28] Five years on, this sum is well under the current value of the flat.

[29] Continuing a strategy of delaying resolution he had already pursued before. Thus he had failed to answer questions the Strasbourg Court had put to him regarding the value of the house, which contributed to the Court being unable to decide on just satisfaction in 1999.

[30] The European Convention gives the Committee of Ministers the task of supervising the execution of the judgments of the Strasbourg Court and thus to close cases through the adoption of a 'final resolution'. The Committee has not yet adopted a final resolution in the Brumărescu case. This is because although the Romanian government is considered to have paid the sums awarded by the Court (it placed 42,000 dollars on an account in the Treasury of the Municipality of Bucharest which can be transferred to the applicant at its first request), the government failed to include in that sum the interest which arose from a delay of several days in its payment: Committee of Ministers' Annotated Agenda and Order of Business for the 834th (DH) meeting (April 2003) – CM/Del/OJ/OT(2003)834, at page 77. In terms of execution through general measures, the six-month limit introduced in respect of Article 330.1 of the Romanian Code of Civil Proceedings satisfied the Committee of Ministers.

could change this. As for Brumărescu, he has so far not managed to get the 2001 Supreme Court judgment executed.[31]

THE LIMITS OF INTERNATIONAL JUSTICE

At the heart of the Convention system is the principle of subsidiarity, which means that national systems are primarily responsible for safeguarding human rights, with the Convention system being subsidiary to them (Reid 2004: 37). The Strasbourg Court comes into play only when things go wrong at national level and an applicant comes forward with a complaint. Then the Court can say something, but it is for the national level to draw the consequences of its edicts. The role of the international is thus to guide and influence the national process, not to manage it or to take it over.

The interplay between the national and the international is also complex from a perspective which is not strictly legal. A fine lawyer,[32] Brumărescu accepts the legal limits within which the Court works and does not begrudge either the Court or European human rights law for failing to give him back his house. To him, the Strasbourg Court represents independent justice, built around the great European national traditions of especially the United Kingdom and France. He is wary of the possibility that former socialist states may exercise a corrupting influence on the Strasbourg system, noticeable – he and others say – in certain judges and members of the Registry's nominations. Nonetheless, in his view Strasbourg functions overall *correctly*. His point of comparison is the corruption which everyone agrees engulfs the Romanian judicial system. If only the domestic courts functioned like Strasbourg, Brumărescu feels he would never have needed to turn to Strasbourg. He either does not see or does not wish to comment on the paradoxical character of this position: it is on the basis of a judgment of a Romanian tribunal – moreover, at the bottom of the judicial hierarchy and after expeditious proceedings which lasted a mere few months in 1993 – that he won at the European level!

'Why should the Strasbourg Court act like our estate agent?' This question was put by the (then) Prime Minister Nastase soon after the

---

[31] This has led him to gear himself for further litigation before the Strasbourg Court, which he keeps informed of this (lack of) development.
[32] A former engineer, he has become so well versed both in the relevant domestic regulations and in European Convention law that he now acts as his own lawyer. There is unfortunately no space in this paper to discuss his relationships with lawyers.

second Strasbourg judgment which had valued, and in that sense put a price on, the house at the centre of the *Brumărescu* litigation. Let us leave aside here the fact that, facing a different audience, Nastase might have wished to signify Romania's submission to and/or honour in being part of Europe. The barely disguised slur of Nastase's exclamation appears exactly opposite to Brumărescu's respect for the Court. In an objective view of human rights law, it appears inappropriate: the Court may have valued the house, but it did not say who its owner should be. One can nonetheless understand why the Strasbourg intervention, however limited, could appear to Romanians like an international intrusion by a body which was neither willing nor able to approach the problem looking at all its facets and ramifications. The Court is indeed aware of the difficulty, which is why it often states that a question before it is not best decided at the international level.[33] From a perspective that would expect a judicial institution to settle conflict, the Strasbourg Court could be criticised for having done too little rather than too much about the problem of house restitution in Romania.

A more severe critique could be put in altogether different terms. It could be judged that the Strasbourg litigation has intensified tensions and conflicts in the Romanian political and social arena between tenants and former owners, contributing to the development of a reified representation of the problem. It is perhaps not irrelevant here to reflect upon the way Brumărescu is now viewed in Romania. The wide reporting in the Romanian media particularly of the 2001 Strasbourg judgment has led him to become something of a public figure. As his son put it, 'Dad, you are somebody.' While some applaud him for having 'beaten the Romanian state', many take his victory *against* Romania as a sign of a lack of moral integrity and national commitment.[34] A lawyer representing the Romanian government had asked him at a hearing at Strasbourg years before: 'Aren't you ashamed of yourself for doing this?' Since then there has been a deluge of such questioning. His wife Sanda recalls being asked: 'Listen, dear, are you married to *that one*', to which she had replied 'Yes, I am married to *this person*'. The couple recounts that these kinds of encounters used to happen 'everywhere: in courts, on trolleybuses, in the streets'. 'People still recognise me today,'

---

[33] For a critical analysis of this logic, see Çali (this volume).

[34] A range of moral positions is expressed. One former owner told Zerilli that he would not follow Brumărescu's path because a favourable judicial outcome (compensation for the former or new owner) would have to be ultimately paid by his fellow countrymen, through taxation, which he felt was not a fair way of repairing the injustice he had suffered.

Brumărescu adds, 'even though I have aged, they still recognise me, everybody knows me.'

Either at a personal or at a social level European human rights law has offered no closure. It has certainly failed to promote social cohesion and may have contributed to the development of mistrust between the state and (some of) its citizens. It would of course be naïve to expect that the European Convention could be waved as a magic wand to solve everything in a situation the origins of which lie in traumatic events, a situation that has never been addressed upfront and in a straightforward manner by the legislature at home, which has not made up its mind as to how to handle the situation. Nonetheless it is perhaps too easy for the Court to hide behind the principle of subsidiarity and other legal notions to assert that it can do no more than it is doing, and leave it to the national to clear up the mess – presupposing that the national can or even wants to.[35] This all begs the question of course: what exactly is human rights law for?

What is human rights law for?

A standard representation of human rights law is that it embodies natural rights, conceived as given and universal entitlements; a competing vision approaches human rights law as principles of adjudication, in a model which regards the rule of law and liberal democracy as agreed values to be supported and universalised; a third conception stresses that human rights are primarily a language of protest, which should first serve to give a hearing to the voices of suffering (Dembour 2006). How, if at all, do these representations apply to the *Brumărescu* case?

Brumărescu went to Strasbourg in a quest for justice. To him like to most of us, justice is a large project. In his case, it includes – but is not

[35] To give an example, lawyers generally accept that a system where the Court would be able to address violations which took place *before* the European Convention had come into force in respect of the defendant state would be unworkable. Within this rule, the Court makes choices. In terms of the case law concerning property confiscated under socialism, the Court has decided to consider expropriation to be an instantaneous act (which happens the very day of the expropriation, and that day only) rather than a continuous act (the effects of which would have continued after expropriation had started). The result is that the Court has been unable to take cognisance of any claim concerning such property which had not been the object of a measure (such as a judicial decision, as in the case of *Brumărescu*) by the national authorities after the Convention came into force in respect of their country. This steadfast resistance to engage with the past has led a commentator to criticise the Court for its thoroughly modernist orientation and to fear that the Court's belief in a future which would alleviate the weight of history may prove to be a misguided leap of faith (Macklem 2005, pp. 20–1). By contrast, Macklem approves the decisions of the UN Human Rights Committee which has taken the opposite attitude. But it may not be insignificant that the decisions of the 18-member strong Committee are not binding; one international site is not another.

reducible to – seeing socialism condemned and the house his family unjustly lost being returned to its rightful owner (who happens now to be him). He regards property as a natural right; he does not doubt that he is entitled to the house. The idea that property is first and foremost a matter of social relations, defended both by anthropologists and legal scholars (e.g. Hann 1998; Munzer 2001), would probably sound strange to him. Like less scholarly versed people (including Romanian 'tenants'), he tends to view property as linking a 'thing' to an individual. This is consonant with a view of all human rights (not just property) as entitlement, a notion which suggests substance rather than a way to govern social relations. By suggesting that the house should ideally be returned to Brumărescu, the Strasbourg Court could be said to have endorsed this view. However, the Court could not deliver in practice the entitlement it affirmed in principle. The first conception of human rights, as universal natural rights, may not entirely apply when it comes to explain the Convention or the work of the Court.

Let us turn to the second conception, that of human rights as a principle of adjudication. It is important to recall in this respect that Article 6 of the Convention, on fair trial, is the provision on which the Court primarily based its finding of violation in *Brumărescu*. The Strasbourg judgment hinged on the lack of legal certainty that characterised the Romanian judicial system. This was a problem of procedure. Conor Gearty has argued some years ago (1993) and again recently (2004) that the Court is at its best when it does not seek to resolve substantive questions which are by nature controversial but concentrates on making sure that the democratic process is observed. This view perfectly accounts for the reasoning of the Court in terms of, primarily, Article 6. However, it is not this particular conception of human rights which prevailed in the reception of the judgment in Romania. As we have seen, the national attempted to find a way to give Brumărescu his house back, misunderstanding what the Strasbourg rulings were about and requested from it.

The third conception of human rights, as a language of protest, could seem irrelevant to our account, except that Brumărescu's failure to be thoroughly successful in having the house returned to him has led him increasingly to want to help others in the same situation as he is and to participate in more collective action. Such a 'struggle', however, does not seem directly akin to what Upendra Baxi (2006) has in mind when he uses this term and insists that 'the voices of suffering' are and must be at the forefront of human rights action and theory. Baxi invites us to imagine a different social project. The idea of a more just society where justice refers to a substantive emancipatory project which emerges from a collective struggle against poverty and global capitalism drives neither Brumărescu nor the Strasbourg Court.

Dembour (2006) has identified a fourth approach to human rights, one which takes human rights as a fact of our world. From this perspective, human rights exist because they are 'talked about'. Once discourse gives them existence, they become a resource in political discourse, as they have in our contemporary world, even assuming a position of prominence. This is our favoured approach. It allows distance and sits well with our aim of reporting how different institutional and individual actors (including academics) use (and abuse) human rights and what they think they should be. Other theorists (Kennedy 2001; Mutua 2002) have offered pregnant criticisms of the triangular model of human rights as involving a victim, a violator and a saviour. The supposed straightforward distinctiveness of these three subjects evaporates in the light of ethnography: to what extent does the role of the victim apply to Brumărescu? In what sense is Romania the violator? Can the Strasbourg Court be said to have solved or helped the situation?

CONCLUSION

In conclusion, we would like briefly to say a few words about the three themes which run through this volume. First, justice. We consider it to be beyond our scope to define or even just explore what justice requires. By contrast, we think it possible to record the development of particular views on this question and to offer a critique of particular institutions. This is what we have tried to do through our ethnographic account of Brumărescu. To us, the question 'what is human rights law for?' is not best approached theoretically. We prefer the way of ethnography which concretely reveals both the social embeddedness of 'rights' and the instrumentalisation of law – where instrumentalisation is not meant critically but as a fact of life. Thus law is recognised to have its conventions; one has to accept and work through them in the hope of achieving the results it may be able to deliver. As for the second theme of the international, our account has demonstrated how the international is positioned apart from, but is also completely enmeshed in, the national. On the one hand, Strasbourg is independent from the national; it does not want to interfere with it; it is not interested in the domestic social context, of which it is ignorant (blissfully or not!). On the other hand, the international is imbricated in the national; it is part of the national story, for it is a tool which is activated and indeed appropriated by national actors – including individuals, the domestic courts, the legislative, the media. Finally, on the third theme of 'paths', we simply wish to note that legal justice is not abstract, but comes out of particular social configurations and individual actions which are never entirely predictable in their deployment and results.

REFERENCES

Bârsan, Victor (ed.). 1997. *De la post-comunism la pre-tranziţie*. Bucureşti: Pythagora.

Baxi, Upendra. 2006. *The Future of Human Rights*. New Delhi: Oxford University Press.

Carss-Frisk, Monica. 2001. *The Right to Property. A Guide to the Implementation of Article 1 of Protocol No. 1 to the European Convention of Human Rights*. Strasbourg: Council of Europe.

CeFRes, 1997. *Anciens et nouveaux propriétaires. Stratégies d'appropriation en Europe centrale et orientale. Cahiers du CeFRes* (n. 11f: mars 1997). Prague: Centre français de recherche en sciences sociales.

Cosma, Doru. 1995. Hotărârea nr. 1/1995 a secţiilor unite ale curţii supreme de justiţie: o analiză critică. In *Revista Română de Drepturile Omului* 8: 8–32.

Dembour, Marie-Bénédicte. 2006. *Who Believes in Human Rights? Reflections on the European Convention*. Cambridge: Cambridge University Press.

Gearty, Conor A. 1993. The European Court of Human Rights and the Protection of Civil Liberties: An Overview. In *Cambridge Law Journal* 52: 89–127.

2004. *Principles of Human Rights Adjudication*. Oxford: Oxford University Press.

Geertz, Clifford. 1983. Local Knowledge: Fact and Law in Comparative Perspective. In *Local Knowledge. Further Essays in Interpretive Anthropology*. New York: Basic Books, 167–234.

Gluckman, Max. 1963. Gossip and Scandal. In *Current Anthropology* 4(3): 307–15.

Halley, Janet. 2004. Take a Break from Feminism? In *Gender and Human Rights* (ed.) K. Knop. Oxford: Oxford University Press, 57–81.

Hann, Christopher M. 1998. Introduction: the Embeddedness of Property. In *Property Relations. Renewing the Anthropological Tradition* (ed.) Christopher M. Hann. Cambridge: Cambridge University Press, 1–47.

Haviland, John B. 1977. *Gossip, Reputation and Knowledge in Zinacantan*. Chicago: Chigaco University Press.

1998. Mu`nuk jbankil to, mu`nuk kajvaltik: 'He is not my older brother, he is not Our Lord'. Thirty Years of Gossip in a Chiapas Village. In *Etnofoor* 11(2): 57–82.

Kennedy, David. 2001. The International Human Rights Movement: Part of the Problem? In *European Human Rights Law Review* 3: 245–67.

Latour, Bruno. 2002. *La fabrique du droit. Une ethnographie du Conseil d'Etat.* Paris: La Découverte.

Leach, Philip. 2005. Beyond the Bug River – A New Dawn for Redress Before the European Court of Human Rights. In *European Human Rights Law Review* (2): 148–64.

Llewellyn, Karl N. and Adamson E. Hoebel. 1941. *The Cheyenne Way: Conflict and Case Law in Primitive Jurisprudence.* Norman, OK: University of Oklahoma Press.

Macklem, Patrick. 2005. Rybná 9, Praha 1: Restitution and Memory in International Human Rights Law. In *European Journal of International Law* 16: 1–23.

Munzer, Stephen R. (ed.) 2001. *New Essays in the Legal and Political Theory of Property.* Cambridge: Cambridge University Press.

Mutua, Makau. 2002. *Human Rights: a Political and Cultural Critique.* Philadelphia: University of Pennsylvania Press.

Nicol, Danny. 2005. Original Intent and the European Convention on Human Rights. In *Public Law* (Winter): 152–72.

Offe, Carl. 1997. *Varieties of Transition: the East European and East German Experience.* Cambridge: The MIT Press.

Paine, Robert. 1967. What is Gossip About? An Alternative Hypothesis. In *Man* 2(2): 272–85.

Pena, Lelioara. 1998. Sinteză a legislaţiei privind restituirea sau compensarea bunurilor naţionalizate, expropriate ori confiscate abuziv, în fostele ţări comuniste europene. In *Buletin de informare legislativă* 1: 7–36.

Petzold, Herbert. 2000. Epilogue: La réforme continue. In *Protecting Human Rights: The European Perspective. Studies in Memory of Rolv Ryssdal* (eds.) Paul Mahoney, Franz Matscher, Herbert Petzold and Luzius Wildhaber. Köln : Carl Heymans Verlag, 1571–87.

Popescu, Corneliu-Liviu. 2000. Comentariu asupra Hotărârii Curţii Europene a Drepturilor Omului din 28 octombrie 1999 in Cauza Brumărescu c. România. In *Revista Română de Drepturile Omului* 18: 8–34.

Popescu, Livia. 1998. *Structura socială şi societate civilă in România interbelică.* Cluj-Napoca: Presa Universitară Clujeană.

Reid, Karen. 2004. *A Practitioner's Guide to the European Convention on Human Rights.* London: Sweet and Maxwell.

Stychin, Carl F. 2004. Same-Sex Sexualities and the Globalization of Human Rights Discourse. In *McGill Law Journal* 49: 951–68.

Van Vleet, Krista. 2003. Partial Theories. On Gossip, Envy and Ethnography in the Andes. In *Ethnography* 4(4): 491–519.

Vasiliu, Adrian. 2001. O nouă expropriere. Legea imobilelor naționalizate. In *România liberă* (9 February 2001).

Verdery, Katherine. 1991. *National Ideology Under Socialism. Identity and Cultural Politics in Ceaușescu's Romania*. Berkeley, Los Angeles, London: University of California Press.

2003. *The Vanishing Hectare. Property and Value in Postsocialist Transylvania*. Ithaca and New York: Cornell University Press.

Woolf, Lord. 2005. Review of the Working Methods of the European Court of Human Rights. Available on-line at www.echr.coe.int/ECHR/Resources/. Accessed on 25 June 2006.

Zerilli, Filippo M. 2006. Sentiments and/as Property Rights. Restitution and Conflict in Postsocialist Romania. In *Postsocialism: Politics and Emotions in Central and Eastern Europe* (ed.) Maruška Svašek. New York and Oxford: Berghahn Books, 74–94.

CHAPTER 9

ENTWINED PATHS TO JUSTICE: THE INTER-AMERICAN HUMAN RIGHTS SYSTEM AND THE PERUVIAN TRUTH COMMISSION

Lisa J. Laplante

In the last thirty years, truth commissions have become a mechanism of choice for addressing violent and arbitrary pasts and promoting democratic transitions.[1] They arise out of the basic assumption that uncovering the truth about the past favours reconciliation and paves the way for a better future (Kritz 1995; Minow 1999; Hayner 2000). But truth commissions are not necessarily a panacea. Indeed, they have commonly been criticised for favouring 'truth' over 'justice' – where justice is conceived as retributive and enacted in criminal proceedings. Thus, 'transitional justice' is perceived as all too often ready to sacrifice individual rights to domestic political expediency (Rotberg and Thompson 2000; Wilson 2001). In contrast, international human rights purport to protect individual rights. This chapter explores both the tensions and the potentially mutually beneficial relationship between an international human rights system and a national truth commission. It does so in the context of the transition process in Peru.

[1] The author's observations come from more than four years of onsite observation as well as more recent interviews with key actors differently situated within the context of Peru's political transition, including former truth commission members, victims/survivors of Peru's internal armed conflict, current and former Peruvian government representatives, professionals from national and international non-governmental organisations, as well as a vice president, a former president and lawyer of the Inter-American Commission of Human Rights, with all transcripts on file with the author. The author wishes to thank all those who agreed to meet and talk to her in the course of her research. The author also acknowledges the support of the United States Institute of Peace for funding the study out of which came some of the results shared in this chapter. She is grateful to the British Academy for having financed her participation in the Brighton seminar convened in September 2005. She thanks all participants, and especially Marie Dembour, Tobias Kelly and Richard Wilson, for their helpful comments on earlier drafts.

Peru initiated a process of transitional justice at the end of a twenty-year internal armed conflict (1980–2000) between terrorist groups and the state's armed forces, which resulted in thousands of cases of human rights abuses by both. The transition from abusive governance to peaceful and legitimate democracy unexpectedly became possible when authoritarian leader Alberto Fujimori fled the country in November 2000 upon the revelation of widespread corruption. The transitional government seized this opportunity to address the human and institutional damage caused by the conflict by forming the Truth and Reconciliation Commission (hereafter, TRC) in July 2001.

Unlike other countries around the world who have resorted to alternative justice mechanisms in order to address a devastating history of injustice and human rights abuses, Peru's experience did not take place as part of a negotiated peace settlement: most terrorist leaders had been jailed more than ten years before and many government and army officials had more recently been arrested, albeit on corruption charges. Peru's decision in establishing the TRC represented a general commitment to what Peruvian lawyer and the TRC's former Executive Secretary, Javier Ciurlizza, calls the country's 'reinsertion in the international democratic community' (interview, 1 June 2005). The TRC's mandate included the investigation and clarification of the causes of and responsibility for the armed conflict as well as the consequences of that conflict. The TRC submitted its final report in August 2003.[2]

This chapter shows how the Inter-American system of human rights protection (hereafter, 'Inter-American system') directly impacted on the history of the TRC, from before its formation until after the publication of its final report. The argument is that Peruvian actors – including both survivors/victims and the state – have often relied on the Inter-American system in their lobbying campaigns to promote their particular justice agenda at home, and that they have done so with good effect. This observation holds true despite the turbulent history of Peru's engagement with the Inter-American system. Indeed, the notable event of Fujimori's withdrawal in 1999 from the Inter-American Human Rights Court (hereafter, the Court) testifies that the system has minimal power to enforce compliance with international obligations despite their supposed obligatory nature (Laplante 2004; Neumayer 2005). Rather, in practice, compliance and the evolving

---

[2] Comision de Verdad y Reconciliación, Informe Final (2003), available at www.cverdad.org.pe/.

authority of the Inter-American system depends on what Juan Mendez, a former President of the Inter-American Commission on Human Rights (hereafter, Inter-American Commission or IACHR), calls a 'mysterious way in which countries decide to comply because they want to comply' (interview, 22 April 2005). For example, it was the Peruvian government's own decision to adhere to the Court's judgments at the start of the transitional process that required it to pay high reparation packages. The government now seems to have forgotten the voluntary nature of this act of political good will, and perceives the future 'threat' of new Court orders. One could therefore say that it is an amnesia of sorts which allows compliance to begin to appear politically obligatory. While one may question the motivation of states in beginning to engage with international human rights monitoring bodies (Hathaway 2002), once they do, intriguing developments become possible.

The Inter-American system has exercised a positive influence in building a culture of rights and in setting parameters of justice in Peru. As highlighted by local actors interviewed by the author (see also González Cueva 2004), the annulment of the Peruvian amnesty laws by the Court made retributive justice possible in Peru, as explained below. From this standpoint, it can be concluded that the TRC in particular, and the national transitional process more generally, did not stand in contradiction with the international human rights regime. If anything, their relationship was one of mutual reinforcement. However, there are also unexpected tensions. Specifically, the Inter-American Court has adopted the view that combating impunity requires both holding the state and its agents accountable and also granting victims appropriate reparations. Thus, it has awarded 'full' reparation packages (including both pecuniary and non-pecuniary measures) tailored to the specific harm suffered by the individual victims. By contrast the TRC opted for an integral reparations plan (*Plan Integral de Reparaciones* – hereafter, PIR) aimed at granting reparations to *all* victims, but not at the high level ordered by the Inter-American Court. This dualism creates a 'twin track' where access to legal remedies is unequally distributed, with the bulk of victims – typically from poor, rural zones – never accessing the Court nor individualised reparations. The variations that occur in popular notions of justice reflect the intricacies of guaranteeing justice in a domestic context that is intertwined with an international human rights system.

SHAPING JUSTICE CLAIMS

The Inter-American system began to play a role in the transitional Peruvian process in the decade prior to the establishment of the TRC. Specifically, Peruvian human rights defenders began to enlist its help upon facing domestic judicial remedies that were wholly ineffective in dealing with serious human rights violations. Up to this time, the late 1980s, the Inter-American system had not been considered useful in promoting justice at home; however the Peruvian human rights movement now recognised the potential value of resorting to this international mechanism. A slow trickle of cases began eventually to form a river of complaints submitted for the Inter-American Commission's review.[3] As a result, the Peruvian situation attracted heightened international scrutiny, with the Inter-American Commission itself publishing two country reports (IACHR 1993; IACHR 2000) as part of its general monitoring functions.[4]

Together, the local human rights movement and the Inter-American system helped to chip away at the legitimacy of Fujimori's policies and practices (Youngers and Peacock 2002). In particular, the latter substantiated the claims of the former, thus lending it legitimacy and backing in the national struggle against the incumbent authoritarian regime. While Fujimori continued to ignore its recommendations, the Inter-American Commission began to pass emblematic cases to the Court, which called attention to particular areas of concern such as forced disappearances, prison massacres and the arbitrary and unjust imprisonment of people under the state's anti-terrorist legislation.[5] These efforts to compel the Peruvian government to align its policy and practice with international human rights obligations, particularly those found in the American Convention on Human Rights (hereafter, Convention) seldom resulted in substantial political changes during the dictatorship. They nonetheless shaped national

---

[3] The Inter-American Commission filters cases to the Inter-American Court; applicants do not have the right to bring a case directly to the Court under the American Convention on Human Rights (signed in 1969 and entered into force in 1978). For accounts of the Inter-American system of human rights, see Harris and Livingstone 1998; Pasqualucci 2003.

[4] These functions were developed under the Charter of the Organisation of American States (1948) after the Inter-American Commission was established in 1959.

[5] See for example: I/A Court H.R., *Case of Castillo-Páez v. Peru*, 3 November, 1997, Series C, No. 34 (on the forced disappearance of a university student); I/A Court H.R., *Case of Loayza-Tamayo v. Peru*, September 17, 1997, Series C, No. 33 (on arbitrary imprisonment and torture under anti-terrorism law); I/A Court H.R., *Case of Durand and Ugarte v. Peru*, 16 August 2000, Series C, No. 68 (prison massacre at el Fronton).

concepts of justice, thus laying out a roadmap for change once the dictatorship fell.

In particular, the Inter-American Commission and Court have defined justice as encompassing both retributive and restorative aspects. Inter-American jurisprudence upholds the principle that when a state's acts and/or omissions amount to human rights violations, they trigger an obligation to guarantee criminal investigations and prosecutions as well as integral reparations and institutional reform.[6] This approach supposedly combats impunity by restoring the rule of law based on a culture of rights that treats all individuals equally and thereby prevents future harm (Roht-Arriaza 1999). The author of this chapter adopts the overarching vision of the Inter-American system, but recognises that justice may in fact depend on what each victim/survivor needs in order to satisfy his or her need for acknowledgment. In conversations with the author, some victim/survivor groups have insisted only on criminal prosecution, others prioritise integral reparations and many hold out for both.[7] All seem to demand that the state take responsibility for the suffering it caused or permitted.

The Inter-American system exists to encourage (not replace) the development and efficacy of domestic justice measures which enforce human rights on the ground (Hesse and Post 1999: 19). For that reason, the Inter-American Commission and Court call on states to conform with international standards without specifically dictating *how*: this question is left to the discretion of the sovereign state in order to strengthen local means of redress. For example, the Inter-American Commission called on Peru to establish an integral response to systematic patterns of human rights violations (IACHR 2000: paras 125–32) but never specifically mandated the formation of a truth commission. While approving of the various truth commissions formed over the years in Latin America, including that of Peru, the IACHR never holds them to be an absolute requirement for compliance with international obligations.[8] At best, truth commissions are a crucial step towards such compliance since they do not normally enjoy a remit to hold

---

[6] See for example, I/A Court H.R., *Case of Velasquez Rodriguez v. Honduras*, 29 July, 1988, Series C, No. 4, at para. 174.

[7] For an unprecedented and interesting study which sought to discover what victims wanted and what outcome satisfied them most, undertaken in the Czech Republic, see David and Yuk-ping 2005.

[8] See for example, IACHR Press Release, 'The IACHR Concludes Its Visit To The Republic Of Peru' No. 27/03, 1 September 2003; also see for general comment, Report on the situation of human rights in Venezuela, OEA/Ser.L/V/II.118 doc. 4 rev. 2, 29 December 2003, para. 97.

criminal trials or distribute reparations, but only recommend such justice measures.

DECIDING TO CREATE THE TRUTH COMMISSION

As the legitimacy of his internal politics came under close scrutiny, Fujimori, unlike many of his Latin American cohorts, did not opt to ignore the Inter-American Court. Instead, he engaged in a cantankerous battle with it.[9] His government only reluctantly adhered, and then only partially, to the Court's orders. When perceiving the Court to have gone 'too far', Fujimori rebelliously withdrew from the Court's jurisdiction in July 1999, a decision declared invalid by the Court.[10] His act of defiance put him under greater scrutiny, which further increased when the Organisation of American States (OAS) questioned the legitimacy of his 2000 re-election.[11]

Fujimori tried to undermine the Inter-American system's authority through his highly publicised acts of protest; this engagement, however, only raised its profile within Peruvian society. In this sense, he established it as a force to be reckoned with rather than an irritation to be ignored. Albeit not intentionally, Fujimori helped to bolster the validity of the Court, and thus laid the groundwork for the Inter-American system to play an important role in the cascade of events that eventually ousted him from office and set in motion the formation of a truth commission to investigate the consequences of those very policies that the Inter-American Commission and Court had so amply criticised.

Peru's new government, led first by Valentín Paniagua and later by democratically elected Alejandro Toledo, sought to legitimise itself as is typical in political transitions (Ní Aoláin and Campbell 2005). Given Peruvian society's high regard for the Inter-American system, the Peruvian Ministry of Justice (hereafter, MINJUS) sought to mend its relations with the Inter-American system for both juridical reasons and political motivations. Conforming to the Inter-American system's recommendations, which directly challenged the previous regime, was

---

[9] In the *Case of Cesti-Hurtado v. Peru*, I/A Court H.R., Series C, No. 56 (Judgment of 29 September 1999).

[10] See for example, I/A Court H.R., *Case of Ivcher-Bronstein v. Peru. Competence.* Series C, No. 54 (24 September 1999).

[11] For international press coverage, see for example: Andres Oppenheimer, 'Watchdog group may condemn Peru election', *Miami Herald* (25 March 2000); 'OAS strikes deal with Peru over election probe' CNN (6 June 2000), available at: http://archives.cnn.com/2000/WORLD/americas/06/06/peru.elections/.

a way of distinguishing itself from its predecessor and improving its international image by fulfilling its international obligations. Thus, in the same month that Fujimori became a fugitive, MINJUS formed a special working group to re-establish relations with the Inter-American system, in particular by rejoining the contentious jurisdiction of the Court. In response, César Gaviria, then Secretary-General of the OAS, applauded the decision and praised the leadership of the transitional government for running 'a clean and democratic government that respects the rights of everyone and is clearly committed to honouring the country's international obligations'.[12]

In seeking to forge a new image, the government considered it 'imperative' to resolve the hundreds of cases which were already far advanced in the Inter-American system (interview with Javier Ciurlizza, who participated in the MINJUS working group). The government was aware, however, that case-by-case resolution would be ineffective if not impossible; thus in February 2001, the government presented a proposal to the Inter-American Commission to resolve dozens of cases. In particular, it accepted a friendly 'package' settlement of more than half of the cases against Peru, all related to forced disappearances and extrajudicial executions.[13] In addition, the government established the Inter-Institutional Working Group for Follow-up on the Inter-American Commission's recommendations, which monitored the implementation of the recommendations adopted in the settled cases and hosted Inter-American Commissioners during several visits. Pointing out that international cooperation and international lending agencies often request compliance with international human rights obligations, the MINJUS special commission convinced the Minister of Economy and Finance of the importance of 'investing' against further liability, leading to the payment of reparations ordered by the Court in a handful of landmark judgments. Many of these judgments concerned the very issues which the transitional government needed to address in

---

[12] See Press Release, 'Peru Restores Relationship with Court' (April 2001), available at www.oas.org/oasnews/2001/English/March_2001/art4.html.

[13] A friendly settlement is an agreement between the parties to settle the case without the Court deciding on its merits. With reference to the 159 settled cases, see IACHR, Press alert (without date), www.cidh.org/comunicados/spanish/2001/PERU.htm. The package settlement, signed on 22 February 2001, is referred to in Report of the Permanent Council on the Observations and Recommendations of the Member States on the 2001 Annual Report of The Inter-American Commission on Human Rights, Oea/Ser.GCp/Doc.3612/02 (23 May 2002), Part VI., available at http://scm.oas.org/Reference/english/INTER-AMERICAN%20COMM.%20ON %20HUMAN%20RIGHTS%20(CIDH)/REPORT%20CP%20OBSERV-RECOMMEND%20 ANNUAL%20REPORT%202001%20CP09961.doc, Part IV. For an explanation of the mechanism, see Standaert 1999.

order to turn a new page in Peru's history.[14] These judgments in hand helped the new government justify, especially to the internal opposition, the need to address and redress the past as an international obligation rather than a mere political imperative (González Cueva 2004).

In the process of addressing the many examples of pending cases in the Inter-American System, MINJUS began to recognise the need for a more comprehensive solution. It became clear that the small universe of cases before the Inter-American system would leave unaddressed the far larger number of potential cases, especially by victims who would learn of the reparation payments and settled cases and want the same. On a very practical level, the government felt it was necessary to create an alternative to a judicial venue for responding to each of these thousands of victims. Following the consistent lobbying of the national human rights movement, MINJUS selected the truth commission model.

EXPANDING THE PARAMETERS OF TRANSITIONAL JUSTICE

Truths commissions have widely been criticised for sacrificing the victim's right to see violators pay for their crimes (Dugard 1997; Lansing and King 1998). For example, Guatemala's fragile political conditions allowed only a diagnostic clarification of the past with no potential for criminal proceedings. South Africa allowed the majority of human rights violators to seek amnesty in exchange for full public disclosure – with prosecution in only the most egregious cases (Rotberg 2000; Villa-Vicencio and Doxtader 2003). The Peruvian case shows another path is possible: a truth commission that neither included amnesties nor placed limits on future prosecution, but on the contrary supported their eventual realisation.

In 1995, one could hardly have predicted such an outcome. That year saw Fujimori promulgating self-amnesty laws which not only delivered sweeping immunity for all state agents involved in human rights violations but also resulted in the release of those who had already been convicted. These laws generated serious concerns for the truth commission planning committee. With no prospect for any prosecution, how could the TRC meet the newly raised expectations of the victims who had

---

[14] See for example I/A Court H.R., *Case of the Constitutional Court v. Peru*, 31 January 2001, Series C, No. 71 (the reintegration of Constitutional Court's judges previously suspended by Fujimori); I/A Court H.R., *Case of Castillo-Petruzzi et al. v. Peru*, 17 November 1999, Series C, No. 59 (the reform of Fujimori's draconian anti-terrorist laws); I/A Court H.R., *Case of Ivcher-Bronstein v. Peru*, 6 February 2001, Series C, No. 74 (protection of the freedom of the press).

sometimes waited as many as twenty years for justice? Moreover, if the amnesty laws forbade all types of investigation, how would the TRC work?

A legislative solution was unlikely, since the Peruvian Congress was still dominated by representatives of parties which benefited from the amnesty law. The highest Peruvian Court suggested in its 1997 opinion that the amnesty laws were unconstitutional but in subservience to the authoritarian regime avoided issuing a final sentence on the matter and declared itself to lack jurisdiction.[15] Even if the Inter-American Commission had consistently questioned the appropriateness of amnesties during the wave of Latin American transitions which had begun with Argentina and Chile in the 1970s and 80s (Roht-Arriaza 2001), it never adopted a binding decision on the issue. Thus, Peru sought clarification by requesting the acceleration of the *Barrios Altos* case. The case concerned a massacre by the death squad Grupo Colina, linked to the army, of fifteen people attending a private fundraising party on 3 November 1991 in a poor district of the capital Lima. Peruvian human rights groups purposely sent it to the Inter-American Commission to challenge the amnesty laws. Susana Villaran, currently Vice-President of the Inter-American Commission and at the time Executive Secretary of the National Coordinator of Human Rights, a broad coalition of Peruvian human rights organisations (Youngers and Peacock 2002), remembers exerting pressure on the IACHR for it to submit the case to the Court instead of simply publishing a final report (interview, 17 July 2006). While the Inter-American Commission feared that the Court might depart from its own (the IACHR's) evolving jurisprudence against amnesties,[16] the gamble turned out to favour both the IACHR and the Peruvian human rights movement when the Court ruled against Peru's amnesty law. Villaran considers the decision arose out of a wave of 'coincidental' factors that made the issue ripe, yet it had great significance to the truth-versus-justice debate in the transitional justice movement.

The Court issued the *Barrios Altos* decision in March 2001,[17] i.e. exactly a month before the MINJUS working group concluded its negotiations regarding the TRC's mandate. However, it remained unclear if the judgment offered a general pronouncement, so Peru requested the

[15] Sentencia Del Tribunal Constitucional, Exp. N° 013-96-I/TC (28 abril 1997).
[16] Such as in Uruguay, Chile and Argentina (Pasqualucci 1994).
[17] *Case of Barrios Altos v. Peru*, Judgment of 14 May 2001, Inter-Am Ct. H.R. (Ser. C) No. 75 (2001).

Court for an interpretation. Just as the TRC was to begin its work, the Court clarified that self-amnesties laws are contrary to the American Convention, and thus are generally invalid.[18] This decision provided the TRC with the green light not only to start its investigations but also to collaborate with the Attorney General's office.[19] The procedural impediments in pursuing criminal justice as part of its transitional justice scheme were lifted (González Cueva 2004: 62).[20] Indeed, upon concluding its two year investigation, the TRC presented the General prosecutors with forty-three of the most emblematic cases based on evidence it gathered (González Cueva 2006). It also recommended prompt criminal investigations and prosecutions in hundreds of other cases of human rights violations. Encouraged by the clear commitment to criminal justice, the human rights prosecutor in the Andean highlands district of Ayacucho, where the greatest brunt of political violence had occurred, initiated investigation and prosecution in some 300 cases of human rights violations after going into rural communities to interview victims. She named ex-president Alan Garcia among the suspected perpetrators, charging him with genocide. Meanwhile, in the capital Lima, domestic criminal trials against the paramilitary Grupo Colina began, including in the Barrios Altos and Cantuta cases, in which the Inter-American Court ordered criminal investigations and trials. As a result, some fifty-six persons were indicted, including a military general and a top intelligence advisor to ex-President Fujimori. In this way, Peru is complying with the recommendations of both the TRC and the Inter-American system, reinforcing the idea that retributive justice is a cornerstone principle in international law while responding to popular demands for such justice.

However, avoidance of accountability still occurs. For example, the Ayacuchan cases were transferred to Lima, far from the evidence and witnesses too poor to travel. Delays in the Colina trial run the risk of suspects being released after passing the maximum of thirty-six months allowed in pre-trial detention.[21] Still, the Peruvian case shows that

---

[18] I/A Court H.R., *Case of Barrios Altos v. Peru.* Interpretation of the Judgment on the Merits. Series C, No. 83 (3 September 2001).

[19] In its Final Report, the TRC acknowledged the important precedent established by the Court, see Hatun Willakuy: version abreviada del informe final de la Comisión de la Verdad y Reconciliacion (Lima, Peru: 2003), 31–2.

[20] By contrast, in South Africa, victims could not resort to an international tribunal when they lost their challenge against amnesty laws before the highest national court (Roht-Arriaza and Gibson 1998).

[21] For more details on challenges of criminal justice post-Truth Commission, see Defensoría del Pueblo 2005.

truth commissions do not have to sacrifice retributive justice. There is no talk of 'forgiveness' in Peru, in stark contrast to the transitional discourse of 'reconciliation through truth' developed in South Africa which greatly circumscribed principles of justice (Tutu 1999; Fullard 2004; Ross 2004). Instead, the Peruvian transitional justice experience revolves around a rights-based approach, as reflected in victims'/survivors' demands for criminal justice as an unequivocal entitlement.

For Giselle Ortiz, an applicant in the *Cantuta* case and now an active campaigner for justice, the right to the truth and the right to criminal justice are two clearly separate objectives. She acknowledges that the TRC investigations, through its assemblage of different sources – testimonial, journalistic, historical, sociological – gave a number of families clarity on what happened to their loved ones and who the likely perpetrators are. But even if 'the truth consolidates and is a part of justice', Ortiz and her fellow co-petitioners 'cannot feel satisfied only knowing what happened or by finding the remains of [their] loved ones' (interview, 8 June 2005). In her words: 'As the family we are clear that the right to justice will be fulfilled only when *all* those responsible are sanctioned.'

Ortiz's brother was 'disappeared' in 1992, while he was a student at the public Cantuta University in Lima. Grupo Colina removed him, eight other students and one professor, from University dorms on the night of 18 July 1992. Journalist investigations helped eventually start a criminal case that led in 1994 to the conviction of paramilitaries, but the convicted were amnestied and released a year later under Fujimori's 1995 law. However, in the wake of the TRC's recommendations, the alleged perpetrators have now been recaptured and face a new trial.[22] Yet, Ortiz and her co-petitioners hold out for criminal prosecution and conviction of the high command and intellectual authors, including Fujimori and top generals, which means resorting to the Inter-American system since these cases were 'archived' by the military court.

Convicting the top gun may not be entirely impossible. At the time of writing, an extradition petition pending against Fujimori, detained in Chile since November 2005, includes twelve criminal charges. All but two relate to corruption charges, with the *Cantuta* and *Barrios Altos* cases relating to human rights – no doubt chosen because of their high profile within the Inter-American system and through the TRC. The positive decision in the *Cantuta* case also sends a clear message to newly

---

[22] Including Martin Rivas, the Intelligence leader of Colina.

elected president Alan Garcia (Pancho Soberon, recent Executive Secretary of the National Coordinator of Human Rights, Public Lecture, Lima, 16 July 2006). Peruvian refugees filed a criminal complaint against Garcia for the 1988 prison massacre of el Frontón that resulted in 119 deaths during his last presidency.[23] The massacre is also the object of a case before the Inter-American Court.[24]

Under the influence of the Inter-American system, the Peruvian TRC established Peru's formula for political transformation as 'national reconciliation requires Truth, Justice and Reparations', as read on banners, publications and other proclamations. Whether mere slogans or new social pacts, these formulas set the direction of political transition towards the rule of law. They communicate both that no one is above the law and that everyone has access to justice, addressing the sense of worthlessness many victims felt when they were first left vulnerable in the conflict and then saw their justice claims ignored for years by the state.

REPARATIONS COMPLETE TRANSITIONAL JUSTICE

Once it had clarified the issue of amnesties, the Inter-American system adopted a 'watch and wait' attitude, not intervening in the TRC's work. Nevertheless, its authority continued to influence Peru's transitional justice process, particularly in the creation of the Integral Reparations Plan (Plan Integral de Reperaciones, PIR), which is one of the most inclusive and integral truth commission reparation plans to date (Laplante and Theidon 2007). Significantly, PIR justifies reparations as being not merely moral but also legal in nature, due to the precedents set by the Inter-American Commission and Court.

Indeed, the absolute standards promoted by the Inter-American system shaped the demands – and expectations – of Peruvian victims and survivors, who learned from the Inter-American system that reparation is a right, and thus the obligation of the state, and not a 'favour' or a 'gift'. Encouraged by unequivocal human rights jurisprudence, victims and the human rights professionals assisting them studied the international reparations standards and then lobbied to ensure that these standards would be included in the final report. Not surprisingly the victims who had either directly engaged with the Inter-American

---

[23] Jueza chilena acepta querrella contra Alan, *La República*, 4 July 2006, at 3.
[24] *Durand and Ugarte v. Peru*, supra. n. 5.

system or had read its decisions made the most adamant and rights-based demands upon the TRC. Peruvian sociologist Eduardo Gonzalez, who directed the TRC's public hearings office, reports that the TRC 'didn't meet with victims who were ignorant of their rights or ignorant of the international standards. That is why survivors' organisations were in the position to be genuine partners of the commission' (interview, 22 April 2005). Here, the TRC could manage victims' expectations by engaging them in the development of PIR, including discussion of the political need to 'work within the system' to create a feasible programme of reparations. According to Gonzalez, by contrast, survivors' organisations with little experience of the Inter-American system often had 'unmanageable demands'.

Victims with prior experience of the Inter-American system tended to have clear and concrete proposals reflecting the Inter-American Court's concept of 'integral' reparations. They expected not only economic compensation but also collective and social programmes with moral and symbolic significance, for example promoting health and education, which the Court has ordered in the past (Pasqualucci 1996; Rodriquez Rescia and Victor 1999). They also adopted the Court's concept of 'beneficiaries' to include not only direct victims but also families.

Gonzalez Cueva is convinced that the Inter-American system played a central role in setting the TRC's justice parameters. Working now with the International Centre for Transitional Justice (ICTJ), he compares Peru's truth commissions to others in the Middle East, Southeast Asia and Africa, concluding that 'if you don't have a supranational system that sets the standards then commissions are basically working in a void, without clear normative yardsticks of how to direct their work and how to interpret their mandate' (interview, 22 April 2005). Human rights provide this benchmark since they are 'aspirations' and 'identify the features or qualities every society should embody', while also providing 'standards for criticising and transforming political and legal structures' (Fiss 1999: 266).

WILL JUSTICE BE ACHIEVED?

The Inter-American system has shaped the parameters of Peru's formula for transitional justice in many ways. The real value of this influence, however, depends on the Peruvian government's political will to implement the TRC's recommendations contained in its final report of 2003.

Knowing that governments are renowned for delaying the implementation of a truth commission's recommendations, the Peruvian TRC sought ways to involve the Inter-American system throughout the duration of its truth seeking project, if only peripherally. It invited Inter-American Commissioners to attend its first public hearing, and sent TRC commissioners to Washington DC to tell the IACHR about its progress.[25] Even after the TRC's mandate expired, ex-commissioners still requested hearings with the Inter-American Commission to report on the implementation of its recommendations, in turn prompting the government to attend and initiate such meetings.[26] In fact, on 7 March 2007, the CIDH held a special hearing to be informed on advances and setbacks with the recommendations issued by the TRC, during which state representatives and members from Peruvian human rights organisations participated.[27] Continuous interaction helped the TRC contend with opposition during its work, and later the government with the implementation of the results. Not surprisingly those under investigation, typically in political parties and in the armed forces, have attempted to undermine the TRC at various stages of its work, including after its dissolution. Invoking the authority of the Inter-American system became a way of neutralising the controversy: the TRC could affirm that it was working towards bringing the nation into line with international human rights standards, and that the state was promoting universal standards of international law.[28] This tactic diluted political accusations intended to undermine the TRC's legitimacy and authority. Moreover, while Peruvians still continue to debate over the veracity of the TRC's Final Report and its allegations, few try to deny that state must repair the victims of the conflict.

Peru and the Inter-American system shared two reasons for monitoring the state's transitional justice initiative: one a matter of principle, the other practical. On the one hand, since the content of the TRC's recommendations echo those of Inter-American jurisprudence specifically relating to Peru, it would demonstrate that the state was complying with the orders of the Inter-American system. On the other hand, it

---

[25] Press release, IACHR concludes its 114th regular sessions, No. 12/02, 15 March 2002, at para. 14.

[26] See, Reports of the 119°, 121° and 122° Ordinary sessions of the IACHR.

[27] In I/A Court H.R., *Follow up on the Recommendations of the Report of the Commission of Truth and Reconciliation of Peru*, 127th Period 7 March 2007. Audio available at www.cidh.org/AudieniasAudios%20hearings%20127%20PS.htm.

[28] For a critical approach to the 'universal' character of this project, however, see Clarke (this volume).

would help avoid a deluge of new cases. An estimated 70,000 people died in the war; thousands more were disappeared, tortured, raped, unjustly imprisoned, displaced or incapacitated (TRC 2003: conclusions). The fear is that if all of these victim-survivors find local redress to be unavailable and ineffective they may resort to the Inter-American system. Indeed, the IACHR continues to receive to this day cases relating to violations which occurred during the repressive regimes and 'dirty wars' of Chile (1973–90) and Argentina (1976–83) – the same could potentially occur with Peru.

Victims do not lose their right to seek justice in the international forum just because a state establishes a truth commission. Giselle Ortiz displays the subjective desire that arises out of this legal entitlement: 'We do not have to give up our struggle for justice as long as our rights are not attended to' (interview, 8 June 2005). Admittedly the risk that all victims would resort to the Inter-American system is not a realistic one (Laplante 2004). Many victims, especially rural residents, are not familiar with how to access the Inter-American system, and have no resources to do so anyway. Moreover, family and work obligations, as well as geographical constraints, prevent the great majority from dedicating themselves to pursuing a legal claim.[29] At the opposite end, procedural obstacles (such as exhaustion of domestic remedies) would stem the flow of cases. Moreover, limited resources force the Inter-American system, which was not established to manage the high number of claims arising out of prolonged, massive and systematic human rights violations, to be selective as to the cases it will accept. For instance, at present the I/A Court H.R. has approximately 1,200 cases involving Peru, but in 2005 it made a decision (regarding admissibility or precautionary measures) on approximately 100. Significantly, that same year the IACHR presented only ten cases to the Court.[30]

Yet, most, including the state, do not know or consider these factors. Thus, the Inter-American system serves as a lobbying tool to exert pressure on the government to comply with the TRC's non-binding recommendations. Political will decides implementation policies,

---

[29] Furthermore, Wendy Coxshall (2005) has documented the refusal by a group of Andean villagers to participate in the Peruvian TRC for reasons shaped by gender and racialised identities which made it too difficult for them to narrate the pain of state violence.

[30] The Petition and Case System. Annual Report of the Inter-American Commission on Human Rights 2005, OEA/Ser.L/V/II.124, Doc. 5 (27 February 2006), at Chp. III., available at www.cidh.org/annualrep/2005eng/chap.3a.htm. See also, Perú busca reducir casos ante CIDH *La Republica*, 6 March 2007. Available at www.larepublica.com.pe/component/option.com_contentant/task.view/id.146165/Itemid.0/.

making the Inter-American system once again 'useful' for pressuring the government. Peru's culture of compliance through the state's previous engagement with the Inter-American system aids this lobbying. Even state representatives use the 'threat' of the Inter-American system as a form of deterrence. For instance, a former secretary of a presidential commission formed to follow up the TRC recommendations invoked the possible risk of victims resorting to the international forum in order to persuade the government to approve reparations measures. He argued that payment of a few Inter-American Court orders will cost more than a comprehensive domestic administrative plan (Jaime Urrutia, former Executive Secretary, Comisión Multisectorial de Alto Nivel, personal conversation, 24 June 2006). Such warnings gain credence given that Peruvian victims, who often perceive the Inter-American system as the only path to justice, vociferously communicate this threat in public forums and in meetings with state representatives. Their patience in waiting for a concrete response from the state is limited. Indeed, the Inter-American Commission receives at the time of writing at least one complaint a day from individuals in Peru, far exceeding the average submission from other countries (phone interview with former IACHR attorney Pedro Diaz, 7 July 2005). This pressure undoubtedly contributed to the Peruvian Congress promulgating a law on reparations on 29 July 2005 to the delight of surprised victim-survivors and their defenders.

UNEXPECTED TENSION: THE DOUBLE STANDARD OF REPARATIONS

While positive overall, the involvement of the Inter-American system in the national process has also had a notable shortcoming. The co-existence of the international and national mechanisms creates inequalities with respect to the level of reparation awarded to victims. The government has paid the high level of reparations ordered by the Inter-American Court to a handful of Peruvian applicants who resorted to the international tribunal.[31] By contrast, the PIR aims at providing a comprehensive solution ensuring that all victims can receive some measure of reparation, although not at the level awarded by the Inter-American Court. Here, transitional justice mechanisms create tensions with universal standards when promoting political pragmatism. While

---

[31] For information on compliance with the Court orders, see 'Supervision of Compliance of Judgments' on Court's official website, available at, http://www.corteidh.or.cr/cumpli_ing/index.html.

this dilemma is usually debated with regard to national amnesties and the right to retributive justice (Zalaquett 1995; Wilson 2001), the same tension arises now with reference to reparatory justice. A pragmatic solution through PIR involves political compromise rather than the full respect of individual rights.

The same *Barrios Altos* case that annulled the Peruvian amnesty laws also included payment of US$175,000 to each of the twenty victims or their heirs.[32] Such a significant amount in the history of civil reparations in Peru caught the public's attention. Immediately sensing the potential implications of such a precedent, the government asked the Court if it could fold the Barrios Altos victims into a nationwide reparation programme. The Court denied this request: the awards had been carefully calculated to reflect the individual damages suffered. Its original order was non-negotiable and non-retractable. In a parallel move, the Peruvian state also requested that all cases before the Inter-American Commission be suspended during the search for a domestic solution. This request also met with refusal. The Inter-American Commission made clear that the formation of the TRC could not be used to avoid or delay compliance with the state's obligations arising out of the American Convention.

The Inter-American system's refusal to dilute or suspend victims' legal rights created in practice a two-track approach to reparations. Victims who successfully bring their cases before the Inter-American Court can expect to win reparations which correspond to (what the Court assesses are) their actual damages; others can only hope to receive a fixed amount in an administrative plan, by definition not tailored to respond to the individual's specific situation. Lisa Magarrell, Senior Associate with the International Centre for Transitional Justice (ICTJ) warns of perceptions that 'urban victims [who are more likely to access the Inter-American system] are worth more than rural victims' (interview, 22 April 2005). Doris Qaqui echoes this concern. Hers was one of the 159 Inter-American Commission cases settled by the transitional government, and she now receives non-pecuniary benefits such as health insurance and access to other public services. She sympathises with the victims who were not included in the Inter-American Commission's 'package deal' and observes: 'Many believe ours are privileged, special cases. They feel theirs have not been considered to be important because

---

[32] I/A Court H.R., *Case of Barrios Altos v. Peru*. Reparations, Series C, No. 87 (30 November 2001).

they come from small towns, faraway places even though they made their local denouncements long before we did' (interview, 4 October 2005). She tries to compensate for this inequity by travelling widely to teach and organise fellow survivors and victims and has founded the Asociación Nacional de Familias de Desaparecidos, Ejecutados Extrajudicialmente y Torturados (ANFADET-CIDH).

Indeed, until now, the state has paid reparations only to a few victims, reflecting a general policy of paying reparations only if it feels obliged. A double standard arises when the state manages to locate funds to pay Court judgments, while insisting it has no money for individual economic reparations under PIR. Giselle Ortiz won reparations in 1994 as a result of the domestic criminal trial against the perpetrators who 'disappeared' her brother.[33] Like Qaqui, Ortiz has taken the route of the Andean mountains to advise peasants of their rights. She finds herself in the awkward position of having to defend her 'luck' in winning reparations to other victims confused as to why their claims for justice do not enjoy the same priority. She then has to explain the long legal battle and the tenacity needed to win reparation.

The reparation law which was passed in July 2005 further entrenches the development of double standards, notably through the 'exclusion clause' provided in Article 4. This provision stipulates that any person who was a member of a 'subversive organisation' will not be considered to be a victim for the purposes of PIR; yet people in this situation retain the right to use the 'judicial venue' to present claims.[34] If their civil damage suits are denied by the Peruvian courts, they will have satisfied the prerequisite (exhaustion of domestic remedies) for resorting to the Inter-American system if they were also subject to human rights violations such as torture. Ironically, this international 'track' may award them better reparation packages than if they had been part of PIR. The resentment generated by this situation could cause more conflict in Peruvian society, undermining the TRC's goal of national reconciliation. In fact, Peruvian society already perceives many of the cases that have reached the Inter-American system to favour people whose innocence is suspect. A general complaint is that there is justice only for 'terrorists', creating bitterness among victims who feel their innocence

---

[33] In the original *Cantuta* case, the Military Courts ordered 300,000 soles (approximately 100,000 US dollars) to be divided among the ten families of the victims. This amount was paid by the government and not the individual perpetrators.
[34] See Plan Integral de Reparaciones Ley No. 28592. Published in the official legal gazette *El Peruano*, No. 9173 (29 July 2005), p. 297798.

increases their claim to justice. This sentiment can be seen most clearly during the polemic decision in the Court's *Castro Castro* decision, in which the country rebuked the idea of paying reparations to extra-judicially killed prisoners being held on charges of terrorism. [35] They question why only some people – perpetrators but also the rich[36] – win. Controversy is bound to ensue if national law is interpreted to require victims benefiting from national reparations to waive their right to international recourse. In this case, the Inter-American system may have to determine whether this right can be renounced.

A second potential object of contention is that the reparation law limits economic reparations to only three categories of victims.[37] As Ortiz says, 'victims have the right to equality with regard to economic reparations [so that the exclusion of some from economic reparations will] continue to be a pending theme'. If victims submit petitions in the face of national administrative reparations that do not satisfy their expectations, the Inter-American system will have to determine the legitimacy of reparation programmes not specifically tailored to respond to the actual damage and suffering of every potential claimant, but which signal, even if symbolically, that the government has been held to account.

These issues raise the question of whether an administrative reparations plan helps strengthen the rule of law. Such an aim would not be achieved if, for example, reparations were paid to victims but the judicial system still failed to facilitate future claims through civil remedies and criminal trials. In this situation, victims might continue to perceive an international tribunal as the only viable option. At the opposite extreme, some Peruvian human rights professionals now feel that bringing cases to the Inter-American system is counterproductive, even 'controversial', and express a preference for the integral administrative reparations programme.

---

[35] I/A Court H.R., *Case of Castro Castro*, Judgment, Series C, No. 160 (25 November 2006). See also, Del Castillo, 'Se obliga a todos los peruanos a pagarles a terroristas', *La Republica* (12 January 2007). Available at www.larepublica.com.pe/component/option.com/_contentant/task.view/id.138400/Itemid.ø/.

[36] The payment by the state of reparations ordered by the Court to a news station owner also created great controversy among victims who complained that only the wealthy enjoy justice. I/A Court H.R., *Case of Ivcher-Bronstein v. Perú*, 6 February 1997, Series C, No. 74. See María Elena Castillo, CIDH no ordenó pagar 20 millones a Baruch Ivcher, *La Republica*, 11 February 2006, available at http://archivo.larepublica.com.pe/index.php?option=com_content&task=view&id=102433&fecha_edicion=2006-02-11.

[37] Reglamento de la Ley No. 28592. D.S. No. 015-2006-Jus. Published in the official legal gazette *El Peruano*, No. 9519 (6 July 2006), p. 323063.

Thus, the state's reparation policy continues to divide the lobbying efforts of different victims groups. At times, petitioners in the Inter-American system distance themselves from the general national movement to implement a nationwide reparations programme. Unfortunately, the national movement thus loses the benefit of the participation of victims and survivors who have experience of the Inter-American system and hence greater information, skills and confidence in pursuing their right to reparations.

DELAYED JUSTICE: WHEN ARE GOOD INTENTIONS NOT ENOUGH?

Despite the described tensions, the Inter-American system continues to view the TRC and the political changes it helped to initiate favourably. Thus, even after the TRC ended its mandate, former TRC Commissioners took it upon themselves to submit an *amicus curiae* to the Inter-American Court in the recent *Lori Berenson* case.[38] The applicant, a young woman from the United States, had been sentenced for life by a military tribunal in 1995 for being a terrorist leader; she was re-tried in 2000 by a newly established non-military court and sentenced to twenty years for the lesser conviction of collaboration, a trial she contended to be unfair. The *amicus curiae* addressed Peru's attempt to normalise its anti-terrorist laws in conformity with international norms so as to provide fair trials for terrorist suspects, and advised the Court not to make a negative ruling which might discourage the ongoing reform initiated by the TRC. The fear was that such a ruling might weaken the Peruvian government's and society's commitment towards change by leading people to think 'well, after all that effort, then better return to the military Court' (interview with Javier Ciurlizza, 1 June 2005). In the hearing, state and civil society representatives testified before the Court about the Peruvian state's efforts to reform itself and meet its international human rights obligations. All made ample reference to the TRC's work, even when it did not relate directly to the *Berenson* case. Such harmony of opinion between the community and the state no doubt persuaded the Court to issue a decision that favoured the government.

Since the end of armed conflict and repressive government, Peru is seen as having entered a period of 'normality' and as being on a 'good

---

[38] See I/A Court H.R., *Case of Lori Berenson-Mejía v. Perú*. November 25, 2004, Series C, No. 119.

path', even proactively cooperating in OAS human rights initiatives. For a new government attempting to break from the past, the Inter-American system's endorsement is of great importance in encouraging these changes. This situation arguably makes anything but a supportive stance by the international bodies difficult. Others, however, have communicated to the author that the Court was swayed too much by political considerations and has become too 'soft' on Peru. Victims themselves denounce the breach between the state's promise and practice through a continued flow of petitions to the Inter-American Commission. It is of course in the gap between intention and result, statute and enforcement, 'what we proclaim' and 'what we do' that most human rights activists operate (Ignatieff 1999: 314). Yet, this gap should begin to close in 'normalising' countries. But the question arises: how long will the Inter-American system wait and watch before stating that the good intentions of the Peruvian government are not enough? Will the honeymoon between the state and the Inter-American system, created in great part by the TRC, end? With the new administration headed by Garcia, who has been implicated in serious human rights violations, one already sees new tensions between the state and the international body, leading some to fear that the positive trend may end.[39]

While the state may only have a moral obligation to abide by the 'suggestions' of a truth commission, it has a legal duty to adhere to international human rights standards. Not by sheer coincidence, as this article has shown, the truth commission's recommendations were made to coincide with these international obligations. When a truth commission employs the language of human rights to express its final conclusions, as the Peruvian one did, it creates a critical momentum that helps set in motion the efforts of victims and their allies who have the ongoing task of demanding justice, reparations and reform. It also shifts 'the level of compulsion' in arguments for implementation, since the sense of obligation to implement PIR arises from international standards embodied in the American Convention (Peruvian jurist José Antonio Burneo, former director of the Investigation Unit of the TRC, interview, 24 May 2005).[40]

---

[39] Alan Garcia: Pediremos a la CIDH precisions a su sentencia, *La Republica* (31 December 2006). Available at www.larepublica.com.pe/component/option.com_contentant/task.view/d.136949/Itemid.ø/.

[40] Mr Burneo gave this interview in his personal capacity as a legal expert, and not in his official position as Executive Secretary of the National Council of Human Rights of the Peruvian Minister of Justice.

As the government takes more steps to implement PIR, the Inter-American system may begin to hold the state accountable for TRC's recommendations which, so far, it has only implemented patchily (with one law on reparations, piecemeal reparation programmes implemented by a few committed local governments and ministers, scattered exhumations and a handful of criminal trials). Yet, by assuming the task of implementing the TRC's recommendations, the state validates the TRC's Final Report and in effect assumes the responsibility for the charges the TRC makes in regard to the violation of human rights, which triggers subsequent obligations in the pursuit of justice and provision of reparations.

Considering this last observation, an interesting possibility arises. If the state fails to implement the TRC recommendations, the Inter-American Commission may declare that it is in effect failing to comply with the Convention. Specifically, the truth commission is *how* Peru chose to comply with its international obligations under the Convention. In this sense, complying with the TRC's recommendations may have become a self-imposed obligation. In this scenario, one sees that by engaging with the Inter-American system and proposing a truth commission, Peru helped to strengthen the legitimacy of both justice mechanisms. Moreover, inviting the Inter-American system to follow the work of the TRC also reinforces the idea that the TRC is indeed an international obligation, even if it was formed by the state's own initiative.

CONCLUSION

In comparison with some of its Latin American neighbours such as Haiti and El Salvador which also embarked on a path of transitional justice, Peru presents a positive example of how local actors can make 'good use' of an international human rights system to serve their own transitional justice agenda. By converting the Inter-American system into more than a parallel remedy, Peruvian activists have shown its value as a lobbying tool in their demands for justice. Peru's experience suggests that the work of a truth commission and the social movements it sets in motion may be positively affected by the presence of a supranational human rights monitoring body.

Indeed, through its repetitive and consistent engagement with the Inter-American system, which changed in nature with each administration, Peru connected with an outside source that informed the development of a counter-political culture. The international system helped develop a new understanding of rights and the relationship between the individual and the state. At a certain point, human rights standards began to become absorbed as imperatives in popular notions of justice. At this point political transformation became more possible, solidifying and taking hold, through small, incremental changes in political and social movements (Stammers 1999).

In the transitional justice setting of Peru, this national-international dyad became stronger when the state became motivated to engage with an international human rights system in order to seek legitimacy. Civil society and the state began to work in tandem and not in opposition. With the state publicly declaring its new commitment to international norms, civil society saw the possibility of challenging these stated commitments and of holding the state to account. It remains to be seen whether Peru will continue to worry about its legitimacy in light of international scrutiny, and thus finally respond to popular demands for justice and accountability.

While different paths of justice reflect the different realities of each country, the experience of Peru may also reflect a growing international consensus led by the norm-setting of international human rights monitoring bodies. This trend supports the idea that provision for some form of criminal justice must occur (Méndez 1997; Greenawalt 2000). Through the *Barrios Altos* decision, the Inter-American system directly shaped what it is that justice would entail for Peru, by ensuring that truth would not be exchanged for immunity. It also contributed to an international dialogue on the questionable value and validity of amnesties in transitional justice settings. Peru's case has shown how the state can no longer justify sacrificing the right of its citizens to proper criminal justice in the name of political necessity.

However, while the Inter-American system may have helped shape concepts of justice in Peru and influenced the TRC's work, it may also inevitably have put the TRC in the position of disappointing the high expectations of victim-survivors, its main beneficiaries. In particular, a double standard – and dual levels of justice – generate resentment not only between victims but also between victims and the state, ultimately undermining the aims of reconciliation. This rift is especially pronounced when the double standard highlights the problem of two classes of citizens with the poor and the rural continuing to suffer marginalisation and discrimination, reflecting the very conditions that the TRC has sought to change in order to avoid future episodes of violent political conflict.

Here, Peru faces the challenge of balancing political realities characteristic of political transitions with pristine concepts of justice. Peru's experience suggests that perhaps the most a truth commission can hope to do is to establish a justice formula, with the help of a human rights monitoring system, which upholds these international standards. In this way, it can direct domestic grassroots political movements towards a stronger culture of rights, whose constant clamour against injustice will legitimise the universal ideal of 'nunca mas'.[41] It is in helping to formulate this counter-ideology that a truth commission can help put a nation on the path to justice.

REFERENCES

Coxshall, Wendy. 2005. From the Peruvian Reconciliation Commission to Ethnography: Narratives, Relatedness, and Silence. In *Political and Legal Anthropology Review* 28(2): 203–23.

David, Roman and Susanne Choi Yuk-ping. 2005. Victims in Transitional Justice: Lessons from the Reparation of Human Rights Abuses in the Czech Republic. In *Human Rights Quarterly* 27(2): 392–435.

Defensoría del Pueblo. 2005. *A dos años de la Comision de la Verdad y Reconciliación: Informe Defensorial No. 97*. Lima, Peru: Defensoría del Pueblo.

Dugard, John. 1997. Retrospective Justice: International Law and the South African Model. In *Transitional Justice and the Rule of Law in New Democracies* (ed.) James McAdams. Notre Dame: University of Notre Dame Press.

Fiss, Owen. 1999. Human Rights as Social Ideals. In *Human Rights in Political Transitions: Gettysburg to Bosnia* (eds.) Carla Hesse and Robert Post. New York: Zone Books.

Fullard, Madeleine. 2004. Dis-placing Race: the South African Truth and Reconciliation Commission (TRC) and Interpretations of Violence. *Race and Citizenship in Transition Series*, available at www.csvr.org.za/res/pubsrctp.htm.

González Cueva, Eduardo. 2004. The Contribution of the Peruvian Truth and Reconciliation Commission to Prosecutions. In *Criminal Law Forum* 15: 55–66.

2006. The Peruvian Truth and Reconciliation Commission and the Challenge of Impurity. In *Transitional Justice in the Twenty-first Century* (eds.) Naomi Roht-Arriaza and Javier Mariecurrena. Cambridge: Cambridge University Press.

---

[41] The popular slogan used in various Latin American countries with truth commissions signifying 'never again'.

Greenawalt, Ken. 2000. Amnesty's Justice. In *Truth v. Justice: the Morality of Truth Commissions* (eds.) Robert I. Rotberg and Dennis Thompson. New Jersey: Princeton University Press.

Harris, David and Stephen Livingstone (eds.). 1998. *The Inter-American System of Human Rights*. New York: Oxford University Press.

Hathaway, Oona A. 2002. Do Human Rights Treaties Make a Difference? In *Yale Law Journal* 111(8): 1935–2042.

Hayner, Priscilla. 2000. *Unspeakable Truths: Confronting State Terror and Atrocity*. London: Routledge.

Hesse, Carla and Robert Post. 1999. Introduction. In *Human Rights in Political Transitions: Gettysburg to Bosnia* (eds.) Carla Hesse and Robert Post. New York: Zone Books.

IACHR [Inter-American Commission on Human Rights]. 1993. Report on the Situation of Human Rights in Peru, OEA/Ser.L/V/II.83, Doc. 31. Available at www.cidh.oas.org/countryrep/Peru93eng/toc.htm.

2000. Second Report On The Situation Of Human Rights In Peru, OEA/Ser.L/V/II.106, Doc. 59 rev. Available at www.cidh.oas.org/country-rep/Peru2000en/TOC.htm.

Ignatieff, Michael. 1999. Human Rights. In *Human Rights in Political Transitions: Gettysburg to Bosnia* (eds.) Carla Hesse and Robert Post. New York: Zone Books.

Kritz, Neil J. (ed.). 1995. *Transitional Justice: How Emerging Democracies Reckon with Former Regimes*. Washington DC: United States Institute of Peace.

Lansing, Paul and Julie C. King. 1998. South Africa's Truth and Reconciliation Commission: the Conflict Between Individual Justice and National Healing in the Post-Apartheid Age. In *Arizona Journal of International and Comparative Law* 15: 753–89

Laplante, Lisa J. 2004. Bringing Effective Remedies Home: the Inter-American Human Rights System, Reparations and the Duty of Prevention. *Netherlands Human Rights Quarterly* 22(3): 347–88.

Laplante, Lisa J. and Kimberly Theidon. 2007. Truth with Consequences: Justice and Reparations in Post Truth Commission Peru. In *Human Rights Quarterly* 29(1): 228–50.

Méndez, Juan E. 1997. Accountability for Past Abuses. In *Human Rights Quarterly* 19(2): 255–82.

Minow, Martha. 1999. *Between Vengeance and Forgiveness: Facing History after Genocide and Mass Violence*. Boston: Beacon Press.

Neumayer, Eric. 2005. Do International Human Rights Treaties Improve Respect for Human Rights? In *Journal of Conflict Resolution* 49(6): 925–53.

Ní Aoláin, Fionnuala and Colm Campbell. 2005. The Paradox of Transition in Conflicted Democracies. In *Human Rights Quarterly* 27(1): 172–213.

Pasqualucci, Jo M. 1994. The Whole Truth and Nothing But the Truth: Truth Commissions, Impunity and the Inter-American Human Rights System. In *Boston University International Law Journal* 12: 321–70.

1996. Victim Reparations in the Inter-American Human Rights System: A Critical Assessment of Current Practice and Procedure. In *Michigan Journal of International Law* 18: 1–58.

2003. *The Practice and Procedure of the Inter-American Court of Human Rights.* Cambridge: Cambridge University Press.

Rodriquez Rescia, and M. Victor. 1999. Reparations in the Inter-American System for the Protection of Human Rights. In *ILSA Journal of International and Comparative Law* 5: 583–600.

Roht-Arriaza, Naomi. 1999. The Need for Moral Reconstruction in the Wake of Past Human Rights Violations: an Interview with José Zalaquett. In *Human Rights in Political Transitions: Gettysburg to Bosnia* (eds.) Carla Hesse and Robert Post. New York: Zone Books.

2001. The Role of International Actors in National Accountability Processes. In *The Politics of Memory* (ed.) Alexandra Bahrahona de Brito. New York: Oxford University Press.

Roht-Arriaza, Naomi and Lauren Gibson. 1998. The Developing Jurisprudence on Amnesty. In *Human Rights Quarterly* 20(4): 843–85.

Ross, Fiona. 2004. *Bearing Witness: Women and the Truth and Reconciliation Commission in South Africa.* London: Pluto.

Rotberg, Robert I. 2000. Truth Commissions and the Provision of Truth, Justice, and Reconciliation. In *Truth v. Justice: The Morality of Truth Commissions* (eds.) Robert I. Rotberg and Dennis Thompson. Princeton: Princeton University Press.

Rotberg, Robert I. and Dennis Thompson (eds.). 2000. *Truth v. Justice: the Morality of Truth Commissions.* Princeton: Princeton University Press.

Stammers, Neil. 1999. Social Movements and the Social Construction of Human Rights. In *Human Rights Quarterly* 21(4): 980–1008.

Standaert, Patricia E. 1999. Other International Issues: the Friendly Settlement of Human Rights Abuses in the Americas. In *Duke Journal of Comparative and International Law* 9(2).

TRC (Truth and Reconciliation Committee). 2003. Final Report. Available at www.cverdad.org.pe.

Tutu, Desmond. 1999. *No Future Without Forgiveness.* New York: Doubleday.

Villa-Vicencio, Charles and Erik Doxtader (eds.). 2003. *The Provocations of Amnesty: Memory, Justice, and Impunity.* Trenton, NJ: Africa World Press.

Wilson, Richard A. 2001. *The Politics of Truth and Reconciliation in South Africa: Legitimising the Post-Apartheid State.* Cambridge: Cambridge University Press.

Youngers, Coletta A. and Susan C. Peacock. 2002. *Peru's Coordinadora Nacional de Derechos Humanos: a Case Study of Coalition Building.* A Wola Special

Report. Washington: Washington Office of Latin America. Available at http://www.wola.org/andes/Peru/Peru_Coordinadora_eng.pdf.

Zalaquett, Jose. 1995. Balancing Ethical Imperatives and Political Constraints: the Dilemma of New Democracies Confronting Past Human Rights Violations. In *Transitional Justice: How Emerging Democracies Reckon with Former Regimes* (ed.) Neil J. Kritz. Washington DC: United States Institute of Peace.

CHAPTER 10

SAME OLD STORY? GYPSY UNDERSTANDINGS OF THE INJUSTICES OF NON-GYPSY JUSTICE

Sal Buckler

On 18 January 2001, the European Court of Human Rights (hereafter, 'the Court') ruled on five cases that had been instigated by Gypsies claiming they had suffered a violation of the European Convention on Human Rights (hereafter, 'the Convention') through decisions and actions adopted by officers in the UK.[1] The five cases[2] concerned the eviction of families from land they owned and had indeed bought with the intention of living there in their trailers. The cases all failed from the Gypsies' point of view. This chapter argues that they were also unsuccessful from the perspective of a normatively proper understanding of what human rights are and/or should be.

No one – not even the UK Government – contested that the Gypsies' right to respect for private and family life (as laid down in Article 8, para. 1 of the Convention)[3] had been interfered with in the

---

[1] Thanks to Mariella Marzano, Anselma Gallinat, Colin Clark and Len Smith for comments on the initial drafts of this paper, to Marie-Bénédicte Dembour and Tobias Kelly for their efforts and assistance with editing this final version, to participants at the September 2005 Brighton workshop for comments, suggestions and encouragement, to Marie Dembour for inviting me to participate in this project and to the Gypsies I worked with who allowed me to see things I took for granted from another perspective.

[2] *Chapman v. United Kingdom* (application 27238/95); *Beard v. United Kingdom* (application 24882/94); *Coster v. United Kingdom* (application 24876/94); *Lee v. United Kingdom* (application 25289/94); *Jane Smith v. United Kingdom* (application 25154/94). See also the previous case of *Buckley v. United Kingdom* (application 20348/92), judgment of 25 September 1996 and the subsequent one of *Connors v. United Kingdom* (application number 66746/01), judgment of 27 May 2004.

[3] The full wording of Article 8 states:

(1) Everyone has the right to respect for his private and family life, his home and his correspondence.

reviewed cases. The Court nonetheless considered this interference to be 'in accordance with the law' and within what could be considered 'necessary in a democratic society' in order to protect the rights of others (so that Article 8, para. 2 applied and the interference was justified under the Convention): the action of the officers entailed no violation of the Convention. Leaving aside legal technique, the rulings raise many questions for the non-lawyer: how can it be deemed necessary for a democratic society to interfere with Gypsies' private life, family life and/or home? What is the impact of this line of reasoning upon Gypsies? How can it be said that the action of the authorities protected the rights of others? Most importantly, how does the resulting case law affect our understanding of human rights?

At the time the cases were heard I was conducting fieldwork amongst Gypsies in the North East of England and was employed as a development worker for Gypsies by a local charity. None of the Gypsies I worked with discussed the cases that were going through the Strasbourg Court. Given that they were not concerned with the ins and outs of the cases, I am not in a position to create an ethnographically informed reading of their feelings and thinking about them, and I shall not attempt to do this. The Gypsies I worked with were nonetheless engaging with human rights issues: they were interested in the possibility of affirming and asserting their humanity and their right to be considered to *have* human rights. What they also articulated, both implicitly and explicitly, was a sense that any decision by Strasbourg or another mainstream system of 'justice' would fail to convey a sense of their humanity, in that it *would not treat them as fully human*. As it is at this level that the Gypsies I worked with engaged with debates about human rights, it is also the level at which I shall consider the five cases that were decided in January 2001.

The argument I develop in this chapter is built around the fact that what constitutes 'family life' is not understood and experienced in the same way by Gypsy-Travellers as by the law. The Gypsies who relied on Article 8 of the Convention to assert their right to family life were therefore working with a concept of the family which was very different from that used both by the lawyers who presented the cases and the

Footnote 3 (*cont.*)
  (2) There shall be no interference by a public authority with the exercise of this right except such as is in accordance with the law and is necessary in a democratic society in the interests of national security, public safety or the economic well-being of the country, for the prevention of disorder or crime, for the protection of health or morals, or for the protection of the rights and freedoms of others.

judges who decided upon them. This fact is not a mere curiosity of Gypsies' conception of life that can be brushed aside as a cultural idio-syncrasy of little significance. This is because Gypsies' profoundly dif-ferent experience of family also leads them to experience what it is to be human in a way very different from that which underpins rights law discourses. Thus, if Gypsies are to feel respected and treated as equally human under rights law then any understanding of the nature and implementation of human rights needs to reflect more fully their expe-rience of being human (as the dissenting judges in the Strasbourg cases implicitly recognised).

In this chapter, I assert that the Strasbourg cases fail not only the Gypsies but also a coherent notion of human rights (upon which we must assume the Convention and the judgments of the Court wish to be based).[4] My argument rests on the conviction that there are com-monalities in experiences of being human which cut across 'cultures'[5] and which can form a moral ground upon which to build an under-standing of human rights. In my view, such understanding has the potential of being universally applicable in that it provides a vision of how human rights could or should be enacted and achieved. This per-spective is rooted in the idea that the purpose of human rights is to enable human agency to flourish and to protect the ability of human beings to act as moral agents. This reading of human rights may not appear particularly controversial. It may even inform the concept of human rights with which lawyers and judges at Strasbourg think they work. The problem is that the view of human moral agency upheld by the decisions of the Court is, I argue, too restricted because it is based upon a singular understanding of human moral agency that supports a vision of an absolute and objective international law. On the other hand alternative experiences of human moral agency support a vision of a relative and subjective sense of interpersonal justice that is not reflected or supported in the decisions of the Court.

I contend that the perspective I offer in this chapter not only has the advantage of sitting well with the experiences and arguments of the Gypsies I worked with, but that it also provides a path towards inter-national justice which accommodates rather than denies their wider

---

[4] Otherwise we must accept that human rights law is divorced from the idea of human rights, a view that Dembour (2006) attributes to those she calls human rights 'protest' scholars and which I personally (as a 'deliberative' scholar in Dembour's classification) would wish to resist.
[5] I put the term in inverted commas in order to stress that cultures are neither bound nor uncon-tested (see e.g. Carrithers 1992; Bhabha 1994; Erikson 2002).

experience as well as that of other members of groups whose moral agency is typically denied in standard human rights law.

THE CASES

Though the five cases originated in separate applications, the Court considered them together because of their common features. All the applicants were claiming that their evictions by officers of UK local authorities from land which they had bought and on which they had been living in caravans, or trailers as they are more often called, constituted an infringement of their human rights as guaranteed by the European Convention, especially Article 8 (right to respect for private and family life) but also Article 14 (prohibition of discrimination) and, in some of the cases, Article 1 of Protocol No. 1 (right to peaceful enjoyment of possessions), Article 6 (access to court) and Article 2 of Protocol No. 1 (right to education).

The Court found that in all five cases there had been an interference with the rights provided by Article 8. Article 8, however, does not provide a right to family life (as well as rights to privacy and home) that is absolute. Instead it lays down relative rights. In other words, it accepts that the guaranteed rights have to be put in balance with other interests which democracy also deems valuable. To phrase it yet differently, the right to family life does not simply 'inhere' in human beings considered in their individuality, it is rooted in, and supportive of, their participation in a democratic society. For the majority of the Strasbourg judges, the interference with the right of the applicants under Article 8 was neither sufficient nor serious enough to entail a violation of the Convention. It is upon this crucial ruling that all the other decisions hinged: the initial finding of non-violation in respect of Article 8, adopted by a majority of judges, led the Court to hold, this time unanimously, that there had been no violation of Article 14 in any of the cases, no violation of Article 1 of Protocol No.1 in the cases of *Chapman, Coster, Jane Smith* and *Lee*, no violation of Article 6 in the cases of *Chapman* and *Jane Smith* and no violation of Article 2 of Protocol No. 1 in the cases of *Coster, Lee* and *Jane Smith*.[6]

What can anthropology offer us in the way of understanding these judgments and their impact upon and implications for Gypsies in the

---

[6] These findings were adopted only in the cases where the applicants had claimed a violation of these articles.

UK? First, it may be worth pointing out that any critique inspired by a cultural relativist position (commonly attributed, though arguably wrongly, to anthropology)[7] would not be very salient in these cases: the Court did indeed seem to accept that for Gypsies to live as Gypsies they needed to conduct their lives in ways that the mainstream population of the UK did not.[8] Indeed, at various points through the judgments attention is drawn to the fact that Gypsies, as a minority cultural group, should be afforded special or particular attention in order to ensure that they are not disadvantaged by their differing cultural needs not being taken into account. To quote one passage:

> The Court considers that the applicants' occupation of their caravan is an integral part of their ethnic identity as gypsies, reflecting the long tradition of that minority of following a travelling lifestyle. This is the case even though, under the pressure of development and diverse policies or from their own volition, many gypsies no longer live a wholly nomadic existence and increasingly settle for long periods in one place in order to facilitate, for example, the education of their children. Measures which affected the applicants' occupation of their caravan had therefore a wider impact than on the right to respect for home. They also affected their ability to maintain their identity as gypsies and to lead their private and family life in accordance with that tradition. (*Coster v. UK*, para. 87)

Given that the Court appeared to find it important to ensure that Gypsies' (changing) cultural practices are respected, why and how did it end up ruling against the applicants, in all five cases? What were the reasons given by the Court for deciding that although the applicants' rights had been interfered with, the inferences did not amount to violations of their rights under Article 8?

The pivotal point in deciding the cases turned around whether or not the actions by the government had been 'necessary in a democratic society': if they were then the government had been justified in interfering with the applicants' rights and therefore there was no violation of Article 8.

In arguing that the actions of the government could not be considered necessary in a democratic society the applicants appealed to the suffering they experienced in being prevented from living a traditional

---

[7] For a recent review of the way in which anthropology has been taken to approach cultural relativism, see Goodale (2006).
[8] This is what led commentators to celebrate the decisions as a victory for minority rights. See e.g. Benoît-Rohmer (2001).

lifestyle as Gypsies. They also expressed their desire to live a more settled life than they had previously been able to in order for the children of their family to attend school. Interestingly, all these arguments can be summed up as having expressed their desire to be better able to participate in the democratic processes of the state in which they lived, though this was never phrased in such a way.

In response, the Government of the United Kingdom maintained that the authorities had acted the way they had in order to protect the rights of others. The argument here was that by ensuring the respect of planning regulations, the environment was protected for the benefit of the entire community. The Government also argued that the Gypsies did not need to live on the contested piece of land to continue to live as Gypsies and that they had a number of options available to them. In particular, they could – so the Government said – move to one of the official sites provided by the Government. This argument was made even though it was established that some of these official sites had no available pitch, were often located some distance away from where the applicants lived, and could not always provide a congenial and peaceful atmosphere and that this would be especially detrimental to young children.

As for the Court, it sided with the Government. The following statement is representative of the tone found in its five judgments:

> In the circumstances, the Court considers that proper regard was had to the applicants' predicament both under the terms of the regulatory framework, which contained adequate procedural safeguards protecting their interest under Article 8 and, by the responsible planning authorities when exercising their discretion in relation to the particular circumstances of their case. The decisions were reached by those authorities after weighing in the balance the various competing interests. It is not for this Court to sit in appeal on the merits of those decisions, which were based on reasons which were relevant and sufficient, for the purposes of Article 8, to justify the interferences with the exercise of the applicants' rights. (*Coster v. UK*, para. 127)

This passage makes it clear that the Court sees its task as managing the interface between individuals (the applicants in this case) and the structures of the world they live in, for instance those of the planning authorities. Underlying this vision is a recognition that there exists a tension, which is not easily resolvable, between the needs of people from a minority group and the needs of the society in which that group lives. The structures and processes of the wider society have to be capable of taking into account the needs and expectations of all the people who live within it. It is down to the officers of the state in that society to enact – within their so-called margin of appreciation – the necessary decisions which allow this to happen. One could surmise that this, in turn, encourages the kind of national stability which Ignatieff (2003: 161–73) suggests is necessary for there to be an international notion of human rights. It is arguably upon this basis that the Court decided that the interference in the human rights of the Gypsies had been both within the law and necessary, having accepted that the officers of the state were in a better position to appreciate what was necessary than it itself did (but for a critique, see Çali, this volume).

This section has briefly presented the relevant case law, discounted a cultural relativist critique as irrelevant, and highlighted how the cases can be read as referring to the perennial debate concerning the accommodation of minority rights. What I contend is needed to understand the cases from a perspective which makes justice to the Gypsies' point of view and, beyond that, to the very idea of human rights, however, is an analysis which focuses upon the nature of agency and its articulation in a democratic society. To anticipate my conclusion, most human rights analyses and debates accept a vision of human agency as providing the moral ground for these rights however they may be theorised and enacted. Despite its apparent, general acceptance, this notion of agency is far from unproblematic; it is not at all clear what it refers to. I shall show that at the root of the judgments of the Court is an implicit assumption that the nature and experience of moral agency is shared, that it is something of substance that human beings have. My understanding of the moral universe of the Gypsies tells me that this assumption is unwarranted. It is at this fundamental level, I suggest, that anthropology has a particular contribution to make to the critique of human rights law.

BEING GYPSY

For a time immediately after the ECHR decisions were adopted my email in-box was hot with messages from people far and wide commenting on the implications and sending commiserations to the families who had effectively lost their homes. None of these emails came from the people that I was working with who were, in the main, semi-literate and not especially interested in the workings of the Court and law of what they perceived as a foreign country. Even if the decisions might eventually impact upon them it was not a matter of their concern: the way they prefer to do things is to turn away from the 'imagined' (Anderson 1999) world of the news and the courts in order to maintain a face-to-face world in which their Gypsiness is both sustained and valued. In this section I lay the ground for examining later how this way of being in the world interfaces with the systems and discourses of human rights law.

> What I love about the Gypsies I spend time with – once they've decided that you can be accepted then the acceptance is unconditional. It's a bottom-line rule of relationships rather than the state. It is wonderful to be in, it is enormously stressful to be unable to commit 100% – but like I said to Sarah the other night in Whitby – I wish I had been born into Gypsy life, as I wasn't I don't feel I can fully commit to it and I don't think they can fully accept me. (Fieldnotes, 22.08.01)

Where we are born and who we are born to makes a difference; as many psychological studies have shown, human beings are not born fully formed – the final bit of making us human happens in an intensely social context, thoroughly shot through with 'culture' (Trevarthen and Aitken, 2001; Decety and Chaminade, 2003). We are taught how to be fully human by people who have been taught before us. Through inter-actions with others we learn how to be in the world, how to understand the world, how to care for one another and how to express that care in a way that another person will understand.

This is a crucial point and one which must be taken into consideration when considering human rights. In a sense, it was made by Jeremy Bentham in his response to the *Declaration of the Rights of Man and the Citizen* which had been issued in Revolutionary France in 1789 and had asserted that 'all men are born and remain free'. Bentham responded:

> All men are born free? All men remain free? No, not a single man: not a single man that ever was, or is, or will be. All men, on the contrary, are born in subjection, and the most absolute subjection – the subjection of a helpless child to the parents on whom he depends for his existence. In this subjection every man is born – in this subjection he continues for years – for a great number of years – and the existence of the individual and of the species depends upon his so doing. (Bentham 2000 [1843]: 398)

I do not wish to draw the consequences drawn by Bentham and claim that what we now call human rights are 'nonsense upon stilts'. Instead, my intention is to argue that it is precisely because we are not born free that we have rights and that those rights spring from, and aim to

250

recognise and protect, the freedom we do manage to achieve – the freedom to act as a moral agent. To return to my specific case, I assert that the rulings of the Strasbourg Court have not recognised, let alone protected, this freedom of Gypsies in the UK, with the result that Gypsies have not been afforded the same rights as others and thereby have not been recognised as equally human.

Consider the following excerpt from my fieldnotes:

> Sitting in a trailer on Metz Bridge Site with Susan, Johnny, Charlie and Robert. Annie is here too – matriarchal grandmother figure. Outside it is grey and drizzly, cold as well. I am struck by the way the children are confined by the space.
>
> This is the site of socialisation, it is the location of habitus, of learning 'body techniques'. It seems obvious to me that this has so much to do with social aesthetics and the way people learn to carry themselves, the reason why they run wild when they do get out, the reason why houses feel so wrong, the reason why the children won't sit at school and why schools find them so difficult to handle. (Fieldnotes, 30.01.01)

Clearly, culture is encountered, experienced and taught first and foremost as an intersubjective consciousness and responsiveness to other human beings. This is articulated as a sensed way of being in the world – a perspective noted in various observations regarding 'social aesthetics' (e.g. MacDougall, 1999; Highmore, 2004). It is this social aesthetic sensibility that informs how we perform social acts and interactions that reinforce (or not) a feeling of 'rightness' or 'fittingness'. Jackson (2002) has demonstrated how such acts come to have moral value and so inform the ethical systems that underpin any culture's rationalised systems of law or justice. Hence the intersubjective and aesthetically sensed experience of being human becomes the grounds for acting as a moral being. This is because, in a very fundamental way, human beings *matter* to one another, we need other human beings in order to be fully cognisant of our own humanity.

In the mainstream worlds of the literate West we are taught to base our sense of what is right or fitting, the standards of our moral agency, on the standards of a wide world, many members of which we will never meet – as Anderson has called it, an imagined community. For the Gypsies I worked with, their way of being in the world is rooted in face-to-face interactions with known others (Buckler 2006) and this informs their sense of justice and law.

Many scholars concerned with Romany studies have shown how quite different notions about responsibility operate in diverse Gypsy

251

cultures; studies of the *Kris* have emphasised the importance of this as a system of law directed specifically towards what is right in a given situation amongst people who are known to one another. Blood feuds are concerned with two groups of people (families) who are known to one another maintaining or retrieving from a situation a sense of balance in the relationship between them (Acton, Caffrey and Mundy 1997; Sutherland, 1997). At the root of these observations is an emphasis on loyalty, honour and maintaining relationships with known others upon whom one depends, not just economically but also for a sense of psychological and social security. Okely provided an excellent example of how such loyalties informed a sense of the 'right' thing to do when she noted how a group of Gypsies would join together to help one of their number hide from the police (Okely, 1983: 42). Such a course of action is taken not because the culprit has done nothing wrong but because it is more important for those Gypsies themselves to manage the means by which a wrong-doer is sanctioned without allowing a stranger into the midst of the very heart of what keeps their culture alive – their personal and intensely intimate relationships with one another.

Expressed by the Gypsies that I worked with in the UK, this aesthetically sensed moral rightness becomes articulated in the ways that people would speak of those not belonging to their known group as 'not a proper person' or 'not proper people'. Indeed it is in just such phrases that Gypsies articulated their own experience of agency and what was necessary in order for a person to be recognised and to act as fully human. It is important to note that what is articulated in such phrases is a judgment about the grounds upon which people act as moral agents – it is not a means of denying humanity or personhood to non-Gypsies. 'Proper people' are those who are known to ground their moral responsibility and actions in a sense of mutual responsibility to others in the group. 'Not proper people' are those who rely upon imagined structures such as states to guide their moral decisions and actions – in other words whose understanding of moral responsibility is grounded in a sense of responsibility to an ideal or imagined norm as opposed to mutual and contingent experience.

As I remarked in the fieldnotes above, the Gypsies' preferred grounds of moral action is a bottom-line rule of relationships rather than the state. The European Court of Human Rights, on the other hand, has its foundations firmly rooted in a perspective whereby the aesthetic sense of sociality is mediated by the written word and other forms of generalised interaction. Indeed this is necessary to allow the imagining of an international community and a universal sense of justice and law rather than a particularised sense of rightness. This is in stark contrast to the preferred approach of the Gypsies described above and is a bottom-line rule of absolutes, of 'right' or 'correct' rather than appropriate or fitting. These different ethical senses can be glossed as an 'ethic of care' and an 'ethic of right' following work by Heidegger, Gilligan (1982) and Faubion (2001).

BEING FAMILY

> Sylvia's mother's family originated in Ireland – she's not sure where. But she can say them back – down on the diagram. Also says how she grew up speaking Romany and that she has uncles and aunts in Eastpool who still speak it. I ask if she gets worried about the culture dying out – or if her uncles and aunts do. Her answer is very simple – 'No, because you can't get out what's been bred into you.'
>
> Sylvia laughed at women who were starting their families now – she would tease them and took great pleasure in telling me just how she was teasing them. We talked about what it is like to have children around and how it 'tears you apart' if they start fighting with one another. As Sylvia put it 'I can take anything from them, they can do what they like so long as they don't start taxing my mind.' By this she meant fighting and bickering amongst themselves. Spoke about how she would have liked to have girls as they would have helped her clean. (Fieldnotes, 09.03.01)

As the focus of the appeals were on applicants' 'right to private and family life', references and appeals to notions of 'family' bear significantly upon my argument. What we assume we are referring to when we use this term is not necessarily the same as what another person thinks; indeed anthropologists have been very successful in demonstrating how 'family' is not a generally transferable concept (Harris, 1969; Collier, Roseldo and Yanagisako 1982; Carsten, 2000). For Gypsies – certainly for all the Gypsies I worked with – 'family' provides the grounds of moral decision-making and the root of a sense of social responsibility. Further, to elaborate on points made above, 'family' refers specifically to an experienced, extended network of people who have shared some experiences and who understand one another as being morally accountable first and foremost to that group rather than to any imagined community or bureaucracy or body of law (Buckler 2006). Of course I do not want to imply that the Gypsies I worked with saw themselves in any sense as above or beyond the law; that would be in no way a fair or accurate representation, although it would bolster the stereotyped attitudes of the wider society in which Gypsies live. Rather, the focus and aesthetic sense of being human and exercising moral agency that Gypsies are taught is found in the extended family network and is articulated more through an ethic of care than an ethic of right. When, then, Gypsies' rights to family life are being interfered with, the very grounds of their moral action and accountability and responsibility towards society are also being interfered with.

The term 'extended family' is not necessarily problematic unless we assume that all experiences of having an extended family are of the same kind. In fact what makes the experience of family different amongst Gypsies I have worked with in the UK is that their extended family network only comprises people who are known on a face-to-face basis. This is unlike the experience in the more mainstream, white, non-Gypsy worlds of the UK where many of us might be dimly aware of distant cousins, uncles and aunts – people to whom we are somehow related but whom we have never met, and who we do not ever expect to meet. Any curtailment of the Gypsies' extensive face-to-face family, whether intended or not, results in a shrinking of their family until 'family' as Gypsies understand it to be is no longer possible.

This is one of the crucial points contested but never made explicit in the ECHR cases. There is an appeal to the right to family life – but what that means is assumed to be a private family life, taking place in a private, discrete location. To Gypsies, on the other hand, family life is not private, it is a semi-public realm, that of the extended family – a family that, in order to be linked into, you need to keep visiting so as to keep the face-to-face or experienced nature of those relationships fresh. This has to take place in spaces that, whilst being familiar and meaningful, are not confined in the ways that houses are. I expect that the applicants at Strasbourg would say that they fought not for gaining permission to put their trailers somewhere so that their family life could take place inside them; nor would I presume that the fight was simply about having somewhere large enough to cope with the coming together and breaking apart of networks of people – many of whom might have trailers. The fight must rather have been about having it recognised that this kind of activity was vital for the Gypsies' maintenance of their family networks and that it could not simply happen anywhere, there had to be some sense of security and continuity. The effect of the Court's decisions would be, whether for economic, legal or planning reasons, to prevent that maintenance of family from happening.

TALKING ABOUT FAMILY

Toivanen (2004) points out that knowledge is not neutral and that discourses about rights are built upon an understanding about what the
world is that carries authority and effectively excludes other discourses
and other knowledges. This is just what has happened in the Strasbourg
cases whereby the aspect of the Gypsies' appeals for justice which was
rooted in their desire to keep alive the very heart of their sense of
Gypsiness – the very grounds of their claims to be human – could not
be articulated without becoming reframed as something else. Within
the framework of the language of human rights there is room to discuss
where Gypsies could or should be able to site their trailers. More
detailed debates regarding the nature of family and the questionable-
ness of a distinction between public and private and the associated
grounds which provide the context of Gypsies' moral agency and articulated humanity get little consideration in a context which considers
only 'the facts' within a very narrow area of concern. For all that the
judges might recognise that there are different understandings and
experiences of family and home that come with different cultural backgrounds, these issues do not form part of the Court's final decision. A
right to family life becomes compressed into a right to respect for a
home.[9] Consider for instance the following point:

> In sum, the issue for determination before the Court in the present case
> is not the acceptability or not of a general situation, however deplorable,
> in the United Kingdom in the light of the United Kingdom's under-
> takings in international law, but the narrower one whether the par-
> ticular circumstances of the case disclose a violation of the applicant's,
> Mrs Chapman's, right to respect for her home under Article 8 of the
> Convention. (*Chapman v. UK*, para. 100)

So in the representations from the Court the cases have shifted to
become about home rather than family. This compresses concerns
about maintaining face-to-face family networks into ascertaining where
some trailers have been sited, and whether there is, reasonably, somewhere else that they can be put. This reframing includes an assumption

---

[9] This same reframing from 'family' to 'home' also proved to be a pivotal move in the decision of
the Lords ruling in the Maloney case on 8 March 2006: *Price & Ors v. Leeds City Council* (UKHL
10) where it was considered that a temporary stop of a couple of days could not be considered
to grant a status of 'home' to a council-owned playing field. Again, home, as a static and private
space, was equated with family life in a way that echoes the assumptions of the mainstream
culture but not the experiences of Gypsies.

that, provided the trailers can be put somewhere, then people will be fairly well able to continue having a family life – expecting that family life is in some way private and taking place within the four walls of the trailer. In fact, for Gypsies, the very idea of associating 'home' with some means of enclosing space is problematic and if home is to be associated with a sense of belonging it is more reasonable to think of Gypsies' 'home' as being that network of relationships which is their experienced family. If this were to be followed up in the Court the question asked might be whether the applicant was in some way – either by the actions or the non-action of the United Kingdom – prevented from maintaining that network of relationships. This is not the course followed and instead it is stated that:

> The Court does not, however, accept the argument that, because statistically the number of gypsies is greater than the number of places available in authorised gypsy sites, the decision not to allow the applicant gypsy family to occupy land where they wished in order to install their caravan in itself, and without more, constituted a violation of Article 8. This would be tantamount to imposing on the United Kingdom, as on all other Contracting States, an obligation by virtue of Article 8 to make available to the gypsy community an adequate number of suitably equipped sites. The Court is not convinced, despite the undoubted evolution that has taken place in both international law, as evidenced by the Framework Convention, and domestic legislations in regard to protection of minorities, that Article 8 can be interpreted to involve such a far-reaching positive obligation of general social policy being imposed on States. (*Chapman v. UK*, para. 94)

That the Court is able to reach such a conclusion is made possible by the relative nature of the rights afforded under Article 8 and the shifting of Gypsies' sense of agency from one frame to another. The rights of Article 8 are, indeed, secondary to and contingent upon other more fundamental rights if you belong to a culture that teaches its members to experience and articulate their sense of moral agency and responsibility as an individual first and foremost and to link one's individuality to an imagined community. However, for Gypsies the rights afforded under Article 8 are the most fundamental rights without which it is not possible for them to exercise their learned sense of moral agency. To expect Contracting States to provide adequate sites for all members of Gypsy families would be to expect those Contracting States to recognise and respect Gypsies' sense of personhood and to thereby enable their full participation, as Gypsies, in the democratic processes of those states. This, I would argue, is necessary in a democratic society unless Gypsies, as Gypsies, are to be denied the capacity to participate in the workings of the states which govern them.

In other words, if the articulation of moral agency is rooted in the ways in which we learn to be in the world and Gypsies learn to articulate that agency in the context of large networks of family, then to deny the opportunity for these networks to maintain and perpetuate themselves is to deny Gypsies the grounds from which their moral agency is achieved. The upshot is, in effect, to deny Gypsies not just their rights but their own experience of their humanity and their ability to exercise fully their sense of moral agency. This in turn engenders a sense that they are not, as Gypsies, accepted as persons and thereby included in the list of those to whom human rights apply – in order for them to become so included they need to stop being Gypsies and accept a more mainstream experience of family and a more mainstream understanding and enactment of moral agency.[10]

THE LOCATION OF RIGHTS?

An understanding of humans as beings who do indeed need to exist in a social context is implicit in the Convention in a somewhat different way – in the appeals to 'democracy' and the underpinning assumption that human rights need to be practised in relation to a democratic state. The implication here is that those humans who have the fullest complement of human rights are those who are able or empowered to participate in such a democratic state. Indeed the ability to participate in the governance processes of democracies has been a major route through which both legal theorists and anthropologists have tried to overcome the difficulties faced by cultural minorities in arguing for a more culturally sensitive implementation of human rights in the light of arguments of cultural relativism and rights to culture noted above (Malik, 2001). This conception of rights as rooted in democracy and linked to the governance of nation-states brings an attempt to separate the arena of rights discourse from that of culture and arrive at a 'multicultural' vision of states and governance. The hope is that this will provide a culturally neutral ground upon which to base the moral decisions required in implementing human rights law.

---

[10] This predicament is shared by groups other than the Gypsies. See e.g. Samson (2001) on the Innu of Canada.

In order for a state to be considered democratic it needs to afford its citizens the ability to make decisions about what should or should not be done, how they should or should not be governed. In short a democratic state needs to recognise its citizens' ability to act as moral agents. In other words, in order to participate in a democratic society people need to be able to exercise moral agency and therefore this notion of moral agency is at the root of human rights law and thinking. So human rights law needs first and foremost to protect a person's sense of moral agency so that they are able to act as a moral agent. Yet there is no single, universal sense in which moral agency is either experienced or enacted. Whilst moral agency itself might be universal – i.e. a mutually recognised and responded to 'universal humanity' along the lines suggested by Carrithers (2005) – the conditions of its being are relative. This might well mean that a differential notion of human rights is called for, one that is dependent upon the context in which people both become and are able to act as moral agents. In this way of thinking about human rights what constitutes a breach of those rights is an action that denies a human being the ability to act as a moral agent. The implication would then be to find a means of actively ensuring that these various social worlds continue, and that those in a position to pass judgments regarding breaches of human rights make their choices based on that. In pragmatic terms, this is an argument, in the end, for a needs-based application of human rights grounded in the question: which decision will most safeguard the sense of moral agency of the people in question?

Read in this light the findings of the Court regarding the successful application of a Gypsy at a later date[11] look somewhat less positive than may have been initially hoped by defenders of Gypsy rights – and indeed I was witness to a certain degree of cynicism regarding the judgment of the Court in this case. Just as with the five cases in 2001 the case of *Connors v. United Kingdom* rested on a claim that there had been a violation of rights under Article 8 and, as with the 2001 cases, it was held that by being evicted from where they had been living there had indeed been interference with this right. However here the similarities end – whilst the 2001 cases discussed whether or not the applicants should or should not site their trailers on the applicants' privately owned land, the *Connors* case questioned whether or not the local authority in question had followed due process in evicting the appli-

[11] *Connors v. United Kingdom* (application 66746/01), judgment of 27 May 2004.

cants from a local authority Gypsy site. The Strasbourg Court found that the local authority had not followed proper procedures; it therefore held the interference with rights under Article 8 to be a violation of those rights. In effect this is a decision *against* the actions of the local authority, not *for* the rights of Gypsies and so a somewhat cynical feeling emerges that, despite the positive ruling, this case would probably not lead to any long-term improvement for Gypsies.

CONCLUSION

The disputes that we see in the ECHR regarding Gypsies v. the United Kingdom are a subtle contest between different ways of seeing, experiencing and framing the world. Further, it is a conflict that results in an impossible situation for people from Gypsy backgrounds as, from their perspective, their rights are not acknowledged because their full experience of themselves as moral agents is nowhere reflected in the discourses of international human rights law. For many Gypsies, the decisions of the Court in the 2001 cases will be perceived as denying them their moral agency. Whilst the Court decided that the human rights of the Gypsy communities in question had not been unjustifiably interfered with, many Gypsies will feel that their claim to have human rights has been denied simply because they are Gypsies.

The circumstances which led to the Strasbourg rulings of January 2001 should pose a stark choice for those who seek the implementation of human rights: *either* be prepared to state that Gypsies' learned ways of exercising moral agency are not considered important enough in forming Gypsies' understanding of their own humanity for human rights to protect them – i.e. there is no requirement to recognise or protect their moral agency and the ground from which that agency develops; *or* recognise the need for states to act in a way which protects this agency and allows Gypsies to exercise it and thus feel themselves to be recognised and treated as fully human.

If we do recognise that the decisions made by courts regarding human rights impact upon cultures differently and privilege certain mainstream and hegemonic ways of being-in-the-world, then we also need to recognise that the exercise of the law is not culture-neutral. So, if it is to protect the humanity and human agency of all human beings, human rights law needs to be applied differently according to the impact it will have upon people rather than its congruence with 'the facts' of narrow legal considerations. In other words, in order for human rights practices to recognise and protect the moral agency of those whose experience of such agency is rooted in an ethic of care then it would itself have to root its decisions in an ethic of care – the arguments I have presented might equally apply to any number of face-to-face cultures, not only Gypsies in the UK. This may well turn out to be too tall an order for a notion that is currently rooted in a legal system and an ethic of right. Indeed, it may well require the development of an understanding of human rights that goes beyond the formalism of human rights law. Nevertheless, this is a path that may be necessary if human rights are to achieve their potential as a source of international justice.

REFERENCES

Acton, T., S. Caffrey and G. Mundy. 1997. Theorizing Gypsy Law. In *American Journal of Comparative Law* 45(2): 237–49.

Anderson, B. 1999 [1983]. *Imagined Communities.* London: Verso.

Benoît-Rohmer, Florence. 2001. La Cour de Strasbourg et la protection de l'intérêt minoritaire : une avancée décisive sur le plan des principes? *Revue trimestrielle des droits de l'homme:* 999–1015.

Bentham, Jeremy. 2000 [1843]. Anarchical Fallacies. An Examination of the Declaration of the Rights of the Man and the Citizen Decreed by the Constituent Assembly in France. In Jeremy Bentham. *Selected Writings on Utilitarianism.* Ware, Hertfordshire: Wordsworth, 381–459.

Bhabha, Homi K. 1994. *The Location of Culture.* London: Routledge.

Buckler, Sally. 2006. *Fire in the Dark: Telling Gypsiness in North East England.* Oxford: Berghahn.

Carrithers, Michael. 1992. *Why Humans Have Cultures.* Oxford: Oxford University Press.

2005. Anthropology as a Moral Science of Possibilities. In *Current Anthropology* 46(3).

Carsten, Janet. 2000. *Cultures of Relatedness: New Approaches to the Study of Kinship.* Cambridge: Cambridge University Press.

Collier, J., M. Z. Rosaldo and S. Yanagisako. 1982. Is There a Family? New Anthropological views. In *Rethinking the Family: Some Feminist Questions* (eds.) B. Thorne and M. Yalom. London: Longman.

Decety, J. and T. Chaminade. 2003. When the Self Represents the Other: A New Cognitive Neuroscience View on Psychological Identification. In *Consciousness and Cognition* 12(4).

Dembour, Marie-Bénédicte. 2006. *Who Believes in Human Rights? Reflections on the European Convention.* Cambridge: Cambridge University Press.

Erickson, F. 2002. Culture and Human Development. In *Human Development* 45: 299–306.

Faubion, J. D. 2001. Introduction: Towards an Anthropology of Ethics and Kinship. In *The Ethics of Kinship: Ethnographic Inquiries* (ed.) J. D. Faubion, 1–28.

Faubion, J. D. (ed.). 2001. *The Ethics of Kinship: Ethnographic Inquiries*. Oxford: Rowman and Littlefield.

Gilligan, C. 1982. *In a Different Voice: Psychological Theory and Women's Development*. Cambridge: Harvard University Press.

Goodale, Mark. 2006. Toward a Critical Anthropology of Human Rights. In *Current Anthropology* 47(3).

Harris, C. C. 1969. *The Family: An Introduction*. London: Allen and Unwin.

Highmore, Ben. 2004. Homework. Routine, Social Aesthetics and the Ambiguity of Everyday Life. In *Cultural Studies* 18: 306–27.

Ignatieff, Michael. 2003. *Human Rights as Politics and Idolatry*. Oxford: Princeton University Press.

Jackson, Michael. 2002. The Exterminating Angel: Reflections on Violence and Intersubjective Reason. In *Focaal – European Journal of Anthropology* 39.

MacDougall, David. 1999. Social Aesthetics and the Doon School. In *Visual Anthropology Review* 15: 3–20.

Malik, Maleiha. 2001. Minority Protection and Human Rights. In *Sceptical Essays on Human Rights* (eds.) T. Campbell, K. D. Ewing and A. Tomkins.

Okely, Judith. 1983. *The Traveller-Gypsies*. Cambridge: Cambridge University Press.

Samson, Colin. 2001. Rights as the Reward for Simulated Cultural Sameness: the Innu in the Canadian Colonial Context. In *Culture and Rights: Anthropological Perspectives* (eds.) Jane K. Cowan, Marie-Bénédicte Dembour and Richard A. Wilson. Cambridge: Cambridge University Press, 226–48.

Sutherland, Anne. 1997. Complexities of US Law and Gypsy Identity. In *American Journal of Comparative Law* 45(2): 393–405.

Toivanen, Reeta. 2004. Contextualising Struggles over Culture and Equality. In *Rethinking Non-Discrimination and Minority Rights* (ed.) M. Scheinin and R. Toivanen. Helsinki: Turku/Åbo, Institute for Human Rights, Åbo Akademi University.

Trevarthen, C. and K. J. Aitken. 2001. Infant Intersubjectivity: Research, Theory, and Clinical Applications. In *Journal of Child Psychology and Psychiatry* 42(1): 3–48

INDEX